Managing To Be Human

*Leading Business Organisations with
Integrity and Effectiveness*

Brian F. Smyth

ORPEN PRESS

Orpen Press
Lonsdale House
Avoca Ave
Blackrock
Co. Dublin
Ireland

e-mail: info@orpenpress.com
www.orpenpress.com

Paperback ISBN: 978-1-871305-45-6
ePub ISBN: 978-1-871305-59-3
Kindle ISBN: 978-1-871305-60-9

Printed in the UK by the MPG Books Group

This book is dedicated to my sister, Margaret Hayes. Throughout a life that has had more than its share of trials and sadness, she continues to grow in her warm humanity, bringing love and joy to so many people's lives. She has truly 'managed to be human'.

Contents

Contents

Preface

I have a few reasons for wanting to write this book and sharing my thoughts with you, the reader.

The first reason is that many people have *asked* me to write it. So often, after courses I have given or events I have run for companies and different organisations, people have approached me and said, 'Where can I read about all this stuff?' I have never been able to adequately answer them; the few times I have recommended books for them to read, I found they were not management books at all. Very often these people would go on to say: 'You really should put it all down in writing.' I finally agreed.

My second reason for writing the book is that I so often find myself talking about isolated, discrete aspects of managing, all of which make some sense on their own, but which would make much more sense if understood in the overall totality. It is difficult to talk about performance in isolation from leadership or to talk about coaching as separate from organisational culture. Here I have tried to bring all aspects of managing together and to see them all, every one of them, as having their roots and meaning in the basic principles of what it means to be human.

Being true to our humanity is critical to our happiness and well-being and our difficulty in achieving this affects every part of our lives and every part of our world. Our frequent failure to behave, lead and manage in a human way is of increasing concern to more and more people and was even raised by speakers at a recent World Economic Forum in Davos. While this book does not pretend to offer itself as a solution to that global issue, it is an attempt to remove the perceived difficulties of managing and behaving in a good and human way in organisations and companies. This, at least, is a beginning. And, of course, the book aims to go further and show that managing in this way leads to greater overall success and sustainable well-being for everybody.

This book is not based on academic research or, indeed, on research of any kind. It is based entirely on my experience of working with companies in many parts of the world and on the solutions I had to find for the various problems I came across. For that reason, you will find nothing in this book that I have not actually practised and continue to practise and apply to the issues and problems I come across in my work with organisations, individuals and companies. The approach outlined in this book works.

Having said all that, the approach is not entirely my own. I owe every insight to the many people with whom I have associated and worked 'for more years than I care to remember'. And I am grateful to more people than I dare to mention for their support, interest, encouragement and patience over the years the book was being written. In fact, its long gestation was due in no small part to my heavy involvement over those years in helping sports teams and individuals reach higher levels of performance and success, and to whom I am also grateful for the many insights I gained.

If there is anything in the book about which you are not clear or you are not sure how to implement, then feel free to contact me or any of the Maybe International team at www.maybe.ie. I can be contacted directly at brian@maybe.ie.

Introduction

'I am a human being. Nothing that is human is alien to me.'

– Terence Roman,
playwright and freed slave

This book will attempt to show that we can 'manage to be human' in how we manage people and situations in work. Furthermore, it claims that if we do that we will actually manage better. This is not the only reward. The greater reward comes from being more human, and the goodness, authenticity and fulfilment that come from working and living in that way.

What do I mean by being 'human'? I mean living in accordance with our fundamental nature as human beings and behaving in a way that is true to 'who' and 'what' we are. I explain this in more detail in Chapter 3. I hope that some of what I say may add to your own rich understanding of the human. Others' experiences and reflections can often add angles and colour to our own.

Much of my life has been spent directly and indirectly trying to help organisations improve their performance and this book will reflect much of the learning I got from that endeavour – from my successes and from my failures. I want to share my struggles, my questions, my breakthroughs, my excitement and my insights with managers of companies who will be at various stages along that same road, even if they are travelling it in a different time and with different companions. But I aim to do all of this while respecting the deep and legitimate needs of the other groups. Failure to include employees, customers, suppliers and society in the overall search would of course doom it to failure by virtue of the limits doing so would put on the search. It is truth we are after, without limits or conditions or censure of any kind, and this truth when we find it will bring enormous benefits to everyone involved.

I will put a lot of emphasis on 'creativity' in this book. I do so because creativity is what lies at the heart of being human and is also a key to successful management in companies and in all organisations. I define creativity as how accurate, fulfilling and life-giving the responses we give to our respective situations in life are. Creativity means doing justice to our world as a place of enormous possibilities and doing justice to ourselves as creatures called to play a real part in shaping and continuing the creation of our universe. This challenge that life gives us is a daunting one, but it is also exciting. If we meet the challenge, it is exhilarating. I will give some examples of both famous and previously unknown people who truly did justice to themselves and to their world, for which we are all eternally grateful.

Of course, I am setting out to look at humanity and creativity particularly in the context of the world of work, in business and other organisations. I will deal with the hindrances to working creatively in organisations in general and in business organisations in particular. I will not focus here on the nature of our business organisations and the global economic system of which they are a part. Notwithstanding the many serious and quite fundamental difficulties this system poses, I will show that it is still possible to behave in a human way within it, and that part of our creative role is to be able to do so. Doing so will, in turn, I believe, have some impact on the nature, values and working of the system itself. Examples of people who found creative responses to imperfect and quite inhumane systems are Viktor Frankl in Auschwitz, Nelson Mandela in apartheid South Africa and Rosa Parks in segregated Alabama. These people show that it is possible to behave creatively and humanely in the particular world system of which we are a part.

However, I will show that, to behave in a rewarding and human way, none of the heroism of the three people mentioned above is required at all. It is relatively easy to be human because we will find it to be so rewarding. It is rewarding in the first instance for the person who manages in a good and human way in terms of peace, satisfaction and fulfilment, but it is also rewarding for the organisations and businesses of which they are a part. It is not only a nicer and better way to manage, but it is also much more effective.

This perspective does require a fundamental look at how we manage and at the role of the manager, particularly as we have traditionally understood, practised and lived it. 'Managing', as we currently understand it and traditionally operated and practised it since the days of the Industrial Revolution, is far from healthy for the manager, for those he or she manages or for the welfare of the organisations in which they manage. An effective manager adopts the traits of a leader. I will show how the two concepts 'manager' and 'leader' differ, and I will provide concrete and practical ways of working towards this new idea of management. The main difference between manager and leader is a difference of power – a shift away from an exclusively hierarchical or positional power to enlisting the power of meaning, of what makes sense; as Benjamin Zander, the conductor of the Boston Philharmonic Orchestra says, 'of what will work for everyone'.[1] By 'everyone' I mean owners, shareholders and managers, as well as those managed or led by managers. This power is not a power over people but a power that is given to people. People become more powerful when they see a purpose to things and when they want to achieve a goal which they see as being meaningful in itself and for them. Having a goal or vision that you really want to realise gives you great energy. By creating, sharing and getting buy-in for such a goal, the manager or leader actually ends up with an empowered and dynamic team. I will explain how this can and should happen right through the organisation, starting off with what I call the 'X meeting' – the meeting where the manager or leader shares the goal with his or her people and gets people 'enrolled', as Zander[2] says, in going after it. Involving people in achieving the goal will make them feel good, included and appreciated, but it will also improve the chances of achieving the goal since everyone's ideas on how to do so will be considered – 'None of us is as clever as all of us' (Japanese proverb).

People will be empowered, then, by having something really worthwhile for which to leave their beds in the morning, by being involved in shaping a plan on how to get there, but also by how they are managed and led on a daily basis. If we manage well, we will have a powerful resource available to us because of our deployment of the enormous and often under-appreciated potential of people. There are many ways in which people block themselves and many ways in which *we* block people. We need to be aware of these and deal with them. Even more importantly, we need to find the keys to unlocking the marvellous potential in everyone who works with and for us. I will put forward what I believe are five keys to unlocking people's potential, freeing them to be, as Zander says, ' the most that they can be', and enabling and empowering them to do what they previously might not have believed possible. These five keys are built around the mnemonic

'COACH' and state that, for people to perform as full and powerful human beings, they need:

- **C** is for Commitment to clear, challenging, shared and exciting goals or vision.
- **O** is for Ownership of the task, job, assignment, project, etc.
- **A** is for Awareness of what is going on or what is needed, or acknowledgment of what has been achieved.
- **C** is for Confidence and trust – in yourself, in others or from others
- **H** is for Healthy relationships.

I will explain what each of these five keys or principles mean in depth and in practice. They are not just disciplines to be practised, but principles to be lived and that colour every part of the organisation's operation – system, structures, ways of working, culture and values. If you want to be a true and empowering leader, all five keys need to be present in all you do and how you operate.

Being an empowering leader is not just something nice and altruistic. In practice, every manager is at the centre of a set of relationships and gets things done through the people with whom they relate. Managers don't make cans or cars or cameras. Teams of people make them and how well they make them will depend to a great extent on how they are managed. It is for that reason I say, 'We are only as good as our relationships.' Because we are the centre of so many relationships as managers and leaders, we have enormous power available to us to make an impact on people and make so much happen. It is a great responsibility to be a manager and a great privilege. Handling that role in line with the five COACH principles will virtually guarantee that we have good relationships and get good results.

While all managers have a big effect on the people around them and on their organisations, senior management has an even greater one. For this reason, senior management need to give special attention to how they manage and lead. However this group, for a variety of reasons, often behaves and performs poorly. In dealing with this problem and in looking for a solution to it, I focus on the dynamics of a group of senior managers when they meet. I provide guidelines to help them work well as a group and to provide the right kind of leadership to inspire and motivate people. Achieving this calls for good thinking and courageous behaviour on the part of all members of the senior team, but in particular on the part of the chief executive officer (CEO) or general manager. Again, it is to the overriding and all-embracing goal that the CEO must turn to find the right kind of power to steer a narrow path between the Scylla of relationships and the Charybdis of tasks and goals. Doing this will override all other goals and give the CEO the real power to help everyone to behave in a way that both maintains and develops good relationships and that ultimately leads to the achievement of objectives. Being truly human as a senior manager is often not easy. I know!

It is the creation and consistent pursuit of a shared and meaningful goal that achieves the same kind of harmonious and honest performance at every level in the organisation. All meetings need to have this goal as the dynamic underpinning all they do and decide. When teams and groups meet to review how they are doing, the measurement used will be the goal or vision that was set and agreed on. Changes that affect the company will be taken into account in terms of how the goal needs to be achieved, given these new circumstances. Problems that arise and setbacks that occur will provide the stimulus to find and create new directions. This twin dynamic of clear and meaningful goals coupled with a changing and challenging reality is what will keep the organisation alive and vibrant. Collapse either one of these and the energy disappears. Creativity, on which I will spend much time in the early part of the book, is the product of the tension between the vision or goal and the existing and challenging reality.

Not only do company, group or team reviews flow from the original vision and goal, but so, too, does individual performance. The approach I will explain and recommend, the Performance Development System (PDS), is based on the people involved – manager and team member – working together to assess how the team member is doing in terms of how well they are helping to make the vision or goal a reality. The assessing, as you will see, is, for the greater part, done by the team member or employee. The manager plays the role of coach, helping the person to assess how they are doing in order to improve their performance in the interests of the organisation and the person themselves. Equally, in cases of unsatisfactory performance, it is the employee's failure to contribute to the overall and shared goal that the manager uses to address the issue and bring about the necessary change. In the case of unsatisfactory or dysfunctional behaviour, the manager should appeal to the employee's sense of contributing to a shared goal. So, even in these quite challenging and difficult situations, it is possible to manage in a human way. This is not in any sense a weakening of management power; rather, it gives the manager a much greater power in terms of helping the employee to take responsibility and realise their own power.

I will spend some time in this book looking at how we can manage other difficult situations, such as managing your boss and dealing with difficult people. I will also discuss dealing with meetings, decision making and managing our own 'bears' – our egos and power. I will provide approaches to help you handle these well – in a good and human way. I hope this will make life easier for you but, even more importantly, I hope it will help make your company a more human place to work.

I firmly believe that managing in a good and human way will also greatly improve the chances of your organisation being more successful in every sense. I have already mentioned the fact that I will not be focusing on the context of a flawed global and economically dominated system. Notwithstanding this, I do believe that every blow that is struck in the cause of the human will play some part in affecting and improving the overall system. So, while I am not claiming that by managing to be human we will right all the wrongs and produce a perfect system, I do hope that the practical approaches in this book will help you and others to play your unique part in making the world a better place. There is no need 'to play small'³ or to sacrifice your legitimate business goals in order to be human. If you manage to be human, you will do better and be better in every sense – in your business, and in your social and personal life. By managing to be human, you will help many others to behave and live in more human way and to enjoy the fruits thereof.

Section I – Foundations

Chapter 1

The Invitation, the Offer and the Challenge to Manage in a Human Way

'A human being is a part of the whole, called by us "Universe", a part limited in time and space.'

– Albert Einstein

Happy and successful or successful by being happy?

Sometimes when working with senior managers in companies on the goals of their organisation, I have a similar experience to that of Tracy Huston. In her book *Inside-Out*, Huston writes of how, during a session she ran for a leadership team in a large corporation, some members of the team suggested that one of the company's core values might be 'happiness'. 'The group gazed on the word in thoughtful silence,' she says, 'as if it were a long-forgotten but beautiful dream; but they then sadly shook their heads and drew a line through the word on the flip chart, for we had taught them to keep only those values they thought the company would live by.'[4] And happiness was not one of those!

This book argues that it should be and will demonstrate in a practical way how to manage successfully while behaving in a truly good, human way. We will take a more detailed look later at what we mean by 'human'. For now, this will be our challenge: Is it possible to manage and act in a business context in a good, human way? Or is it that, yes, it is sometimes possible to do so, but that in many situations it is not and we simply have to park our 'humanity' for the sake of business or results?

My claim is that it is possible to act in a human way *all* the time and that doing so is helpful for everyone involved, *and* it leads to better and more successful organisations and businesses.

Why get into all of this? What is the motivation for managing in a human way?

The reasons are:

1. To make life more satisfying and fulfilling for everyone involved in organisations and businesses, including ourselves.

2. To find new and better ways to manage businesses and organisations so that they are better and more successful.

3. Eliminating well-being and happiness from our list of goals will seriously impoverish our lives and the lives of those we manage.

4. Turning a blind eye to people's welfare will do serious damage to our own well-being and the whole human agenda, i.e. the agenda of creating a meaningful world and meaningful lives for all of us.

Let's take a look at each of these:

1. To make life more satisfying and fulfilling for everyone involved in organisations and businesses, including ourselves

This can be quite problematic because satisfying lives are not seen as core to organisations and businesses and to what they are about. Happiness is seen as being for the birds...and maybe the bees! It certainly is not for business. Sure, you can believe it is valuable and good if happiness and well-being can be achieved at and through work, but happiness and well-being are not seen as really essential or part-and-parcel of what we are about in organisations and businesses. After all, 'Business is business!' Nothing more and nothing less.

I always find this attitude amusing. What we are really saying is that we want to be successful but not necessarily happy. We might make a few people happy, if possible, and if it happens, well and good. But we certainly don't aim to make everyone happy, or even the vast majority of people who work with or for us. If we do manage to make them happy, it's a by-product, incidental.

I guarantee you that if you ask businesspeople if they would prefer to be successful or happy, a huge number would go for the former – to be successful.

In other words, people are saying, 'My happiness is secondary to my success.' And this attitude plays out in their actions.

Like what happened to Tracy Huston, clients often squirm a little when I propose including 'happiness' as a core objective or as another goal or value. It is as if the world of work belongs to a different realm, a realm without feeling, sanitised of emotions, cut off from the rest of our lives. We want to be successful, to grow, to become market leaders, to be profitable, and our happiness is incidental. What a price we are willing to pay to be 'successful'!

The good news is that we can achieve both success and happiness. And my purpose in this book is to show that this is possible.

'There's a man in my street...'

There is a danger that a lack of belief in the feasibility of achieving happiness at work could lead to us giving up on happiness as a goal in life in general and settling for an impoverished life. The Thank God it's Friday (TGIF) mentality, living for and during the weekends only, is very common and accepted. Work is work and has to be done and in many cases suffered. As a result, lives can get frittered away looking forward to weekends and vacations and even retirement, based on a mindset that work is not meant to be good or enjoyable. People spend no less than 50 per cent of their lives at work and to 'settle for' such a large percentage of life being unhappy or even 'just OK' is truly serious and sad.

I read recently that in some countries to smile at a stranger in the street can lead to being arrested for being drunk and disorderly. About a month ago, I was driving down the Fairyhouse Road in Ratoath in Ireland, where I live. It was mid- afternoon. As I drove, I noticed a man walking along the footpath, with a huge smile on his face, laughing to himself. I said to myself: 'He must be a bit odd or a little mad!' All around were very serious people, sporting frowns and really grim faces. Then it hit me – I had no difficulty accepting all the worried and very serious people but a person publicly displaying happiness and joy seemed very strange and odd to me. How sad!

It reminded me of a song by the Catalan singer, Joan Manuel Serrat, called 'There's a Man in My Street Who Has a Friend Who Says He Knows Someone Who One Day Was Happy.'[5] Serrat's song deals with this same tragedy that happiness is the exception or unusual, and is not to be expected.

I purport that happiness is not something exceptional and unusual, but it is the norm. Even more, I believe that work is actually the key to our happiness if it is handled and managed well.

2. To find new and better ways to manage businesses and organisations so that they are better and more successful

In order to find new and better ways to manage our businesses, we need to take a fundamental look at how we manage and organise our work. We are getting a lot of it wrong, since we do not design our organisations with people in mind. We design them for a specific function and based on mechanistic models. It is like designing a car to suit our engineering needs and then trying to get the driver to fit into it.

1.1. Shaping human beings to fit the organisational structure.

To continue the analogy, there are a few bad outcomes from this practice:

- It is most uncomfortable and not helpful or good for the driver.
- The car will not be well driven so we will ultimately get bad results.

A basic premise of this book is that the traditional concepts of manager and managing that we have become accustomed to and take for granted are fundamentally flawed.

When we take the human seriously and base our management structures, systems, philosophy and approaches on the truth of what it means to be a human being, we will end up with:

• A management approach that is helpful and good for people.

• A management approach that delivers the best results.

Our driver now feels better and will drive the car better.

1.2. Shaping organisations to fit with how human beings are.

3. Eliminating well-being and happiness from our list of goals will seriously impoverish our lives and those we manage

If we exclude our overall well-being and other people's happiness and welfare from our goals, then we are seriously impoverishing our lives and those of the people who look to us.

Far too often, doing what is good for the organisation or business, irrespective of whether it is good for society or for people, is accepted as part-and-parcel of doing business. Business is seen to have laws of its own and these are accepted as valid and beyond question. I recently heard a spokesperson for a UK tabloid newspaper defend her paper's right to probe into the private life of some football celebrity. When BBC's David Dimbleby questioned the appropriateness of this, she replied: 'Helloooooo! We're a business!' This answer was intended to dismiss the very basis for Dimbleby's question as if 'appropriateness' or the issue of what is right has no place in the world of business. The good of the organisation or business entity is seen as primordial and super-sedes any other. There is no shortage of examples of blinkered management in the interests of business only, without reference to the greater good.

Narrowly focused management – a smelly business!

In his book, *Voltaire's Bastards*,[6] John Rawlston Saul gives several examples of how industry and private business owners prevented the modernisation of the sanitary and sewage system in France. He describes how in the late seventeenth century, Paris was without a sanitary system – its streets were a gigantic latrine for five hundred thousand people. The terraces of the King's palace smelled so strongly that no one dared go onto them except to relieve themselves.

One hundred and fifty years later, in 1844, very little had changed. Six hundred thousand of the 912,000 residents of Paris lived in slums. At Montfaucon, in the north of the city, transport-ers of excrement, who had been collecting door-to-door during the night, dumped their loads into great swamps of the same matter. Men spent their lives living on these shores and wading out every day in search of small objects they might sell. At Lille, in the 1860s, in the working-class district of Saint-Sauveur, 95 per cent of the children died before the age of five.

The famed Paris sewer system was created over a long period in the second half of the nineteenth century. The long delays were largely due to the virulent opposition of the property owners, who did not want to pay to install sanitary piping in their buildings. These people, Rawlston says, were the New Right of their day. In 1900 the owners were still fighting against the obligations both to put their buildings on the public sewer system and to co-operate in the collection of garbage. In 1904, in the eleventh *arrondisse-ment*, a working-class district, only two thousand out of eleven thousand buildings had been piped into the sewer system. By 1910 little over half of the city's buildings were on the sewer system and only half of the cities in France had any sewers at all.

The free market opposed sanitation. The rich opposed it. Most of the educated opposed it. That was why it took a century to finish what could have been done in ten years. Put in contemporary terms, Rawlston Saul claims that the market economy angrily and persistently opposed clean public water, sanitation, garbage collection and improved public health because they appeared to be unprofitable enterprises which, in addition, put limits on their individual freedom. I say all this because an overly narrow version of the role or mission of companies as consisting of making profits or returns to shareholders is both damaging to the real mission and welfare of the company, and damaging to the efforts of all to manage and live in a more human way.

Just doing what I was told

There are many other extreme examples of what can happen when we regard human considerations as extraneous to the cause of organisations, and probably none are more striking than the awful crimes during the Holocaust. At his trial, the Nazi Adolf Eichmann explained his role in the Holocaust as an act of loyalty to the system and obedience to his superiors.[7] Gone was any consideration of the destruction of the human. The highest goal of his life, he said, was to serve his superiors.

Franz Stangl was the first head of Sobibor and then ran Treblinka. 'Of course thoughts came,' he said, 'but I forced them away. I made myself concentrate on work, work, and again work.' His assistant said: 'I think what he really cared about was to have the place run like clockwork.' And, despite all the awful things he saw and did, Stangl said the worst experience of all was waiting to hear how his superiors would respond on hearing there was a revolt in his Sobibor camp.[8]

Don't rock the boat

We don't need to go back so far or to such extreme situations to find examples of how business and putting loyalty to our organisations above everything else can lead to ordinary, 'good' people doing or allowing terrible things to happen. In the 1950s and 1960s, government officials in the US were given the task of overseeing occupational health and safety in uranium mines. However, critical environmental dangers to workers were ignored because certain officials and scientists went along with the general organisational drift of the institutions that paid their salaries. Scientists of the Atomic Energy Commission (AEC) kept virtually silent about the effects of radioactivity on workers in mines long after the dangers were known: 'We did not want to rock the boat... We had to take the position that we were neutral scientists trying to find out what the facts were, that we were not going to make any public announcements until the results of our scientific study were completed.' One US Public Health Service scientist admitted: 'By the late 1940s there was no question in anybody's mind that radiation in the mines was a real problem...But nobody in the AEC wanted to pay attention.'[9]

Sometimes we need not do very much to do a lot of harm.

Our failures as human beings are enormously conditioned by the circumstances and systems within which we operate. Dynamics still exist which allow us to murder our fellow human beings and to do other inhuman and cruel things to our fellow man. But, while I am aware of this issue and of its importance, my aim in this book is primarily not to question and analyse the overall ethics, values or morality of the world of business and the economic system in which we find ourselves, critical as they are. My aim is essentially constructive: It is to look at how we as managers can behave and manage in creative, human ways that are in stark contrast to the existing system. Every time we have a chance to behave in a good human way, and we take it, this will have a positive effect on the overall system, however great or small that may be.

4. Turning a blind eye to people's welfare will do serious damage to our own well-being and the whole human agenda

Every time we behave in this way, we are doing damage, serious damage, to ourselves. As we will see in a bit more detail in the next section, being human is not an arbitrary, take-it-or-leave-it, whatever-you're-having-yourself choice with only marginal consequences for ourselves and others. Our fundamental happiness as people depends absolutely on our ability to be true to our nature as people, as human beings.

A study of the behaviour of Rhesus monkeys involved an experiment in which six Rhesus monkeys were trained to pull on a variety of chains to get food. When they pulled on one chain, they got a big helping of their favourite food and if they pulled on another chain, they got a smaller helping of a less appetising food. Naturally, the monkeys very quickly learned to pull on the chain that gave them the large helpings of their favourite food.

After several weeks of this very satisfactory and rewarding experience, something happened. One monkey pulled on the 'good' chain and, at the same time he saw that another separate monkey in a different cage got a painful shock from a jolt of electricity. The other five monkeys saw this happen too and heard the shriek from the monkey who got the electric shock. They saw the effect on the poor monkey who grimaced and cowered in fear. What happened then? Well, four of the monkeys immediately stopped pulling on the 'good' chain that gave them the big helpings of their favourite food. They were prepared to settle for less and inferior food to avoid hurting another monkey that they did not 'know'. A fifth monkey stopped pulling on either chain for five days and a sixth stopped pulling for a whole twelve days. They starved themselves so that a monkey they did not know didn't suffer![10]

The roots of our humanity and goodness also go very deep. We cannot turn a blind eye to them. Unfortunately, other so-called 'goods', such as the success of the organisation, or a too narrow version of success, can override these very basic instincts in us. They can be regarded as not relevant to business or, while important, have to be sacrificed for the so-called good of the business. 'I know it's tough but business is business' – such mantras can be used to override values and what is right. I hope to show in this book that there is no need to take such a stance and no real benefit to doing so.

But, true as all this may be, the feasibility of going after this new way of working may still not be clear, especially when times and economic conditions are tough.

Let's take a look at this and some other questions before looking at how we can manage to be human in work.

Chapter 2

My Uncle Pat and What Happened to Work

'When I work, I relax; doing nothing or entertaining
visitors makes me tired.'

– Pablo Picasso

Why get into all this...especially at this time?

At a time when it is estimated there will soon be one billion people
unemployed internationally, it would seem a luxury to begin talking of whether work is meaningful or not. The general sentiment
might be along the lines of 'Just let's get on with it. We have
things to do. Tough if people don't like it!'

One simple and clear reason why it is worthwhile exploring working in a human way is that, in fact, it will make a big contribution
to improving the *performance* of your company or organisation.
You will get many insights into what is really going on in your
company that will throw a lot of light on how your organisation is
being managed and led, hence helping you manage it even better.
Yes, insights. Have you ever been in a room or place where there
was no light? You feel your way around, you grope and you bang
against some things but you cope. But then, when the light is
switched on or daylight comes, you see everything in a very different light. It is the same room or same place but it is transformed
by the light. Now you *see* what you have been stumbling over or
banging against. I want to do the same for your organisation and
working life. I believe that many have been working in the dark
for a long time and I want to throw light on some of those hitherto
unclear or hidden-from-view areas.

You may already be spending a lot of effort and money on
developing your people and your organisation. The approach I am
putting forward will not only add to those efforts but will leverage

them to help you get even better results. It will also make it easier for you to get those improved results.

And, apart from making it better and easier, I want to make work more enjoyable and satisfying. As I already mentioned, we spend at least half of all our lives at work and we will fail ourselves and others if we don't take on the challenge of transforming work into something richer and more meaningful. Pie in the sky? Not at all! It's well within our grasp.

And it is for this reason also that I am connecting work with being human and with happiness, because I see it as a powerful and, indeed, critical vehicle to help us live happier and more fuflfilled lives. What I mean by this is that, not only is the improvement of management and work worth exploring because they are or can be problematic for people's happiness and fulfilment, but also because they offer unequalled opportunities for realising both of these. Management and work are powerful platforms for restoring meaning to centre stage in our world.

Is this not a little far-fetched?

The purpose of this book is to show how attainable this is. For now, do you know that there are many people for whom the word 'work' does not exist or has very different meanings from the negative one many of us give it?

My Uncle Pat worked all his life and yet never 'went to work'. In fact he never knew he was 'working' at all! My Uncle Pat was a farmer and I lived with him for a period in my life. Like many people then and now, he would never have described what he spent his time on as 'work'. It was simply his life, what he did from morning to night – getting up, milking cows, counting and looking after cattle, cutting and 'saving' hay, planting fields of turnips. It was all simply living. To ask him if he was *working* would have made no sense to him. Equally, to ask him if he enjoyed it would have been meaningless. It was simply life and a life that was, for him, full of meaning and fruits . I will come back to this later in the book but for now let's assume that it is possible to make work truly meaningful and to integrate it into the totality of our lives, because it was once the case, for Uncle Pat and many others.

The parable of the carpenter and the bank official

I have two neighbours who both go off to work at more or less the same time in the morning, albeit in different garb and vehicles. One is a bank official, the other a carpenter and cabinet maker.

They both arrive home in the evenings at different times but with the same sense of urgency and excitement. They both look forward to their evenings but for different reasons. The carpenter/cabinet maker is taking night classes in Business Management. The bank official is big into his hobby, which is woodwork, and he has his garage converted into a workshop where he spends every free hour he can get, often *working* to midnight and past it. Do you see? The question is why is it that the bank official can't wait to get home to his woodwork when his neighbour two doors away can't wait to get away from it? And the one who wants to get away from his day job is, in addition, getting *paid* for doing it! They are both doing the same thing, but one loves it and the other hates or tolerates it. OK, we can make the point that when a hobby becomes a day job, perhaps it loses all its interest, and so on. But the reasons for their different feelings go deeper, as we all know. Let's take a quick look at why this should be so before we get on to looking at what we need to do about it.

What's wrong?

What is the problem with work as we now have and see it? What's wrong that we need this kind of correction?

I do not want to go into a long history of work as that is not the purpose of this book, and it is more important to spend our time agreeing on how to change it and what we can get out of it rather than on analysing it. I do want to examine what we have done to work that has turned it from being simply part of what we do and who we are, as it was for my Uncle Pat, and something as enjoyable like a hobby, into a chore, as it has become for our carpenter/cabinet maker. And, more importantly, I want to put forward practical ways of correcting this situation. But for now, here are a few points that may help to clarify what has gone wrong and to point us in the right direction to correct it.

One company, many players

In work situations, and certainly in the more problematic ones, there are six main players: Owners, managers, customers, suppliers, employees/workers and society or the community. A major part of the problem arises from these six players becoming separated or fragmented because they each have their own goals, independent of the others' goals and needs. While what they are after could be called 'goals', all of these goals are underpinned by one thing – dissatisfaction.

Dissatisfaction is what most characterises each of these groups. Owners and shareholders can rarely, if ever, express satisfaction. There is always more to be gained – higher profits, better share value, increased dividends. Customer dissatisfaction is both real and fabricated. In some cases, customers' need for something new or better is real. Often it is created by companies who want to offer them new products. Customers are never allowed to feel satisfied. Suppliers can never be *seen* to be satisfied. Naturally they want better prices and stronger guarantees. Employees or workers never experience or feel real satisfaction for lots of reasons, which we will see later. And managers manage performance on the basis of an endless dissatisfaction with what is currently being achieved in the interests of pushing for even more – more output, more efficiency, more profits, better quality. This creates the wherewithal for infinite tension and unhappiness between all these conflicting and unsatisfied needs, and an environment of endless struggle and conflict.

A vacuum of shared meaning

Quite apart from the potential for conflict or lack of collaboration and harmony between the various parties, what dissatisfaction also produces is a lack of an overall shared meaning and a break-up of relationships between the parties. Each of these parties has a different version of what the company or entity is and what it means for them, and it is for these reasons that we need management to pull it all together and ensure things happen. In the absence of an overall meaning that all parties can identify with, management has to coordinate and manage the various parties and their different and conflicting needs. We will come back to this aspect of the management role later. For now, let us go back to my Uncle Pat. All six parties and interests came together in him. He was the owner. He was in direct contact with his customers who bought cattle and turnips from him and whom he knew personally. He bought his supplies and machinery from his local suppliers whom he also knew personally and whom he in turn supplied. Any labour he needed was either given voluntarily by neighbours or, if not, became an integral part of the farm and its endeavour. In a sense, the farm managed itself or drove itself. The needs of the farm were obvious to everyone and neighbours responded naturally. If rain looked likely, help descended on the fields to help him 'save' his recently cut and drying hay. When the enormous threshing machine came, in threshing time, it brought in its wake a host of help from surrounding farms and houses. The system virtually drove itself. A mere word or mention of rain, or 'hay down', or threshing was enough. Everyone understood, and shared the overall meaning of what it was all about.

Of course it is not possible to return to these times, and nor would we want to. But it is possible to recreate a similar sense of integration and meaning in our work and we will look at how to do this later, especially in Chapter 17. What has happened is that work and culture have become separated to the detriment of both. This comes from the emphasis on the individual at the expense of the communal. The latter, the communal, is merely a possible and occasional support for the former, the individual, who is primordial. It is all about me as an individual, as an isolated, independent and stand-alone individual. Until relatively recently, a person, like my Uncle Pat, was identified within the community with his work – not that he got his identity from it, but his persona and role in society was very much tied into the service he provided and the role he played in a community. In this way, work had a special meaning for people and had a value beyond the simply commercial return one got from it, important as this was too. But, over and above that, there were the notions of service and value in the context of the community that were integral to the work. Relationships and the human could not be separated from work. The butcher, the baker and the candlestick maker were part of a community, and the role they played and the service they provided were a critical part of the community to which they belonged. Neither had meaning without the other. Morality and ethics were, then, built into the work, as were motivation, meaning, commitment, quality and all the other concepts we are attempting to build back into work today. The absence of these qualities from work, as it is currently designed, puts a huge weight on organisations that have to replace the inherent meaning in my Uncle Pat's work with management. While it is not possible to go back to the past, we do have to be cognisant of what it is we are calling 'work' and what it is we are asking of people. This calls for innovative ways of building the human back into work and making the workplace or organisation some kind of community, replacing the previous geographical community. In a large part, this book deals with what this means and how it can work.

Help! We need some management around here! Or do we?

One of my favourite cartoonists, Gary Larson, has a cartoon of a cocktail party of sheep. The sheep are standing around chatting with cocktail glasses in their hands. There are sheep everywhere in great disorder. A dog is coming in the door and the caption on the cartoon has one sheep saying: 'Ah good. At last, here comes a border collie to put some order on things.' It is the absence and lack of integration and meaning that creates the need for managing and managers (and border collies), and restoring integration and meaning is the central focus of this book. Hierarchical structures take the place of integration and meaning as binding and driving forces. In other words, because work is broken up between all six aforementioned players and because it has only partial meaning for these players, especially for the employees who actually do the work, there is a need for someone or some mechanism to provide the organising and driving force to ensure things get done.

But reliance on this mechanism of management, institutions, and institutional and hierarchical power can block authentic human performance and behaviour. By institutions, I mean both state and business and other societal institutions. What happens is that we transfer the responsibility from ourselves for doing the right thing to an institution and, in so doing, remove the deepest and strongest force for good there is – our own conscience and sense of what is right, meaningful and makes sense. This happens easily and often goes unnoticed. The whole notion of being policed is the prime example of this, whereby I come to believe that I should not do certain things, not because they are unfair or stupid, but because they are against the law and I may be caught.

The existence of a body that is there to ensure people do the right thing means that people no longer feel the onus on themselves to do it. This pervades everything we do and may date from childhood when our parents established a set of rules, backed up by some form of authority, be it religious, legal, or whatever. From an early age we learn that the 'right thing' is something external, divorced from us. The muscles for thinking things through for ourselves and deciding what the right thing is are pretty weak and flabby by the time we reach adulthood.

Many work situations and organisations are built on this premise. People consciously and unconsciously do things, not because they make sense in themselves and are meaningful, but because management says so. This has become so accepted that we no longer even see anything wrong with it.

Uncle Pat's farm is an example of a form of cooperative living, where people did things because they made sense and the whole scheme of things worked on the basis of cooperation. Where there is a failure of cooperative living, such as that created by the existence of six separate parties in a company, huge weight is placed on other institutions to intervene and make up for this lack of common sense and commonly agreed codes of conduct. As a result, we put much more faith in institutions and institutional solutions and on hierarchical forms of power than in cooperative living. It is now inconceivable to leave people 'unmanaged', and, even if the manager is absent for short periods, temporary or acting managers step in. It is as if this takes the onus from us to behave properly and well, and so we don't. Gone are the days of verbal agreements and hand-spitting deals. People have learned the hard way that these do not work. Now no transaction can take place without the involvement of some institution or department, such as Human Resources, Government agencies, the Labour Court and trade unions.

The sacred institution

Every company and all management, like every institution, in theory at least, is oriented towards adding value to what is already there. They are there to help people do what they cannot do on their own. In this sense, all companies, like all institutions, are intended for the sake of people towards the welfare of people, the performance of people and the real freedom of people. Institutions come from human cooperation, are the result of human cooperation and are there to support human cooperation. Unfortunately, this is very far from the reality, where the institution becomes primordial and is to be protected at all costs, even at the cost of the greater good. Loyalty to the company or institution, irrespective of what it is doing or how it is doing it is what matters. The culture of cooperation gets replaced by power and authority, and cooperation is reduced to playing a minor part in how the whole thing works.

The view of institutions as limiting, as being a curtailment on people for the sake of some other good, can be held both by those running them and those working in them. This paradigm leads to all kinds of problems and falsity and to a negative attitude to work among employees, which is one of the main challenges I confront in this book. To go back to our parable, this is one reason why our carpenter friend lacks the love of his work that his neighbour, the bank official, has of the same work.

The managers of an institution or a company have a deeply felt suspicion that ultimately the interests of the business are not really in line with the interests of the people in the company. This often arises from the understanding that they have their jobs as managers or supervisors because people are in some way lacking and need managing; they need border collies to keep order and to perform well. Because of this, managers have a natural nervousness and mistrust of people and feel some guilt as a result. They are, in a sense, against people and not at the service of people. They believe they are at the service of the institution, whose goals may not be or not be seen to be in line with those of the people who therefore need managing. Because they hold this view and have these feelings, they then resort to activities to win commitment, maintain support, increase morale, share objectives, etc. This approach to managing, then, becomes a whole new language and level of dialogue. Layers of management get put in place, procedures, rules, practices, communications, etc, and relationships between people are conducted through these layers. Everything gets institutionalised to deal with a problem that should not be there in the first place, but which actually comes from guilt and inadequate thinking, and maybe from dishonesty around the goals of the organisation and how they benefit the people.

Commodification of everything and human resources

The significance of this is that we have turned the world and everyone in it into commodities to be used by us and bargained and exchanged. Houses are not homes; they're properties. People are not human beings; they are resources. Everything, including people and people's work, is seen and treated as a resource of little or no value until it gets turned into something else. Things and people are not valuable *per se* but simply as contributors to and components of something else, to be discarded when their use has been exhausted or worn out. This is creating an alienated world where nothing is of value but is only seen as either a part of something greater or as an item to be exchanged. Managers make this very clear when they say or infer, 'Your personal problems are of no interest to me', meaning that they are only interested in the result of the act or work and not in its value as a human act.

If we treat people like commodities then we will pay a huge price in terms of the riches we will lose, the damage we will do and the value we will waste. Being paid for work should not take from the real value of the human endeavour, the effort and creativity of the work. We must reawaken this awareness and have it at the forefront of our decisions, guiding us based on what is truly valuable. We must put people first at all times, as it is people who are behind all of our projects and enterprises. Putting people first, as we will see, does not mean that the goal of the enterprise is put in second place. There is no need for a dichotomy. We will deal with this later.

Getting out of this mess

To get out of this damaging approach to managing, we need to work for the integration of the needs of all six groups: Owners, employees, customers, suppliers, management and society. We need to refuse to sacrifice any one of these six..

I am tackling the issue at the level of management because here there is power to influence, change and improve things. As we will see, managers are very much in the middle or at the centre of the relationships between all six players and so are ideally positioned to take initiatives. I know they are often caught in a bind by virtue of being in the middle and feel powerless, but we will come back to this and to the great power they do have.

As well as that, I see managers as a group that has both needs and opportunities knocking at their door. A trillion dollar industry built on management training and development is testimony enough that some needs exist in this area. So much time and money is spent on training managers because of perceived needs or deficiencies. They do need attention.

The notion of management is a relatively new one. It is also one that does not operate in every area of society and life and, while there is much about it that needs to be changed and improved as we will see, there is a unique richness and power in the concept also that can be put to much greater use in virtually every aspect of life. We will be linking it to or identifying it with leadership, creativity and responsibility. We see how the management function has changed in the world of sport, where the role of former trainers or coaches has evolved into a much more comprehensive role of 'manager'. This new role of manager has taken on a much greater and wider responsibility for the overall performance and well-being of teams of all kinds. It is because the role of manager has the possibility of embracing so much responsibility that I believe it has the power to initiate a major change in bringing about a more human and more successful environment in companies; the kind of environment my Uncle Pat enjoyed without even knowing he was doing so. A more human environment.

The next chapter will deal with what we mean by 'more human'.

Chapter 3

What Do I Mean by the Word 'Human'?

'The true rebel is motivated by outrage against the diminishing of human life.'

– Albert Camus

British comedian Rowan Atkinson, in the series *Not the Nine O'Clock News*, used to talk of the blind man...in a dark room... looking for a black cat...that isn't there!

Looking for or trying to pin down what it means to be human may not be quite as difficult or as fruitless, but it does present its challenges.

According to the literary theorist and critic Terry Eagleton, toads know exactly how to behave in order to be toads. They simply do what toads do and follow their toad-like nature. So, being toads is not an achievement. Toads, Eagleton says, do not win medals for being toads. For us human beings, it is different. Whether we are lucky or unlucky, we have to work fairly hard to be full human beings and so we can indeed be congratulated when we make it, when we manage to act as human beings.[11]

If I am proposing to show in this book how we can 'manage to be human', then I need to explain what I mean by 'human'. More than that, I need to get some level of agreement with readers on what that word means, and an agreement that is soundly based on reason. No easy task! Virtually every book that has ever been written has either been an attempt to deal with what being human means or had some implication for our understanding of the notion of the human. I have no ambition to add significantly to that wisdom. Rather, I intend to select from it a range of insights and views on what being human means, which will, I hope, both engage and make sense to readers. Far from arguing a position here, I simply want to present my understanding of what being human means so that you, as the reader, will know what I mean by 'human' for the purpose of this book.

I present my understanding of the human within what many experience as an often 'inhuman' environment, that of the office and work. The reader's role in defining the human lies in both *exploring* and *testing* the various insights I offer on what being human at work means. By 'exploring' I mean looking for the meaning and validity in my arguments and extending these through your own thinking. You can then test the practical applications of what I am proposing.

Human?

If asked for examples of occasions when you behaved in 'a human way', I wonder what examples you would come up with. Would they be times when you behaved in a sympathetic way? When you had pity or compassion for someone? When you went with your feelings as much as your head? When you were soft? If you heard someone say that someone behaved in a human way, what would come to mind? If you heard someone saying that so-and-so was very 'human' in how they handled something, what would you assume they meant? That the person was very understanding? That, for example, they refused to apply the letter of the law when someone made a mistake or misbehaved in some work situation? That they made the effort to understand why a person had a bad absentee record rather than play things by the book?

I think these examples of 'being human' are valid, but they are far from giving a full understanding of what the words mean. To get closer to what I believe being human involves, I want to look at three different life situations:

1. Where we take some initiative to address a problematic situation.

2. Where we find ourselves trapped in some difficult situation.

3. Where it is an ordinary day-to-day situation.

1. Where we take some initiative to address a problematic situation

There are situations that cry out for a big response. Take, for example, apartheid. Now, we might say that Mandela, with his soft tones and warm smile, is a good example of what it means 'to be human'. But would we use the same word to describe his long fight against apartheid and against the regime supporting and promoting apartheid? And what of his involvement in the

3.1. Nelson Mandela © Getty Images (www.gettyimages.com).

formation in 1961 of a new specialised section of the liberation movement, Umkhonto we Sizwe, as an armed nucleus with a view to preparing for armed struggle? Would we offer this as an example of what being human means? We might admire Mandela's courageous and firm opposition to apartheid, but still not name it as an example of being human. Here in this book I *am* naming it as being so. I will be doing so by applying the criterion of authenticity, i.e. giving a truly authentic response to a particular situation. Who knows if this action of Mandela's was truly authentic or the best response in that situation? Mandela believed it was. At the Rivonia Trial, in 1961, he explained:

> At the beginning of June 1961, after long and anxious assessment of the South African situation, I and some colleagues came to the conclusion that as violence in this country was inevitable, it would be wrong and unrealistic for African leaders to continue preaching peace and non-violence at a time when the government met our peaceful demands with force.[12]

Mandela's strength, courage and confrontation in addressing a problematic and serious situation is an example of what being human means.

2. Where we find ourselves trapped in some difficult situation

Sometimes we can find ourselves in unpleasant and painful situations from which there is, for a time anyway, no escape. Viktor Frankl's situation is an example of this.

He spent three years in four different concentration camps in truly horrific circumstances. He tells how he was awoken one night by the groans of a fellow prisoner, who was throwing himself about in his sleep, obviously having a horrible nightmare. 'Since I had always been especially sorry for people who suffered from fearful dreams or deliria,' Frankl writes, 'I wanted to wake the poor man. Suddenly I drew back the hand which was ready to shake him, frightened at the thing I was about to do. At that moment, I became intensely conscious of the fact that no dream, no matter how horrible, could be as bad as the reality of the camp which surrounded us, and to which I was about to recall him.'[13]

3.2. Viktor Frankl © Getty Images (www.gettyimages.com).

'One thing I beg of you,' an older prisoner told him one day, 'shave daily, if at all possible, even if you have to use a piece of glass to do it. You will look younger and the scraping will make your cheeks look ruddier. If you want to stay alive, there is only one way: Look fit for work. If you even limp, because, let us say, you have a small blister on your heel, and an SS man spots this, he will wave you aside and the next day you are sure to be gassed.'[14]

Notwithstanding all this, Frankl shows that even in the most awful of circumstances a man can still lead a meaningful life. 'When a man finds that it is his destiny to suffer,' he writes, 'he will have to accept his suffering as his task; his single and unique task. He will have to acknowledge the fact that even in suffering he is unique and alone in the universe.... His unique opportunity lies in the way in which he bears his burden.'[15]

I am using Frankl's extreme story as an example to show how someone can behave in a creative and empowered way, a human way, in a situation of extreme suffering. Of course, most of us are not called to such depths of effort in our ordinary lives, but we all have our own particular challenging situations and, as Frankl says: 'No situation repeats itself, and every situation calls for a different response', and 'suffering, like a gas, completely fills the human soul and conscious mind, no matter whether the suffering is great or little.'

In any situation on any day we have a multiplicity of situations open to us, some good, some bad, some OK and some great. It is the quality of our response to a situation that I am linking to being human.

3. Where it is an ordinary day-to-day situation

Sometimes life just rattles along and there is nothing big on the horizon. It was like this in the 1950s in the Southern states of the US. At that time, the code of the capital city of Alabama, Montgomery, required that all public transportation be segregated. Drivers were required to provide separate but equal accommodations for white and black passengers by assigning seats. This was accomplished with a line drawn roughly in the middle of the bus separating white passengers in the front of the bus and African-American passengers in the back. When an African-American passenger boarded the bus, they had to get on at the front to pay their fare and then get off and re-board the bus at the back door. When the seats in the front of the bus filled up and more white passengers got on, the bus driver would ask black passengers to give up their seat.

On 1 December 1955, a bus which had some black passengers in their allocated space began to fill up and the driver noticed that there were several white passengers standing. He stopped the bus and moved the sign separating the two sections back one row and asked four black passengers to give up their seats. Three complied, but one, a woman called Rosa Parks, refused and remained seated. The driver demanded, 'Why don't you stand up?' to which Rosa replied, 'I don't think I should have to stand up.' The driver called the police and had her arrested. Later, she recalled that her refusal wasn't because she was physically tired, but that she was tired of giving in.[16]

The police charged Rosa with violation of Chapter 6, Section 11 of the Montgomery City code. That evening, a boycott of Montgomery buses commenced and the Civil Rights movement was under way.

3.3. Rosa Parks © Getty Images (www.gettyimages.com).

Rosa Parks found a different way to respond to her situation. Her refusal to give up her seat is an example of someone finding a creative response to a problematic situation, which is what it means to be human.

I am not saying that all our behaviour and responses to our daily situations need be as great as those of Mandela, Frankl and Parks. I am saying that we have many options open to us in terms of how we respond to challenges. In choosing the positive and active route, we are behaving as true human beings and, in the process, developing and fulfilling ourselves as real human beings. And, based on how good and truly human our actions and responses are, we will make a great difference to the world and those around us. No less importantly, we will achieve fulfilment, satisfaction and deep happiness for ourselves.

Is there a criterion for what is human?

How does one estimate what is human? What are the criteria or qualifications?

This is difficult to pin down, as it is difficult to explain why we find a particular painting beautiful or a Mozart piano concerto so wonderful, or why a lily can take our breath away. But it is really as simple and clear as that – we know deep down and have no doubt why we love Mozart and lilies and so, too, we know and have no doubt about what being truly human means and why it feels and is so good. It is right. It is appropriate. It is filling and fulfilling.

The criterion I am putting forward for behaving in a human way is that, for each situation in which we find ourselves, we act in a way that respects the truth of the reality and respects ourselves and our own calling as human beings. So it is about being true – true to the reality of a particular situation and true to ourselves. This is relatively easy in many situations of our lives. Imagine that a friend has had an accident and is in hospital. You have a few options:

1. Drop what you are doing and go and see the friend. The situation is calling for an act of unselfishness or generosity on your part and you respond to that reality in an authentic or true way. Equally, you feel good about what you are doing because it is in line with your own nature and desire to be good, attentive and responsive.

2. You are very busy and can't really find the time to visit your friend. You decide that you will call to see them when they come home and you phone and leave a message for them. This is a different kind of response, which is still attentive and is the best you can do at the time.

3. You might feel very sorry for your friend, visit them and offer to take the friend to your house to help them convalesce.

4. You could go further still and go and see them, offer to look after them when they come out of the hospital and also offer to pay for their hospital bills or for additional and expensive treatment because they have no medical insurance.

All of these different responses are to the one situation. I am not saying that any one of them is wrong or that any one is worse than the others. I am saying that there is a difference in the quality of the responses and I am naming that quality of response – being human. Without turning life into a tortuously scrupulous examination of conscience at every turn, we do have the option and the opportunity in every given situation to respond in a variety of ways, some better and more human than others.

Being human and being happy

Even though managing to be human in different situations does feel good, that is not what it is really about. Happiness and being fully human are not synonymous. There is more to being human than being happy. There is and has to be a better criterion or touchstone for being really human.

3.4. George Best © Getty Images (www.gettyimages.com).

We are all familiar with George Best's story of the hotel waiter who, on finding him in his hotel room in bed with Miss World and downing caviar and Champagne, asked: 'Where did it all go wrong, George?' Best told the story as a joke against the poor hotel waiter who, according to Best, was missing the point of what was actually going on, i.e. that, far from anything having gone wrong, he was having a great time and was just enjoying life. In fact, it was Best who was missing the point because the point was not and never is just about having a good time. Yes, he may have been enjoying himself but enjoyment is not all we are about and for and, in reneging on his real calling and innate skills as a footballer, he was failing to be truly himself. He was failing to be the full person he could have been, failing to be fully human as

George Best. Fulfilment or being truly human is more important or fundamental than being happy or having a good time.

We are so accustomed to aiming for goals in life that we see everything, including being human, as a means to an end. But there is no reward for being virtuous apart from that, in itself, it fulfils our nature. Aristotle saw acting well and being well as a reward in itself. Sometimes, acting well, behaving well and being human may even bring unhappiness, but it also brings fulfilment. Robert Frost said, 'All great things are done for their own sake.'

Jack Houlahan, in his book *A Ghost in Daylight*,[17] sees addiction as a flawed attempt to find fulfilment because it is a flight from life as an ongoing and vain struggle or effort to find meaning. A struggle may be required for us to be really human. A child could decide not to bother getting off their all-fours because it is comfortable and safe where they are, and standing up and walking is fraught with hazards, bumps, falls and pain. But the avoidance of pain is not the answer, and the absence of pain is not the sole indication as to how we are doing. Helping our children to grow in every sense may actually involve them experiencing some miseries. It is wrong to always agonise over tribulations that befall those close to us and to try to shelter them from all such experiences. Our role, as parents, etc., is not to protect others and shelter them from pain, but to help them to grow as human beings. As managers, as we shall see below, we have a similar obligation.

So far so good, but there is more. We have to be careful of providing too narrow a definition of what being fulfilled, being happy, being human is. It is impossible to arrive at a version of what is truly human unless we take into account the species, the totality of human beings, our world and not just what is good for me or for one person. Since we are relational beings, nothing can be good or meaningful in isolation from the whole, and so being human equally means being true to the greater-than-I at all times. This too could seem like a brake on what we want to do, on our happiness, but it is actually the opposite. We become part of something greater and thereby gain more freedom to experiment with and be ourselves; Margaret Wheatley says that 'I want to surrender my care of the universe and become a participating member...in an organization that moves gracefully with its environment, trusting in the unfolding dance of order.'[18] I don't want to stray into the larger issue of how human or inhuman the social systems are, of which individual organisations are a part. However, we will find neither true happiness nor fulfilment as human beings if how we think, what we do and how we are do not contribute to the greater good.

Eckhart Tolle says that 'sin originally meant to miss the mark rather than do wrong things.'[19] So when we fail to do what is right and best in any given situation, it is a sin in the sense that we are missing the mark of what is really best for us. In this book I try to show how we can be true to ourselves, and how we can be 'on the mark' in work and business situations.

In this book, I use the word 'human' in the sense of 'being on the mark' or hitting a true note. We do this when we behave in ways that best allow us to flourish as individuals and as people in society. We succeed in doing this when we are able to find truly good and creative responses to or ways of behaving in whatever situation we find ourselves.

I want to turn to the subject of creativity now in terms of describing how we can be human in the context of work and organisations.

Section II – Creativity

Chapter 4

Creativity – What Makes Us Human

'The uncreative mind can spot wrong answers, but
it takes a creative mind to spot wrong questions!'

– Anthony Jay

Creativity is often understood to refer to the arts. It is frequently
seen as belonging to leisure and what is peripheral, and not as
a core aspect of how we live our lives. It can be seen as a luxury,
something to take away the drudgery of daily life. Because it gets
identified with and is seen as belonging to the arts, fun and adventure, it is not seen as being part of real day-to-day living and is
certainly not seen as an *essential* element in how we live our lives.

Here I am going to spend some time going over why I believe
creativity is critical to our lives, our happiness and welfare, *and*
why it is the single most important element in how we manage our
organisations and companies. I am using the word to refer to and
capture a whole variety of attitudes, behaviours, practices and
philosophies that are at the heart of everything we do in companies and in our daily lives. I hope to persuade you that paying
attention to this aspect of how you manage will reap more benefits
for you than any other. In the context of being more successful
overall, I cannot think of anywhere better to focus than on your
creativity. I cannot think of a better question to ask yourself than:
'How creative am I being in how I am handling my situation, 'my'
people and my company?' As we will see, how well you and the
people you manage handle the situations that you encounter will
rest ultimately on how creative you are.

I hope that the various topics I cover under creativity are all
useful and of interest to you. As well as insights, I will also cover
some guidelines. Towards the end of this section on creativity I

will offer some practical processes you can use to help you work and lead in a more creative way.

Born to be human – born to be creative

If we want our organisations to be successful and great places to work then we must have our people operating as full human beings. When they are, both goals are achieved, *and* people will experience fulfilment and will enjoy their work.

Creativity is of the essence of what it means to be human. It is to be identified with what most makes us human. We humans are the point where the universe emerges into reflective consciousness. Every positive thing we do, every decision we take is to a greater or lesser degree a creative act – our unique contribution to the evolutionary process. We are truly human to the extent that what we do and the decisions we take are genuinely creative, enhancing our own and others' lives. Creativity is about what enhances life. We were born for this, for endless searching, reaching and growth. As human beings, we are, by nature, agents of change and betterment. This is our vocation.

A hand-axe was discovered in the Olduvai Gorge in Kenya that is reckoned to be over a million and a half years old. That far back humans began to shape our world. But we don't want to shape our world any old way. We want it to be beautiful. The Acheulian axe had qualities and workings way beyond practicality. It was made with a craft, symmetry and elegance that speaks of real

4.1. Acheulian hand axe (150,000 years to 1.5 millions years ago).

pride in creation. And this was not confined to Kenya, as similarly designed tools from the same era were found all over Africa, the Middle East and Southern Europe.

We continue this heritage today. Creativity is simply the endeavour to follow this example of our ancestors of a million and a half years ago to continuously shape our world. By shaping my world I am, at the same time, shaping myself. We know this from the ordinary ventures we take on, from building a house to planting a garden. Building a house or planting a garden can change the world and make it better. This is essentially what all our work is about or should be about – changing our world. But we, too, are changed and made better in the process, despite the blisters and calluses.

But what *is* creativity?

In this section of the book, I offer ideas on creative processes, creative systems, how to unlock creativity and other aspects of what I believe is required to develop a truly creative organisation and culture. As we have seen already, creativity can mean many things and the danger exists that what I cover in the following sections might appear a flimsy and superficial version of creativity. To counter that, I would like to list eleven principles that show what I mean by the word creativity, when I use it in this book:

1. Creativity arises from an understood dissatisfaction with how things are, compared to how they could be and should be. It consists of attempts to express in different ways the truth and beauty of the universe, whether that is through describing how it is or can be, or in calling attention to the deficiencies in current attempts at shaping our world and lives.

2. Many creative people – writers, painters and musicians – express in their works an unhappiness with some thing or event or with how things are. Such an attitude can appear negative. While the plays of Eugene O'Neill or Arthur Miller might appear negative, they are not. In a sense they are displaying a real unhappiness with how things are compared to how they believe they should and can be. By focusing on what is wrong, and naming and identifying it, they draw our attention to how it could be right. In this sense, far from being depressing, they are inspirational and empowering. This unhappiness with how things are in the world is important because it is a refusal to just go along with

or accept how things are. In this sense, creativity is a hunger for something better and a refusal to settle for what is seen as being 'good enough'.

At work, the human can yearn for something which he or she knows is missing. Often when someone points out things that are wrong in a work situation, it can often be misinterpreted as negativity. But it is critical to the improvement of companies and organisations that people do this, and we will come back to this later on in the course of the book.

3. Creativity is about seeing the beauty and potential in things that is there to be revealed and released.

    Creative people have the ability to see the hidden but real beauty in all kinds of things and want to give expression to that beauty. Michelangelo could see the angel already in the stone he was going to work on, wanting to be released, to be given form. A painter can see an object, scene or situation and see a beauty in it that we can't see. This does not have to be something beautiful, as we can see from Picasso's *Guernica* or Goya's *The Third of May*. But they have the ability to find and express what is already there and make it real and true for us.

    We will see how this works in organisations through managers and leaders doing the same thing by creating and sharing powerful visions with their people.

4. Creativity is about seeing things in fresh and more accurate or more comprehensive ways, without the limitations of language, habits, comforts or fear.

    As I have said, we see strong links between creativity and the arts and justifiably so. To some extent, all the arts express something through different media – painting, music, poetry, etc. – which cannot be expressed as well in any other way. What an artist expresses lies to some extent outside the boundaries imposed by normal day-to-day language and conventions. Shakespeare could have made a list of the key points he wanted to make in *Hamlet*, but what he wanted to say could not be captured in a list of points, or even straightforward theoretical prose. Creativity is about making the ordinary look extraordinary, which, in essence, it is. In this sense, creativity is questioning, stretching or breaking out of the normal boundaries we impose and live within.

    We will see how creativity in work and in organisations calls for the same ability to escape from existing constraints of habit, custom, routine and comforts; how the new idea or concept equally does not fit within existing frames of reference and so can run the risk of being rejected as not making sense.

5. Creativity is part of our nature, part of the whole evolutionary process. Our evolutionary creativity as human beings is not based on instinct and so we do have the choice to either opt out of it or to play an enormously cooperative part in the whole process.

    I was made to feel a little guilty recently, probably of my own doing, when my wife bought herself, or 'treated herself' as she said, to an orchid. It was around St Valentine's day but I am sure she had no hidden motives in asking me to take a long look at the beauty of the flower. It was incredibly beautiful, even through the eyes of a guilty partner: The silk-like delicacy of the leaves, the seemingly careless structure of the growth, the uniqueness of each part of the little flower. A miracle of beauty, one could say. But this is only one small example of millions of other miracles happening every day around the world as the evolutionary process continues its inexorable way.

    We are part of that evolutionary process and we have a choice as to how and whether we play our part. The same spirit of life that is present in the evolutionary part of nature is at work in us too. We have the added advantage and thrill compared to other creatures of being able to reflect on and admire our work and that of others. We can also, by virtue of our enormous power as human beings, play a unique part in this whole evolutionary process.

6. Creativity consists in responding to the truth, meaning and beauty of the universe, or of the particular reality which we find ourselves facing, a beauty which is always there to be seen, discovered, released and developed.

    When we are creative we are acting in tune with the deepest truth of the universe, which is aching to be expressed and finds that expression through us. It is a beauty or truth that is there to be discovered or brought into relief and reality. This means that we will find it everywhere we look. If this is valid, it will give us the assurance and the confidence that we can find answers and truth in every situation.

    We will come back to this when we look at creative processes in work.

7. In this sense, it is our role, our vocation as human beings in the world, to be creative and play our part in co-creating the world with everyone and everything else.

This is a constant theme in both the Old and New Testament in the Bible – that we are called to take part in God's creation. It is probably for this reason that nothing gives us the deep satisfaction that creative work does. We feel as if we are being really true to ourselves, as part of something greater. Eckhart Tolle says that being truly present and aware as part of the overall and underlying consciousness is what we are about. He says that this in itself is what matters, even more than what our creativity produces.[20]

8. Creativity involves difference.

    The ability to hear the different opinions of others, and to hold different opinions to others, is a sure path to reaching a bigger and deeper truth beyond all and any one of those opinions. We will come back to this later and show how it works so well in the organisation and business context. We each have a unique perspective on things and on the world. We often take that perspective to be the only one. When we are able to hear other perspectives and use them to enrich our own then we find that our own perspectives, far from being dismissed or lost, have been actually endorsed and enriched. The wonderful secret is that, instead of a single opinion or 'truth' prevailing, one gets to a truth that embraces and goes beyond all the other versions. We will look at techniques for working in this way in a work situation.

9. Creativity is present in our approach to problems. Problems are our friends. We can live and feed off problems and use them as pointers to what needs attention and is not yet perfect but is asking to be made perfect or helped to perfection.

    It is natural to dislike and avoid problems. Sometimes we can't avoid them. When this happens, we can bemoan our situation, blame whomever or whatever caused the problem, or life in general. Or we can just solve the problem. Alternatively, we can use the problem as a pointer to something more fundamental that needs addressing. Nature, again, is replete with examples of this dynamic, where creatures encounter problems and, over time, develop the wherewithal to overcome those problems. My cat developed its uncanny speed and endless patience from years of failure in hunting. Its beautiful, if deadly, skills only got honed from the problems the speed of other creatures gave it. We will come back and look at how this key dynamic works in business development.

10. Creativity is about looking for the oneness in all things and in all of us. It is about enjoying harmony, and, dare I say it, love.

    Could this be it? That creativity is all about love? A desire for oneness, for connections, for unity?

    We will look later at how creative working is such a marvellous way to build teams and develop team working.

11. Creativity consists in finding a truly human and powerful response to any situation in which we find ourselves.

    We referred to this earlier in the examples of people who, in very different and trying situations, managed to live truly meaningful lives. At the outset of this section, I said that I was not referring to creativity as a luxury or as being confined to the arts. This is core because every day in every situation we have the opportunity to be creative and find a truly creative response, one that does justice to the reality in front of us and to ourselves as human beings.

These are my principles and truths about creativity. Let's now take a look at what they mean in practice and how to put them to good use.

Making the most of our situations

Living our lives is about dealing with situations in life, the realities in which we find ourselves. We tend to talk of our lives as being governed by these situations. We talk of fortunes or misfortunes that befall people. People lose money or win lotteries, get promotions or lose jobs. The implication is that it is the situation, the so-called 'reality', that is what really matters. But I wonder. On the programmes I run in companies, I often ask groups to imagine if we assembled all the people in the world and drew a line down the middle and said: 'Happy people on this side and unhappy people on this other side.' I believe that we would find exactly the same kinds of people on both sides: Rich and poor, young and old, black and white, sick and healthy. The message is that it is not the actual situation that makes the difference as to whether we are happy or not but how we handle the situation. Graphically it looks a bit like figure 4.2. It is the arrows that really matter – how we handle what comes our way.

    The quality of our response to any situation I am calling creativity. There can be a wide spectrum of responses and these will vary in quality and effect, and I am using 'creativity' to describe

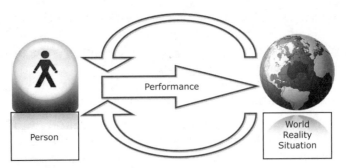

4.2. How you handle situations is what matters.

the quality of those responses – the more creative they are and we are, the better the outcome will be. In that sense, the invitation to be truly human is an invitation to be creative, to respond in a really good and powerful way. It is the wonderful role of the manager to not only find truly creative responses to situations, but to help others find equally powerful and creative responses.

When we do this, everything changes. Going back to the model, yes, the arrows change in the sense that, irrespective of the actual situation, we can handle it in a good way (cf Viktor Frankl above). But, quite apart from not having our happiness or well-being dependent on the outcome of some situation, we become empowered to see and handle the situation in a better way. So the world or situation changes in our perspective too! And we, by virtue of doing all this, feel different and see ourselves differently, i.e. as more powerful and resourceful, and so *we* change too. It is this change, this piece of magic or this miracle that we want to be able to bring off by being more creative. And it is this change, this enormous and empowering change that we achieve when we manage to be human, when we help others to get in touch with and remain faithful to the enormous infinite power of their humanity.

This may sound grandiose but, believe me, it is true. Take a look at where you are today in your company. You may take it for granted but, just for a moment, think of the initial idea someone had to begin that venture. And think of the many other decisions along the way, many of them courageous and creative, that have led to establishing the organisation to which you belong today. All of these people operated with creativity, which is the capacity to shape the future. The future depends on how we act and, indeed, *if* we act. Because of this, creativity needs to be operative all of the time, and in all we do, for the world to be developed and bettered, and for us to develop and be better.

Maybe take a minute to think of your life and what you are doing in your work. Think about how thinking and working in a creative way would apply in your case.

Find out why this is important and what contribution it is making. Deepen or broaden this with some more questions like: 'And why is that important?' 'And why is *that* important?' and so on.

For example: 'I manage a call centre.'

And why is that *important?*
'Because it ensures that people who call in get good service.'

And why is that *important?*
'Because it means that people are more satisfied and our company is seen to be a good company.'

And why is that *important?*
'Because it is good to make people happy and to have a successful company.'

This self-analysis should lead to two things:

1. A greater sense of the importance of what you do and how you can make a difference in the context of work.
2. A greater awareness of how you can make a difference at other levels and in all kinds of ways.

To repeat: You will be successful as a manager or leader depending on how creative your own responses, and those of your team, are to your given situation. And being creative is not something disconnected to how we run our organisations. It is central to it.

Chapter 5

Creativity – A Luxury, or Key to All We Do at Work?

> 'When men carry the same ideals in their hearts,
> nothing can isolate them.'
>
> – Fidel Castro

I first became formally involved in creativity as a topic and theme some twenty-five years ago. In that time, especially in the early days, when I told people I was about 'creativity', eyes would glaze over and I would hear comments like, 'How interesting....I see!' before the conversation moved on to some other more practical, relevant and important topic. Creativity might have a part to play in business but that part was mostly confined to Research and Development, and some areas of Marketing. Things have changed since those days, but it is still important to be clear why exactly we are talking about creativity in the context of work. What has creativity to do with the ordinary day-to-day issues and challenges we all face at work? Just how practical and useful is it to you in terms of what you do and how you manage your company and your people? Is it something nice to have or something critical to your business and company?

To find out, let's check out what *are* the critical or core elements in your company, and in *any* company, and then we will see how creativity fits with and contributes to them.

Would you agree that, for your company, and indeed any company, to be successful, it is important that:

1. There is *real leadership* and a move from just managing to leading.

2. People in the company really *want to work*.

3. There is a *sense of freedom* and people feel a sense of autonomy and ownership.

4. Your organisation is *live, vibrant and dynamic.*

5. You and your organisation can *handle* and indeed *welcome change.*

6. Your company is constantly *beginning new projects* and enjoys a spirit and practice of *continuous improvement.*

7. High performance is achieved through real *empowerment* of people.

8. *Good decisions* are taken and with the good will and cooperation of those involved.

9. *Collaboration* rather than *conflict* is the dominant culture.

Assuming that all, or at least some, of these elements are key to the success and welfare of your company, let's look at each of these and see the part creativity plays in them.

1. Creativity – the key to leading versus managing

'Managers do things right. Leaders do the right things.' This quotation is not meant to be a criticism of managers or managing, but it does describe neatly for me where the difference in focus between the two lies. By 'right' in the case of the manager, I mean ensuring that procedures and operating principles are adhered to and that things go smoothly and as close to plan as possible, and, when they don't, that they are put 'right'. By 'right things' in the case of the leader, I mean the things that will take the company and business forward to new levels of performance. The difference between leaders and managers is covered later in Chapter 15, but the key point to make here is that it is creativity that marks the difference between the two. Leaders are interested in what *can* be and what they *want* to be. This is what creativity is – a refusal to settle for things as they are, a belief in things being better and a brave commitment to work to make them so. This calls for a special way of thinking, seeing the world and, thus, acting. It calls for a creative mentality, creative skills and creative systems and structures. It is the manager who makes things happen and, in the process, becomes a leader. This shift is both subtle and enormous. It is a shift in thinking, in influencing, in organising. Above all, it is a shift in beliefs. Being creative and working in a creative way is dependent on how we see the world, how we see others and how we see ourselves.

I reflected on this one night when I was having a meal in a restaurant in the Plaza Oriente in Madrid. I looked at the manager of the restaurant and imagined that his role was to ensure that everything went well each day and that customers were satisfied with their food and service. A 'leader' in the restaurant, while naturally wanting that to happen, would also wonder and think of and plan ways to make the restaurant even better – offering new menus, presenting a different image, growing, expanding, and so on. We will come back to this restaurant later in the book.

Being a leader means seeing the world as fluid, full of energy and full of possibility. This means leaders see the world as a place where anything can happen and does happen. It means seeing the world as inviting and waiting for our contribution to continue to make it, to create it, to develop it. It is a world full of excitement and change. There is no proof that the world is like this, but it is the mark of every leader – and every artist – that they *believe* it is. So, irrespective of the area managers work in or what responsibility they have, they are leaders by virtue of their commitment to making their area of responsibility better and taking it to new levels of performance and service. Maintaining what is already in place, while important, takes second place to the drive to constantly seek and pursue betterment.

This means seeing others in a special way too – as people who are full of potential that is waiting to be released and put to use. Our potential can get hidden and blocked by our own beliefs and prejudices. Here are some very common ways in which we disempower and block ourselves:

1. Fear – of making mistakes or getting outside our comfort zones.

2. Lack of self-belief and confidence in ourselves.

3. Inadequate skills level and knowledge.

4. Lack of focus on what we really want.

5. Blaming others, the organisation, our manager, etc. for things going wrong.

6. Not spotting or taking opportunities that arise.

7. Poor relationships and turf wars that distract us and waste energy.

8. Lack of real desire and clear goals.

9. Failure to take responsibility for things.

10. Becoming trapped in a narrow world view of what is really possible.

Do you identify with any of these? We will revisit them again when we talk about performance in more detail.

The role of the manager as leader is to help people to identify these blocks to creativity in themselves and to also spot them in their people and take the necessary action.

All ten of these points are dealt with when a manager works and behaves like a leader, in particular by respecting the five principles for high performance as represented by the COACH mnemonic (see Chapter 13). We can discover them through the Performance Development System which we will look at in Chapter 19.

Finally, leading and being a leader will depend on how we see ourselves. It is not enough to see the world and others in a different light; we also have to see ourselves in a new way. This comes back to what Mandela allegedly quoted in his inaugural presidential speech about not playing small, but which was originally said by Marianne Williamson:

> It's our light, not our darkness that most frightens us. We ask ourselves: Who am I to be brilliant, gorgeous, talented and fabulous? Actually, who are you not to be – you are a child of God. Your playing small doesn't serve the world. There's nothing enlightening about shrinking so that other people won't feel insecure around you.

For some, behaving like this comes easy. Some *seem* to be natural leaders, born leaders. Rarely is this so. Virtually always, leaders come to see themselves in a particular way because of the experiences they have had and how they responded to them. Often it was the people around them who 'made' them the way they are, who pushed or encouraged them to be leaders.

The converse is also true. We see ourselves negatively by how we respond to our own situations and by how others see us. But this is not something fixed. We can change it and can come to see ourselves in a new way, a new light. This we can do, not by psyching ourselves up to be what we don't really believe we are, but by staying faithful to the reality and challenges in front of us and responding to them as well as we can. With every step and authentic response, we grow to become who we really are.

Creativity is, then, the key which allows us to switch and move from being managers to being leaders and in the process being more human and more ourselves.

2. Creativity – the key to getting people to *want* to work

All kinds of ruses and approaches are used to get people to work and want to work. Thousands of books have been written on motivation and you have probably read many of them. The simplest approach, however, *and* the most powerful one is to invite them to use their creativity, that quality, as we have seen, which makes them most human and most excites them. This is easy to do. We simply share our problems, challenges and opportunities with them. If this keeps *us* working long hours and thinking and talking endlessly about work issues, why will it not work for everyone?

People love a challenge because they are made for challenges. I heard a man recently talk on the radio about how, when his business collapsed, he went into deep depression. One day he found himself in his car a few inches from a pier and an image of his children stopped him from ending his life. He then told how a friend one day asked him to climb a small nearby mountain or hill. And he did. That challenge commenced his recovery, that little challenge that he faced and overcame. He subsequently climbed Mount Everest and now has five new businesses.

Giving people challenges is so easy to do. We are surrounded by challenges and problems and exciting opportunities. People spend time away from work enjoying artificial challenges such as three-mile races in athletics. At work we have real challenges and some of us don't use them. Some managers can take all the burden on themselves, not just because they are so good and responsible, but because they enjoy the power, the sense of achievement, the ownership and responsibility, and the challenge. But, in the process, they reduce others to playing minor roles, making them feel bored and unimportant.

We can get people to want to work by running our companies in a truly creative and challenging way. We can invite all to help us to identify and take on the issues and problems that arise, and we can invite all to be alert and awake to all the options that surround us. Doing this calls for a different approach to how we structure our businesses and organise our work as well as creating a new version of our role as managers.

It always intrigues me that people can get so excited at weekends by trying to put a small ball into a hole on a green patch of grass, or a slightly larger ball over a net and an even larger one into a basket or between two goalposts. There is no real value being added or any substantial merit in achieving any of these. A self-enforced challenge or target has been met but the world is not a better place because I beat a friend in a game of golf or tennis, enjoyable and valuable as this is in its own way. What these activities have in common is that they fabricate a challenge or competition. Compare this to the enormous value being added by these same people during the five days of the working week, be that in products, in services or in improvements to the system and the organisation. But the reason why many people do not enjoy doing this even though their very livelihood depends on it is that the challenge and competition have been removed and covered over or eclipsed by a bureaucratic system based on hierarchical power. Or it gets eclipsed by the money factor whereby they do it for the money and not for the inherent merit in the thing itself. People get removed and sheltered from the reality of the business, from the real challenge. I am often amused to hear managers, in the midst of a long moan about something their workforce are or are not doing, say: 'Mind you, when we were under pressure some years ago, they were great and did whatever was required to get the show back on the road.' Why was this the case? Because there was a raw challenge, a real and perceived need and people responded with all they had. But, as soon as the crisis passed, things returned to normal and people went back to 'doing their jobs'.

I am not suggesting that we fabricate challenges at work just for the sake of it, which is what we actually do in the world of sport, but that we reveal and expose people to the real challenges and the actual competition that is fully present and part of work in every situation. This is quite easily done. But we need to change how we organise work and give people true responsibility and ownership for what they do and trust them to do it, rather than supervising and managing all challenges and responsibilities. This involves nothing less than creative work, creative thinking and creative responses. The essence of creativity, as we have seen, is seeing a real need and using all our resources to find and give the very best response.

3. Creativity – the key to freedom and autonomous working

To respond well to our particular situations we need to be free to do so, truly free. If we or our people are not free, then we will not really achieve much for ourselves or in general. Creativity and freedom go hand-in-hand. If we are not creative then we are limited, constrained and not free, not able to do the things we really want to do. A person locked up in prison is deprived of certain freedoms, but a person locked up in a prison of his or her own mind is also deprived. Having limiting thoughts, low self-appreciation and restricted views of what can be done in certain situations are all examples of such imprisonment. The more creative we are, on the other hand, the more options we have and the more resources we have at our disposal. In that sense we are able to act out and live up to more of what we are as human beings in the world. People who are limited by routine thinking, addictive behaviours or narrow mindsets are in fact less free to be and do what they want and need.

Human beings can choose not to be free. Being free can be a burden and a challenge. It is full of risk and the unknown. Many people welcome their lack of freedom, be it as children, spouses or employees. It is a kind of relief not to have the responsibility of thinking for oneself, of choosing, of being wrong. This is a flight from life because in life there is no security or certainty. The very nature of life means that we are constantly in the unknown and this is not a comfortable place to be. It is much easier to abdicate one's freedom and responsibility and leave things to others to decide. This way one can't be wrong. But nor can one really live.

The cost of freedom is endless and the risks huge. Freedom means we are exposed to failure and rejection. I recall visiting Chile in 1991 following the return to democracy after the Pinochet dictatorship and asking people how the land reform programme had developed. Many years earlier, I had witnessed how the Christian Democrat Government of Eduardo Frei, and subsequently the socialist government of Salvador Allende, had purchased or taken land from the large landowners and distributed or sold it to the labourers who had worked the land for the great landowners. But when I enquired how the land reform had turned out I was told that in most cases the labourers had given the land back. I was shocked. When finally given their chance to own and farm their own land, why had they passed up on it? I was told that they preferred their earlier lives where they had had enough to live on, plenty of wine to drink and even marihuana to smoke – all of this without any burden of responsibility. They had settled for a so-called life of minimum responsibility and equally minimum freedom.

There is a risk involved in moving away from the familiar, irrespective of how bad that familiar may be. Freedom requires the courage to enter uncharted waters where there are few supports of any kind. Creativity requires effort to get away from 'more of the same' and the comfortable routine that this entails.

Sometimes the call to freedom comes in the guise of disaster or tragedy and life drags us kicking and screaming from stagnant situations of apparent ease and comfort back to real living. This is sometimes a price that we pay for not having faced up to the real problems that we knew were present but which we shrank from confronting.

Every time we invite and encourage our people to go after something new, to find a better way of doing things, to question and possibly dump some existing practice, to find a better approach to dealing with some issue, we are involving them in the process of making the world a better place. In this sense we give them more power and free them up to use more of their potential. People can get blocked, imprisoned and chained by their fears and low expectations. As managers, we have the ability and the responsibility to free people to be better and stronger. We can help people to become free of their fears and doubts and enable them to do things that will surprise themselves and others.

When we do this we create a more alive and vibrant organisation and this in turn generates more freedom and more vibrancy. Let us look at that now.

4. Creativity – key to the need to create live organisations... and live, vibrant people

> 'Billions of people show up for work every day, but way too many of them are sleepwalking.'
>
> – Gary Hamel

What a tragedy if so many people spend so much of their lives at work half asleep or going through the motions, looking forward to 5.00 p.m., the weekend, the next holiday or even retirement. Yet this is how many people live their lives. What is worse is that this is seen as normal, as being 'how life is', 'as good as it gets'.

It need not be so. We have so much scope to create vibrant, live organisations with vibrant, live people who passionately enjoy what they are doing.

I wonder how your organisation would fare if people took the Towers Perrin survey that Gary Hamel talks of?

How many in your organisation would agree with the following statements?

1. I really care about the future of my organisation.

2. I am proud to tell others I work for my organisation.

3. My job provides me with a sense of personal accomplishment.

4. I would recommend my organisation to a friend as a good place to work.

5. My organisation inspires me to do my best.

6. I understand how my unit/department contributes to the success of the organisation.

7. I understand how my role in the organisation is related to my organisation's overall goals, objectives and direction.

8. I am willing to put in a great deal of effort beyond what is normally expected to help my organisation succeed.

9. I am personally motivated to help my organisation succeed.

10. I can personally identify with the values and goals of the organisation and see an alignment between them and the rest of my life and my goals (my own!).[21]

Gary Hamel says that only 14 per cent of people around the world are highly engaged with their work and 24 per cent are disengaged. If this is true or even half true, it means there are a lot of people at work who don't want to be there, aren't happy when they are at work and so must be making a relatively poor contribution to their companies. Hamel says that 85 per cent of those at work are giving less of themselves than they could.[22]

This is so because, as we already said, we do not design our work to fit with how human beings really are. We try to twist and distort and bend and shape human beings to fit with the model of our organisation instead of shaping our organisation around how people really are, as we saw with the image of the car we looked at in the Introduction. After all, people have taken twelve billion years to become what they are and it is not easy to change their essential nature and their basic needs to suit some artificial model that we create.

This does not seem to worry managers in most companies and they appear to have no issue with the gap between the essential nature of human beings and the needs of the organisations in which they work. Their view is that people have to serve the organisation.

Hamel says that the challenge is to reinvent our management systems so they inspire human beings to bring all of their capabilities to work every day.

We pay a big price for not working hard and imaginatively to bridge the gap between what people need and should contribute, and what our organisations give them and require of them.

Hamel came up with a table of the most important human factors in high performance:

- Passion: 35 per cent
- Creativity: 25 per cent
- Initiative: 20 per cent
- Intellect: 15 per cent
- Diligence: 5 per cent
- Obedience: 0 per cent[23]

While you may not fully agree with this table of priorities, I bet that you can see that the top ones were present in moments when *you* performed really well. This is certainly true in my case.

What are the priorities in your company, in your area?

I will put forward new and more creative ways of managing, leading and designing our organisations to help you ensure your people are truly alive and vibrant in all they do.

5. Creativity – the key to handling change

It is a cliché that we live in a time of great change; there never was a time without great change, however perceptible or imperceptible that change was. However, it is important how we relate to change – how we create it and how we deal with it when it comes our way.

There are basically two very general approaches to change at different ends of a spectrum:

- Lead it and make it the norm, or

- React to it as a once-off or exceptional event.

Change will happen and is happening; it is only a question of how we handle it. We can engage and cooperate with it and 'enjoy the ride' or we can fear and resist it and try to sit it out. Like surfing on waves in an ocean, if we adopt the former attitude, it will be great fun and we will make great progress. But if we adopt the latter, we will be buffeted and battered and will possibly drown.

Whichever attitude we develop towards change will determine if it is seen and handled as a transformation process or seen and handled as a crisis.

This attitude will depend to a great extent on how the organisation is structured and managed. If it is managed in such a way that permanence and continuity are seen as the norm, then change will come as a shock and surprise, something that upsets our system and messes up our plans. Many organisations are structured and managed in this way where management roles are seen as maintaining and preserving what *is* rather than moving with life into ever new situations and circumstances. Working in this latter way requires a different type of organisation, an organisation that constantly seeks to renew itself, is in touch with its environment and is able to adjust and respond to it. This calls for special skills and philosophies that are not the usual ones that managers are expected to possess. It calls for a new version of the role of manager as change agent and leader. For this reason, creativity is a core skill for managers, and not something additional or optional. The role of a manager is to make change happen and to live change.

The change programme

In some companies there are formal change programmes. Some years ago I worked on a large change programme with an oil company in Europe. All the managers went through a programme to condition and prepare them for change. 'Change' became the buzz word and an end in itself. Little badges were made and worn which said: 'I am changing, are YOU?' What 'change' meant differed from person to person and 'change' came to be a weapon that people used against each other. People were accused of not trying to change. It may come as no surprise that in this environment no one really changed at all.

Some companies even have a Change Department. In others, Research & Development (R&D) and Product Development departments have this same change role. But this is not enough, not nearly enough. Every department and every manager has to be aware of and working on what is happening in their environment and what they need and want to do better. Every day and every meeting must be used to spot what is really going on, what is changing and what needs to be changed. The response will involve change, but change is not an end in itself.

But what if people don't like change?

People love change. They love variety and excitement. It is what they look for most of all in their personal lives. Watch any road or highway on a weekend and see people rushing around visiting new places, looking for a change of social scene, a change of activity. It is not that people don't like change. It is that they don't like *being changed.* No one likes things being done *to* them, even if they are good things and for their welfare. Imagine if you returned to your office after a meeting and someone had rearranged your desk and office, and shifted things around to new locations. Imagine how surprised and indeed annoyed you would be. Even if the changes were for the better. Very often managers make decisions that affect other people's lives without working to get people's agreement, even to the reason for the decision. The people affected resent this and see it as an abuse of power, which in a sense it is. Very often resistance to change is resistance to management; resistance to the arbitrary power that managers believe they have and which they wield; resistance to plans that people either don't understand or don't agree with.

I worked with a company some years back where this great sensitivity to the arbitrary power of management was strong. As a result, even the smallest of decisions, irrespective of how much sense they made, were resisted by staff. Any small but valuable improvement, such as a better Goods Inwards process or smoother shipping process, was challenged by staff, and had to be discussed and negotiated. This was so because people did not see the change or the actual improvement so much as the power and authority that management wielded over them in imposing the change. Management felt they had a right to introduce changes and resented any challenge to that right or questioning of the rationale for the change.

We can handle change in very different ways and how we do so will make a huge difference and even determine the kind of response we get. Pushing through change without any clear or communicated rationale for it is blind force. Change, with clear and meaningful reasons for it and that involves staff, is stimulating and invigorating. As I have already mentioned, the involvement of people in change will not only get commitment to it but will increase the chances of it actually being a good change, a good decision. This means that we handle the change creatively, and are open to new ideas and improvements to our own ideas and plans. Handling change in a good way and finding the best response to a particular changing environment is an example of creativity in action.

6. Creativity – the key to the need to create new initiatives

All organisms need to be revitalised. Otherwise they fade and die.

Charles Handy, the writer and business consultant, talks of the curves in life where everything has an initial period in which there is no gain or contribution, then there is a long period of growth and contribution until a period of demise arrives.[24]

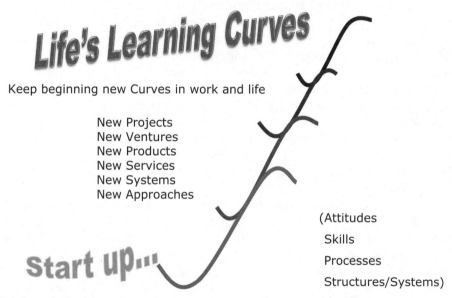

Life's Learning Curves

Keep beginning new Curves in work and life

New Projects
New Ventures
New Products
New Services
New Systems
New Approaches

Start up...

(Attitudes

Skills

Processes

Structures/Systems)

5.1. Learning curves.

All life follows this pattern. We spend nine months in our mother's womb, which is followed by a (hopefully) long life where we grow and contribute and thrive, and then a period of decline until we die.

However, in organisations and in many parts of life this need not be so as we can begin new things and new projects and endeavours. This is the role of the creative in organisations – to begin new curves, new ventures.

This will not happen automatically as in life and in nature. We have to consciously replicate the same dynamics that are at work in nature in our organisations so that new life is constantly being generated in the form of new ideas, projects, directions, products, ventures and services. Sometimes these happen by chance but this is something far too important to leave to chance. We have to shape our companies around a creative dynamic that will ensure the company is constantly being revitalised. This, as has been mentioned elsewhere, is achieved through designing and operating a truly creative organisation where roles, processes, systems, structures, attitudes and skills are all based on a view of the world as changing, full of possibility, dynamic, chaotic and alive.

Earlier I mentioned the time I first became involved in creativity in a formal way. My first encounter was when I was managing director of a General Motors company in Ireland. I came across a company – Synectics – which many years later I joined – and I put all of my management people through a programme in creativity and creative problem solving. The result was amazing. Quite suddenly the routine of production became a centre for new initiatives and change. Problems were actually welcomed by production supervisors because they had come to learn and realise that these problems would be a trigger and source of change and improvement. They had, of course, also learned that they could solve or resolve any problem but not in the sense of getting rid of it, but in the sense of using it to get on to a new level of behaviour and performance.

So why not spend some time taking a look at your area of work to see where you could and maybe should begin a new curve. What things need improving in your area of responsibility? What are the practices or activities that have been around for a long time and may no longer be serving much purpose? What new things could you begin? If you are stuck, get a group of people from your area to help you, to explore new alternative ways of doing things.

7. Creativity – the key to performance and empowerment

By 'performance' I don't just mean hard work, effort, blood, sweat and tears. I mean effectiveness and doing the right things as much as doing things right. Performance does not mean only doing what one is told, however well it gets done. Performance means that, as human beings, people, managers, leaders, we handle the situation in which we find ourselves in the very best way possible for us. We do justice to the event or situation in which we find ourselves and by that we do justice to ourselves.

'Empowerment' can sound like a cliché. This is a pity as it really involves doing what we do every day and what is most important to do every day. Often on my way to work I marvel at the little miracle of parents, mostly mothers, dropping their children off to school. They may not appreciate that, by giving their children an education, they are preparing them for empowerment and for being able to do things in life that they would not otherwise be able to do.

5.2. Peas enclosed in packet.

In summer I marvel at my garden and how I have empowered little seeds in sealed packets to grow into big bean and pea plants. These seeds are full of intelligence and full of potential. They know exactly how to germinate when given the right conditions. They will make use of the heat, moisture and oxygen to grow into big plants that produce food and that reproduce and propagate. But, as they are, sealed in a packet, that intelligence and potential will remain unused. By removing them from their sealed packets where nothing will happen and putting them into an environment of moist and prepared soil, I am enabling and empowering them to be what they really can be.

5.3. Peas freed from packet.

'Empowering' can mean different things, like authorising or delegating or entrusting someone with something to do. But it really means much more than that. It literally means awakening the power in people or giving them the power or making them sufficiently powerful to be able to do something and to do it in a really good way. This is what we do normally as parents, teachers, citizens and friends – we empower and enable people. It is above all our job as managers to enable people to be the most that they can be so that they can do the most they can do.

There is no better way of helping people to be more empowered and more powerful than helping them to be more creative in terms of how they think and what they do. Just like my bean and pea seeds, we release them from where they are contained so they can flourish and grow and contribute. What this means is that we open people up to all of the possibilities that are present to them in

5.4. Rich, blossoming peas.

their environment. We help them to see what is happening and we invite and encourage them to take a positive or proactive attitude towards it. This help is needed because we can and do become stuck in our ways of seeing reality and very often get discouraged from doing anything about it or even thinking we might be able to do anything about it. Substantial change is required then to help people take on a new attitude towards their reality and towards themselves. It calls for new mindsets, new skills, new behaviours and new roles. Our job as managers is to awaken people to who they really need to be and who they really are. When we do this, people are truly empowered. And the key to all of this is creativity – having the attitudes, skills and approaches to give the very best response to any given reality or situation and helping others to do so as well.

You can do this by modelling, promoting and expecting creative performance from your people to the actual situations they face. In so doing you will enable them to be creative. You will be a kind of alchemist – turning the base metal of existing reality into golden opportunities and great outcomes.

Our own belief systems and our belief in people are essential in achieving this. If we really believe in our people, they will begin to believe in themselves. If we really believe in the wealth of possibilities around us in every moment, others will see them too. We can structure and carry out our work to ensure that this belief in people and in possibilities is apparent. We can demonstrate our belief in every situation and encounter with people. One very powerful and simple way to do this is to practise COACH-ing in all our conversations and interactions (see Introduction). By doing this we are giving the message that we believe the other person can find *their* answer, *their* breakthrough and we are *encouraging* them to do so. If we can practise a COACH-ing way of relating to people, we are empowering them to be creative.

8. Creativity – the key to good decision making

I sometimes hear people say with great conviction, 'The buck stops here!' – a phrase that was said to have originated in a poker game and which US President Harry S. Truman made famous. It could be applied to management because decision making is what management is mostly about – deciding on directions to take, responding to situations, finding ways to deal with problems, and so on. If this is so then the quality of our management will rest on the quality of our decision making. We are only as good as the decisions we take, whatever field we work in. Taking good decisions will, in turn, rest on how well we are able to read or understand what is really going on and having the resources to come up with the best possible responses to this. This, in effect, is creativity and for this reason creativity is at the core of all decision making.

Bad decision making is not only about mistakes but also includes making decisions that fall short of all that *might* have been decided or followed. It is relatively easy to not get it wrong. The bigger challenge is to ensure we get it as *right* as possible and do real justice to the actual situation with all its potential. When Ken Olson, chairman and founder of Digital Equipment Corp (DEC), decided in 1977 that 'There is no reason anyone would want a computer in their home', in effect he did nothing wrong but he missed out on spotting a huge opportunity in the situation facing him at that time. DEC, once the second largest company in its industry, is no more, having been absorbed by Compaq, which in turn was absorbed by Hewlett Packard.[25] For this reason we need to take our decision making seriously because every decision we take is one out of a thousand that are possible. The difficulty is, our difficulty is, that we only see one possibility, when there are, in fact, always a myriad of possibilities available to us.

We can underestimate the importance of this very easily and regard decision making as being a fairly clear and straightforward process. It is, but we need to work to make sure we are handling it well. The big danger is to associate being certain with being right. There is little connection, if any, between these two. The day after the Space Shuttle Challenger disaster, a psychology professor named Ulric Neisser got his students to write about precisely where they had been when they heard about the explosion. Two and a half years later he asked them for the same information. While fewer than one in ten got the details right, almost all were certain that their memories were accurate and many couldn't be dissuaded even after being shown their original notes and records.[26] We have all had similar experiences of being certain only to discover we were wrong. While this does not matter in terms of a difference of opinion about a football game, it matters a lot when it is about a decision affecting our company and its staff. We need to doubt ourselves in order to be more reliable in our decision making. Certainty and autocracy is a dangerous cocktail.

Alfred P. Sloan, who was president of General Motors in the 1930s, knew to doubt himself and to doubt his entire team. His practice was to say:

> I take it we are all in complete agreement on the decision here…. Then I propose we postpone further discussion of this matter until our next meeting to give ourselves time to develop disagreement and perhaps gain some understanding of what the decision is all about.[27]

He knew the value of doubting and the danger of certainty.

One obvious and easy way to learn to doubt ourselves is to involve others in our decision making when it is of something of any real importance. This means that we gain as many perspectives as possible on the issue or decision to be made and we open it up to people around us and get their input and reactions. For this to be effective, the people involved need to be trained to respect differences and to respect every perspective and idea.

The story of the blind men around the elephant explains the value of differing.

5.5. Learning and making the most of differences – elephantine thinking.

The story is based on the old myth of the Blind Men of Hindustan who came across the elephant and about which John Godfrey Sachs wrote his poem of the same name.

Each of the blind men touches and explores a different part of the elephant or reality.

They each form a different opinion based on their experience. 'It's a snake,' says one. 'No, it's a tube – water comes out of it!' says another. 'No, it's a hill; I can climb up on it and slide off it,' says another. 'We are in a cave...feel the roof of it,' says the fourth. 'It's not a cave, it's a house. I can hit my stick off the rafters,' says the fifth. 'Sorry, you are all wrong. It's a tree – I can feel the bark and put my arms around the trunk,' says the last one.

So they each have a different opinion of what it is they have come across. But this is more than an *opinion*. Not only do they *think* it is a snake, a tube, etc. but they are all *sure,* they are all *certain* that they are right. They all *know* what it is. And they know the others are wrong.

They are all certain because their view is based on the only experience they have and so they are obliged to believe it is what they feel and think it to be. They are limited and indeed confined to *their* particular experience. So what can they do? Yes, they can remain happy and convinced about their particular version of the reality. Or they can make an effort to advance, to learn more, to see what more there might be.

What does this involve? A lot. It involves sharing their different experiences and views. And sharing involves two things – talking and listening. By far the more difficult of these two is listening. It is not easy to listen to 'nonsense' and people being 'wrong'. Most times, in fact nearly always, people who are 'wrong' in one's opinion are people who have a different perspective than you because they have had a different experience from you.

So, at meetings where decisions are made, each attendee will have a different perspective, and while none of these will necessarily be right on its own, the combination of the different ideas will lead to a rich, more complete and probably better decision – 'None of us is as clever as all of us.' The rationale and process for this is covered elsewhere in this book (and particularly in Chapters 19 and 20) but for the moment suffice to say that group work is a great aid to creativity and creativity is key to good decision making.

9. Creativity – the key to creating collaboration versus conflict

In the game of rugby, for those who are not familiar with it, there is a position called 'out-half' or 'outside-half'. The out-half is a play maker and often gets the ball from the restart of games – scrums or line-outs. Out-halves are often fast and elusive and can break through a defence to cross the opponent's line and score a try. Sometimes they can be too fast and elusive! What I mean by this is that if they go it alone, rarely will they make it across the line as they will get caught and sacked by the opposition. Their best bet is to stay in touch with their team mates, and, in this way, to use the combined skills, speed and numbers to get the breakthrough. They need to bring their team mates with them.

The same is true of decision making in work situations. Even if we do take good decisions on ways forward, we may not always enjoy full support and backing for our decisions. We not only need to take good decisions but we need to bring people with us in order to make things happen and happen well.

In order for decisions to get implemented well we need collaboration and collaborators. For the reasons mentioned above it is fairly easy to see how creativity is an aid to collaboration and will prevent conflict. The focus and engagement on challenges and problems will bind people together around a common goal. The search for better ways of doing things, better products and better services puts the focus on the real problem and gets people cooperating and working together to deal with the challenges and issues. This drags the focus away from internal differences and gets everyone united against the real 'enemy'.

Conflict very often arises from differences of interest and differences of viewpoint. Creativity helps to remove differences of interest by getting everyone looking at what can be improved or at what needs improving or bettering. This becomes, then, a shared interest, a common goal.

Creativity stops people getting stuck in the present and actual situation by giving them the mentality and tools to look for ways out. People then cease feeling stuck and seek new solutions and pathways. Problems stop being a source of dissension and become normal events that need to be handled well out of a shared interest in the betterment of the organisation.

Differences of opinion are also a source of conflict. But when people learn to work in a truly creative way, where all recognise that no one has a monopoly on truth and what is best, conflict dissipates and disappears. The skills and practices to do this do need to be learned and practised.

It is difficult, however, to see how conflict can last long if there is a real spirit of creativity, a joint and united search for improvement and breakthroughs.

So, what to do then? How do we go about being a creative organisation? Chapter 6 deals with this.

Chapter 6

Creativity Is Child's Play, if You Follow the Rules – Practical Steps to Working Creatively

'In the long history of humankind (and animalkind, too), those who learned to collaborate and improvise most efficiently have prevailed.'

– Charles Darwin

Remember – You are only as good as you are creative

So, if it is all about how responsive and creative we are in terms of dealing with our world and the situations in which we find ourselves, what does this mean in practice? How do we go about handling our situations in a good and creative way? It's easy.

The seven steps to tackling problems creatively

Some years back, my wife and I were minding our young grandson, Alex, and one afternoon when he fell asleep we engineered an hour or two of peace for ourselves by taking him to his room and putting him safely in his cot. He went to sleep and we went back to what we were doing. We looked in at him once or twice and he was sleeping soundly. About an hour later, while we were thinking he was safe and sound in his cot, to our great surprise our little Houdini arrived into the kitchen to us. We wondered at his ingenuity but really it was his creativity we should have been marvelling about. In fact, it was easy. He just followed the basic steps of the creative process.

What did he do?

1. Well, first of all he woke up and saw that he was not free but was 'locked up' in his cot.

2. He cried for a little while until he realised this was not achieving much. Instead he accepted he was in fact locked in.

3. Then he got up on all fours and decided he was going to do something.

4. He tried a few things like shaking the sides, squeezing through the bars, throwing things on the ground to call attention.

5. He decided that climbing up on the side of the cot was the best way to go. He stood on some of the clothes in the cot and tried to pull himself up.

6. This did not go too well so he tried other ways of climbing over the side of the cot.

7. He continued to check what worked and what didn't and which side looked most promising based on his various 'failures' until he arrived in the kitchen having 'fallen' his way out of the cot!

What Alex did was to follow the seven basic steps that we can use all the time in working creatively:

1. *Notice* and become *aware* of the situation; see what is or what is not happening, give it attention, get to 'know' it.

2. *Accept* the situation as it is, as a reality.

3. *Decide* to *do something* about it – even if that means doing nothing.

4. *Get working on the issue or situation*, and look for and create good ways to handle it.

5. *Act* on how you have decided to handle it.

6. Constantly *review the results* of your actions in the light of what is happening and the feedback your actions are getting.

7. *Adjust, correct, improve* and change your plan and actions accordingly.

Some of these steps seem self-evident but it is easy to fail at any one of these seven stages, or not do them at all.

This might seem a mechanistic and forced approach to dealing with life, but in reality it is what we do all the time when we encounter any situation or problem. Much of the time when we perform well, we do it automatically.

And yet, in organisations, it is possible to miss out on each and every one of these seven steps.

Let's check it out for ourselves and apply it to ourselves.

1. Notice and become aware of the situation

Do we always spot problems and issues? Sometimes we just don't see or notice them. We don't have the sensitivity of the artist, which I mentioned earlier, to see what is in front of our eyes.

Or how often do we wish problems away, call them blips, wait for the storm to blow over, hope things will get better? Was there *ever* an economic downturn that was not characterised by a refusal on the part of governments and financial institutions to see the writing on the wall long before it actually happened?

And what mechanisms do we have to spot and detect problems and to really check them out to see how serious and lasting they might be?

How do we handle the people who raise these issues and identify problems? Do we just see them as negative individuals, pessimists, naysayers?

How big a factor is group-think in blinding us to seeing problems looming or issues arising?

So the first step to handling reality well is to see it as it is and for what it is. Take a look at some issues in your life or organisation that you might not be spotting, acknowledging or addressing.

We can't handle reality if we don't see it; we may not see it because we aren't really aware enough or because we don't *want* to see!

Take a personal issue like a person suffering from alcoholism. In this case the first step to recovery would consist of recognising that they are drinking too much. But it is easy not to notice that alcohol has become a problem and it is easy to be in denial.

Or take the example of a gradual drop in quality and service standards in a company as a result of complacency. Perhaps this is not picked up on because it is so slow and the situation may have grown comfortable for the employees. We all know the story of the frog in the boiling water. Put a frog into a pot of boiling water and it will hop back out again. But put a frog into a pot of cold water and gently bring it to the boil and the frog will quietly boil to death (only a theory; never tried it!).

6.1. Danger of comfort and not responding to changes.

Why will the frog behave in this stupid way? Because the frog becomes comfortable in the water and its skin adjusts to the small and gradual increases in temperature and so does not notice what is happening. One second feels very much like the preceding one. And so too with us. Things can happen so gradually and so slowly that there is no noticeable discomfort until it is too late. We do this every day. We can live with our eyes closed, asleep to what is happening around us. It is time to wake up.

2. Accept the situation as it is, as a reality

This is not as easy as it may appear. One of our biggest struggles in our own personal lives is to accept reality. We can spend a lot of time wishing things had not happened, blaming ourselves or others for their happening and regretting that they *have* happened. This is not a great use of time or energy but that does not stop us doing it. I bet that when you get a cold, like me, most of your feeling bad comes from the belief that you should not have got this cold: 'I should not be feeling like this.' In reality, your discomfort is not great; it is your annoyance with the cold that gives you the trouble rather than how you actually feel.

In work situations there is no shortage of similar ploys. People don't like making mistakes or being wrong and will go to great lengths to avoid admitting their mistakes. People especially don't like making mistakes that others will criticise or take advantage of and so they use ingenious techniques to cover up.

Accepting reality, even if it is a bad situation, does not mean that we acquiesce and do nothing about it; rather, it means that we accept it now as real and do something about it. Until we accept it, we can't do anything about it. In our heads we are dealing with what should not be rather than with what actually *is*!

Until reality is seen and accepted for what it is, there can be no progress towards handling it well or finding a solution to a problem. We cannot do anything if we are starting off from a place that is not real.

Again, take a look at some issues that you or your organisation may be dismissing or denying or wishing away, and not fully accepting as a reality.

If we go back to our two earlier examples – the alcoholic may actually realise he has a problem but refuse to admit it, to others or to himself. Any attempt by others to raise the issue gets rough treatment and eventually people learn not to raise it at all. So, too, with the problem of the company's dropping standards. Denial or the absence of real recognition and acceptance can be an even deeper part of the problem. And we go to great lengths to convince others that all is well. In a work context, many screens and walls can be adorned with PowerPoint and Excel presentations that bear little resemblance to reality. They are designed to misrepresent, exaggerate, play down, cover over, distract and mislead. The real problem is that we can end up believing them ourselves. Billy Connolly says that the Queen thinks the world smells of paint because everywhere she goes has been painted a few days before she arrives. I am sure visiting General Motors executives in my time working in the company thought company plants were very tidy places with little inventory because this is or 'was' the only world they are were allowed to see. It is bad enough that we fool visiting executives but far worse when we believe our own stories and deny the real problems that exist around us.

3. Decide to do something about it – even if that means doing nothing

This looks obvious but it actually takes courage and some level of faith. Many people wallow in their problems. It becomes a pastime, a way of life. The last thing they want is for their problems to go away. Where would that leave them? 'I become my limp. I love my crutch.'

In organisations there can be people like this too. Even the people who see their role as dealing with problems can form part of this group, and end up not really resolving them or getting rid of them. Many managers can fall into this trap of being problem-solvers or 'problem-entertainers', i.e. they actually enjoy problems and entertaining them. Industrial relations experts or negotiators can also occupy this role and, like militaries or mercenaries, make a livelihood of problems. The last thing they want is that something is really done about them. The Slovenian philosopher Slavoj Zizek talks of 'the joy that people get out of their problems'. The suffering becomes their identity and they will not be separated from it. Partners of alcoholics can play a major part in prolonging the problem because victimhood has become their way of life and they fear for their identity if this cross is taken away from them.

Are there problems and issues that you and the company have known about for a long time but have not really stood up to and decided to do something about? What would be involved in really deciding to take on and tackle some of the big issues that have become part of your reality? Just making this decision will make an enormous difference.

It is easy to postpone dealing with an alcohol problem and to wait for the right moment to arrive to deal with it. Or to cut down a little and fool oneself that you are dealing with the problem. In companies, the very problem of poor service and standards can justify the existence of all kinds of people, make heroes out of them and so make the problem adequately tolerable. In one of my past lives, we had a quality control person residing in the premises of our main customer whose job it was to liaise with key people there so that any problems with our components were caught as early as possible and so were not escalated. This person was a godsend to us and rescued us from many potentially dangerous situations. He was also helping us to live with and do nothing really major about our more fundamental problem. So we carried on as usual and lived with what was a tolerable but unacceptable level of quality. We did nothing.

4. Get working on the issue or situation, and look for, and create, good ways to handle it

Actually beginning to tackle a problem calls for open-mindedness and creativity and we will spend a lot of time on this in Chapter 8. The challenge here is not to let the problem block us from finding a solution because all we know about the problem, or our expertise, can become the greatest obstacle to our resolving it. The oft-quoted Einstein statement comes to mind: 'The way of thinking that led us into a problem will not be the same as the one we require to get out of it.'

If you have a problem, you are like a person who falls down a hole. How you fell into the hole will throw little or no light on how you can get out. But you are going to need something – a rope, a ladder – or someone from the outside to help you to get out of it. This is how we can deal with a problem. Being like a bee at a window pane means we keep returning to the same failed solutions.

6.2. Stuck in a problem.

So we need to go after the problem, even if we do not yet have an idea how we will resolve it. But we will have to explore many possible ways of solving it. Nature and evolution love lots of options and create them. At every stage in the evolutionary process where mutation or a new species is evolving, Nature chooses the best options from a myriad that has been presented to it. She often does this without knowing at all what the next stage will look like and cannot know it until it emerges. We have to do the same and with the same courage and belief. Face the issues and create all kinds of possible ways of dealing with them and overcoming them.

So, how can you go after your problems and challenges in a new way and involve others to help you find fresh approaches for handling them?

The alcoholic, having once decided to do something about the problem, needs to work out a good way of solving it. Good intentions and hard work will not be enough. He may need to come up with an intelligent plan to deal with the problem in an effective and lasting way. Just deciding to quit is unlikely to do the trick. So too with the standards issue in the example of the company. This is a complex issue and simply putting a directive on notice boards or internal websites will fall far short of what is required. A lot of good, intelligent work will be required to come up with a comprehensive plan to deal with the issue. As I said already, I will go through many processes to help do this work in a really good way in the next chapter.

5. Act on how you have decided to handle it

> 'Whatever you can do or dream you can do, begin
> it. Boldness has genius, power and magic in it.'
>
> – Goethe

This sounds easy but it does not always happen. Sometimes the plan, the breakthrough or the strategy can be mistaken for action. But this is less than half the battle. The follow-through, the delivery, the less exciting but disciplined work is what will make the difference and make something happen. It will also give us lots of information on how well our plans are working. Without this, we can remain convinced of the wisdom and beauty of our solution and never test its efficacy.

Today begin and do something that you have been holding off doing for some time. Just do it, begin it. It will take you to a new place where you will see things differently.

Taking the first step may be the key for the alcoholic in our example. Simply doing something concrete about the problem may set in train a whole series of actions that will gather momentum and create the energy to keep going. In companies, paralysis by analysis is well known and the desire for absolute certainty can postpone managers taking action on problems like the one of inadequate standards that I mentioned. Sometimes any action is better than none and, at worst, will lead to some learning.

6. Constantly review the results of your actions in the light of what is happening and the feedback your actions are getting

This can seem wearisome and can be neglected. It is easier to carry on and hope for the best. We get busy with other things, move on to new projects; we can take it as read that all is fine and we can't be bothered checking. Review is critical because we will rarely get things absolutely right irrespective of how right they may appear in our own heads. We have to act on the basis of hypotheses, that what we have come up with is a theory which may or may not work no matter how convinced and certain we may feel about it. We can make our organisations veritable universities, centres of research and learning, by rigorously reviewing the results of our plans and initiatives. These will not lead to academic learning but will ensure the organisation continues to improve every aspect of its performance.

Checking and reviewing what we are doing calls for humility. We need to have the humility, and the common sense, to recognise that we did not and do not always get things right. Unfortunately there is often little time for this in companies. It can be difficult to admit to a mistake for fear of some kind of punishment, even if that is only in the form of a black mark against you which may rule out opportunities for promotion at some future date. Or it may be the punishment that comes in the form of condemnation or point scoring by a smug rival. These all-too-frequent dynamics discourage honest review and so choke the internal learning process in companies.

Apart from projects, where regular reviews are normally built in as part of the project process, what ruthless mechanisms are there in the organisation to routinely and consistently check how well your plans are working? How strong are you in questioning your pet ideas and plans? Are you really prepared to ditch some of your precious projects and initiatives if they don't make sense?

For the alcoholic, the review can lead to learning but it can also lead to encouragement based on an understanding of what *is* working. In this case and in many cases of professional and personal review, carrying out the review with an honest friend will be a great help as they will force or encourage you to be honest. A review is also critical in terms of the organisation working on its standards and improving its service. The feedback from clients and from the system itself will provide critical information on what needs to be continued to be done and what needs to be done differently or better or not at all. But, as in all cases, a review needs to be done formally and it needs to be done well.

7. Adjust, correct, improve and change your plan and actions accordingly

If we have done all the previous six steps then step seven is relatively easy. It may call for the consumption of some humble pie but it goes down easily and does a lot of good! It brings freshness, life and energy, and is rewarding at every level.

Again, it can be a difficult step to take because we do not want to lose face in front of people. But if we can become good at this, we will earn enormous respect from everyone..

Can you find the courage to gather some people around you to question what is going well and what is not going well,and what you are doing that could be improved? Can you do this for every serious activity you engage in?

The alcoholic will ensure flexibility is part of his plan to ensure that he is able to change if what he is doing is not working. Having taken the first steps, he can review how they are doing and make changes if he needs to. So too with the drive to improve standards in the example of the company. There is no guarantee that the initial plan will be the right one or will be right in all its facets. As we say, an aeroplane is only going in the right direction when it lands. Prior to that, it is adjusting and correcting.

It can't fail

All seven of these steps need to be handled well if we want to be responsive to our world and situations. If we are rigorous in following these steps, it is hard to see how we can fail to come up with good ways to handle *any* situation we find ourselves in.

Make this the way you work and after a while it will become easy and natural for you. It will also guarantee you success.

And this is what it means to be a manager and leader – to not just accept situations and cope with them but to respond to them and creatively turn them into fresh sources of life and opportunity. We will look at this in more depth in Chapter 15.

Chapter 7

Blocks to Creativity – The Seven Capital Killers of Creativity in Organisations

'Though we live in a world that dreams of ending,
That always seems about to give in,
Something that will not acknowledge conclusion
Insists that we forever begin.'

– Brendan Kennelly

Question: If creativity is something natural, what's the problem?
Answer: We kill it.

I have said that creativity or finding novel, powerful and appropriate responses to your current reality is the most important aspect of how you manage in an organisation and one that governs all else you do. I have also said that this is the most deeply human way for us to behave. Creativity, in fact, should not involve a huge effort. After all, every human being is a born creator. To be and to be creative are synonymous. It is impossible to exist and not to be creative. It is our nature to be so. So, if this is the case, what goes wrong? Why is it difficult? We need to identify the reasons why our organisations often struggle to be creative and to find out what they are struggling against. We need to find out why something productive and natural, like creativity, gets turned into a problem.

The reason that creativity gets turned into a task is because during the course of our lives we move away from our true natures. We go out of tune with our nature and how we really are. All children are born creative but slowly we damage their creativity by conditioning them to our way of seeing the world. We push them for the right answers and to get things right to satisfy us, and in the process we do serious damage to their imagination and ability to see things differently or even clearly. This natural drive to see and imagine things in fresh and creative ways can weaken as we move on in life, and can be especially diminished at work where we need to get things right, prove ourselves and please others by agreeing with their way of thinking.

What I am offering in this book is the promise and process whereby our innate ability can be recovered and revitalised through working creatively, through consciously pursuing betterment and through constantly facing and tackling problems and challenges that come our way, creatively and in new and fresh ways.

Not as easy as all that

But if it seems to make so much sense to work in a creative way, then why don't more people do it? Why are all organisations not creative places?

Organisations can be creative places but we have to re-learn some ways of being that we had when we were younger and get over some bad attitudes and habits we have picked up along the way. Doing this can be uncomfortable and we can feel we are on shaky ground.

Shaky ground

Creativity necessarily involves some fantasising and imagining. However, the imagination can feel like a very unstable base from which to operate. Not surprisingly, when we fantasise or imagine, most times we look up, our eyes go up. It can feel like this too; that we are leaving firm ground and going into clouds and blue skies and unknown lands of wonder. It can feel insecure. It can also appear unstable and create doubts in *others* around us. It is risky. We can put little forward by way of evidence.

I find that one of the most challenging tasks I give groups to do on my seminars is when I ask people to imagine a far better reality than their existing reality. They first of all look up, then look at me with blank faces and then put their heads down and go to work on coming up with something. I always relieve them of the pressure by explaining why exactly this is not an easy task.

One of the reasons is that, in terms of creating an alternative reality and better future, our sources are not the usual and reliable facts, figures, data and analyses. The basis for our visions of the future has to be built less on concrete, heady facts, than on heart and stomach feelings and on deeply felt beliefs about what will really work and make a difference. We couple facts and experiences from our lives with our dreams, aspirations, hopes and beliefs. We create a new reality. Not a reality that exists in the world, yet, but a new reality in our own heads and in others' heads, which is the precursor for what will eventually become concrete reality in the world.

If right now you were to imagine something really nice that you could do tonight or to-morrow (go ahead and take a minute to do it) you will find that it will remain with you and have a real power over your thinking and maybe over what you will actually do, depending of course on how risqué and adventurous you were in what you chose. But this can be an uncomfortable place to be when we go after bigger things that bring bigger rewards and bigger risks. It can appear like a risky business.

Risky business

With creativity there is always risk. Have you ever seen young boys playing at wrestling each other to the ground? Often there is one strong lad who goes around routinely dumping all the others on the ground. Sometimes a kid who sees him coming his way will throw himself on the ground and avoid the hustle and the risk of losing. It is easier to give up than to take the risk and fail. So, too, with creativity. There is always a risk of failure. We do not know which of the multiple options we have imagined and created will work. We can't answer the challenge to prove what will work. There is little real evidence we can produce apart from an analysis or description of the inadequacy of what we currently have. This is a risk that has to be accepted. There can be no certainty as creativity is never about simply repeating the past; it is about moving forward. The process is not a deductive one. It is not about remembering the past and repeating it. For that reason it is a risky business.

If I asked you to imagine a very different and much better future for your company, or if I painted a picture of it, it is quite likely you might doubt me and give me funny looks. It may seem so pie in the sky, so unreal and baseless, and just wishful thinking. Yet something like this *will* happen. Think about how your current reality is very different from how it was five or ten years ago, and that it would have sounded unreal back then. Now, even though we know the future will be very different from our present reality, we find it hard to imagine it or to believe it will be different. And, of course, by imagining and visualising the future we are already influencing it.

Creativity is risky, too, because we can get it wrong. It is risky because we can lose those around us and fail to bring them with us. We can become isolated, marginalised and be regarded as being out of touch with the real world. It can be challenging to continue to assert that our imagined world is actually more real and true to reality and what is right and good than the actual world we and others cling to. We will always be surrounded by people who will hold us back, keep us on the straight and narrow and prevent us from wishing too much or dreaming at all.

In addition to this, there are other challenges to the creative approach, and I describe these below.

The seven capital killers of creativity

There are seven fairly typical ways in which organisations stifle or kill creativity. Unless we spot them at work, they will block our best efforts to have truly creative and responsive organisations that can adjust to and make the most of any given situation.

1. A lack of a sense of real need; settling for what is or what we have

If we really felt we needed to be creative then we would be so. But we don't because we believe we are doing fine as we are – 'Steady as she goes,' 'Don't rock the boat,' 'If it ain't broke don't fix it?', 'Things could be worse,' etc. We have mentioned this over and over again in this book – our desire to be comfortable and at ease. We grab at any straw that will give us this sense of assurance. It is the role of the leader to prevent this happening and to maintain a sense of need and drive alive in people and in the organisation. If we don't create real need ourselves, reality will do it for us, and unfortunately this will often involve some pain.

A failure or refusal to identify a need for things to be different and better is the single biggest block to creativity. But there always is a need if we want to look for it and we should find it before it finds us.

And so the big sin or temptation is to settle for what we have, simply because it is what we have. We settle for what we have because of the risk of failing if we go after more or better and because it is easier to continue where we are. An example of this is told in the Exodus story in the Bible where Moses takes the people from Egypt off into the desert in search of the Promised Land, or a better life as free people and not slaves. In Egypt they had food and were generally fine, whereas in the desert it was boring, difficult and painful and some wanted to go back to Egypt (and to slavery). In other words, the people wanted to settle for Egypt because it was familiar and therefore 'comfortable'. 'Settling for' is a real 'sin' or mistake as we are here to go after better – a better life, a better world. We have an innate capacity to question everything, to continuously challenge what is, and to challenge whether it is good enough. Moses represents our capacity to creatively shape the future. We are different from the other animals. We have taken 13.7 billion years to become what and who we are and this growth to greater perfection is ongoing. It is our responsibility as human beings to continue this growth and not to stop or settle for what we currently have.

A role I most often play with my clients is that of the 'prophet'. Not prophet in the sense of forecasting what will happen, but prophet in the sense of calling people to be who they really are – disturbing them out of their comfortable existences; getting them to be true to themselves, and to their true calling both as individuals and as organisations.

This involves prompting people to get in touch with their dreams, both the dreams they had when they were young and full of hope, and their current dreams, which may have been dulled by experiences and failures or destroyed by the so-called realism of people around them, some of whom may not want their ordinary lives disturbed by pie-in-the sky wishing. Dreamers challenge the status quo and can be seen as critical of what is currently being done. They do this because most of us have been trained to cope, to accept, to stop questioning and to settle for what is. As managers and leaders, we have to re-awaken the truth and beauty and hope in people, which is always present and has never really gone away. They may have appeared at various times and in various contexts, often ones outside of work. We can resurrect these glimpses and help people to get in touch with them again, and thus become who they truly are.

In organisations the role of prophet is about recalling people to the original vision or goal of the organisation and reminding people of the great achievements it has had along the way. It will be about reminding people of the spirit behind these achievements and helping them to again get in touch with it in the here and now. This will involve confronting them with the reality of their current challenges and opportunities and helping them to find the confidence and energy to again go after them and not settle for the existing plateau, no matter how comfortable and satisfactory that may be. This is a different and special power that will be present in various parts of the organisation, in various individuals in the organisation and in certain teams or groups within the organisation. In each of these there will be a live spirit that can be rekindled and used to move the whole organisation forward. Because this spirit or energy can get taken for granted, it can be forgotten. So bringing it forward again is a role that the outsider can often play better than anyone within the organisation. It is the role of the prophet.

Not all prophets need to be on the outside. Within each organisation there are prophets who are not satisfied or happy that enough is being done or has been achieved. Often these prophets are perceived as negative, as critics, even as trouble makers. We need to identify these people and listen to what they are really saying. Their criticisms can be the shadow side of a dream for, or a hope or belief in the real power of the organisation. Often we, as outside facilitators, identify these people in organisations and give them a real platform where their voice and message can be heard. They become our allies in awakening the organisation to being the most and the best it can be.

As has been said many times already, this is a different place to be and is one that is not devoid of risk. For this reason, leaders are needed. Every good leader is also a prophet. As in every aspect of our lives, the journey to growth often takes place in a desert where we can feel very alone and abandoned and not at all sure of where we are going. People can need assurance and help at these stages and this is the role of the leader as prophet. Every stage in our growth, from learning to walk and talk, to learning to ride a bicycle, is fraught with danger and takes place in the unknown.

It does not always need to be as tough as this and sometimes life gifts us comfortable and easy opportunities for growth. But it is also often the case that refusing to settle involves courage, effort and some pains – growing pains.

Find your prophets. Be one yourself. Don't settle or let others settle.

2. The collective mind – groupthink kills ideas and initiatives

There is great power in groups of people working together and there are equally great dangers. The power of people cooperating in groups has already been covered in various places in this book. The dangers are equally great and even more commonplace. The main danger is the danger of the compromise where the outcome is the lowest common denominator of all the various views. People try to reach agreement above all else, with the result that the ideas that emerge are a mix of all views and the ones most accept-able to everyone. This can lead to mediocre thinking and equally mediocre performance.

What happens in these cases is that people believe that good relationships are primordial and that nothing can be achieved unless good relationships are maintained.

While this may appear to make sense, it is not true that it is impossible to develop good relationships while differing and disa-greeing. Without disagreement, quality thinking and truth suffer and overall performance naturally follows behind. This false philosophy leads to a peace-at-all-costs mentality where people in the group consciously or subconsciously collude to avoid the relentless pursuit of truth in the interests of so-called harmony. Contact with the outside world, the real world, gets lost and even-tually people begin to believe their own stories and confirm them to each other. Great strength is felt by virtue of everyone agree-ing with each other and naysayers or critical voices are quickly silenced.

The problem is that one mind, a collective mind, develops instead of the natural and healthy dynamic of different minds struggling and grappling with a reality in the search for truth and the best way forward.

It takes a real conscious effort to deal with groupthink. While everyone needs to understand the risks of groupthink and the effort involved in not falling into that mode, the leader has a criti-cal part to play in ensuring that a culture of honesty, accurate thinking and frank talking develops and is maintained. Can I remind you again of the elephant? The same principle applies here – stick passionately to your own valid experience and view-point *and* be equally respectful and curious about the stances of others, which are probably equally valid. If you do this well, you will avoid the collective mind.

Be elephantine in your thinking. Embrace, celebrate and combine differences.

3. Conservative tendencies overcome expansionist tendencies

We are each born with a conservative tendency and an expansive tendency. The first will remain but the second will wilt and wane if not cultivated. The motive to engage in creative behaviour is easily extinguished.

These two tendencies are hard at work all the time, struggling against each other, wrestling, tugging and striving. As long as this struggle continues all is well. The danger is that one or other disappears. Most times it is the expansive tendency that wilts and fades or gets suffocated by the conservative tendency.

The conservative tendency in us has many allies outside of us. The first ally we come across is, of course, our parents. They want our well-being and so work hard at protecting us from danger and risk. We need quite a bit of safety in our early days though not as much as most parents actually think. Taking risks and trusting children is as important for their development as it is for the development of adults. It is all too easy to fear too much and become too anxious and, of course, to transfer our own fears to our children. What is most dangerous is that parents often don't know when to stop worrying and protecting and so the need for safety and the conservative tendency in people can be easily over-developed and the person becomes blocked or inhibited forever. Adolescence often rescues children from this excessive caution when they react against their parents and other authority figures. This can also turn into an over-reaction.

Be that as it may, a conservative tendency is a very important trait to have as it protects us from all kinds of dangers. However, it does need to be balanced with the equally important expansive or growth tendency. Just this awareness of what each is doing will be of great help to us in keeping both active, alive and playing their important parts.

The additional factor is the dynamic of the organisation. It too has both of these tendencies at work in the individuals and in the culture of the overall organisation itself. While organisations can be brave, dynamic and creative, they can also be careful, conservative and cautious. 'There is nothing as cowardly as money,' the economist John Kenneth Galbraith said. The natural tendency of an organisation to preserve itself can exaggerate the conservative tendency and lead to the organisation failing to take advantage of its challenges and opportunities to grow in every sense. It is this dynamic that leads to the failure of organisations. The critical source of renewed life gets choked off and the organisation suffers and dies.

An absence of alternatives

This attitude simply refuses to imagine that anything can be different or better than it actually is and so asks what is the point of looking for a better or alternative way? Because it seems that we are doing all that is possible, we see no scope for or point in exploring anything new. (See Chapter 8 on possibilities.)

Adherence to old mental models

Creativity becomes impossible if we stick to models of the past and refuse to look at things in a new or different light but simply impose the old model on to reality so that we always and only see according to that model. Anything that does not fit with our model may not even be given the time of day, not to mention considered or taken on board. Many of our models belong to an old paradigm of managing which limits our thinking and fails to match the true reality of our world. Seeing the world as a static place built on a cause-and-effect philosophy will dampen and choke our creative strengths.

For this reason, there is a need to artificially create expansive mechanisms and models in every organisation, as they will not happen automatically. Routine, the predictable and the need for comfort will all kick in and dominate unless there are equally strong elements working in the opposite direction to maintain the vibrancy and responsiveness of the organisation. These mechanisms and models too are covered in Chapter 8 and need to be cared for so that the innate expansive element in all of us and in life itself is given a chance to play its powerful part. With this in place, organisations can provide the strength and confidence that individuals on their own don't possess and so organisations can do great things that individuals cannot do.

Begin new creative mechanisms and models.

4. Wanting things finished and wrapped up – killing possibility

We like to finish things, get things done with, closed off, tidied up, 'done and dusted'.. We believe in this; we believe that we can finish things and close them off. We reach 'conclusions'. We seek conclusions in order to be able to finish something once and for all. This is very much part of the concept and philosophy of management – getting things completed. But this is a model we superimpose on reality. Life and experience are never finished; they are ongoing. So, while we believe that we are finished with something, it keeps rumbling on whether we know it or not.

Creativity involves seeing the world as unfinished. This is important because it is the reality of things. It is also important because it is a very healthy and happy attitude to have to the world and our affairs. The world is alive. It is beautiful. The unfinished, with its hunger and search for fulfilment and perfection, has a beauty. We can feel this in music. In a sense, every melody is unfinished. Every piece of music is full of yearning for the next note and, even when it is over, the yearning for more music remains.

Developing such an attitude in business is radically different from seeking comfort in practices that look for finality. Decision making is often about seeking this comfort but as the Indian Guru Osho says: 'God's things are never finished!' Learn to tolerate the unfinished, what is not done and dusted, things up in the air, confusion. Things will get done far better when you handle them like this. They will ripen in their own time.

Keep your mind loose and open. Trust.

5. Forcing creativity versus relaxing and letting go

I have stressed that creativity, like all good things in learning and living, calls for effort, hard work and courage. While this is so, it cannot be forced or made to happen. In fact, we have to stop trying in order for creativity to happen. In a sense it does *happen* more than our doing it, though of course there is lots we need to do. But we need to be relaxed and confident. We need to let it happen. The opposite is also true – our efforts, endeavours and anxiety can block it. On occasion, I have been called on to run a creative workshop over a day or two. The agenda, timing, process and pace are all left up to me to decide and design. Sometimes they are not and I am given a full agenda to get through in an action-packed day without a minute wasted. This efficient process is aimed at producing breakthroughs at particular points in the workshop. Sometimes they do happen. But not always.

In fact, the action happens through inaction. We all know this from our own experiences of how ideas and brainwaves can pop into our heads at the strangest times. Our main challenge is to *let it happen*. This does not mean that we do not want something or that we are not searching. It means that we become very clear about what we want and that we begin a real search. Then we trust and wait for the answers and breakthroughs to come.

Creativity comes from consciousness and consciousness is different from the mind. The mind is part of consciousness but is not the same as it. It is in consciousness that creativity arises and for this we need to shut off the mind. All creative artists and writers testify to this – that the creative action comes from a different place than the mind in the sense of rational thinking. It comes

94

from a deep place within us through which we are in contact with the world around us. When we block our thinking or rational mind and get to this deeper place, we get in touch with truth and wisdom. When this insight arrives we are at first unable to give expression to it. Then it gets expressed in some new form, perhaps a painting, book or song, which is the representation and expression of what we discovered in our conscious or subconscious state. We give birth to something but it is not all of our doing. We are partners in it and for this we have to stop our minds to let our other partner – the universe – play its part.

This is not easy. It is not easy to let go of our thinking minds and spend time feeling lost and waiting for something to happen. We want to be always in control and it is uncomfortable not to have answers, not to know. The temptation is for the mind to satisfy this need for control by coming up with answers. The trouble is the answers may come early and may not be good enough or equal to the situation. Instead, we need to get into a state of quiet where we wait, a state of 'no mind' as Eckhart Tolle calls it.

The thinking mind does have a part to play which is to take the work of the subconscious mind and turn it into practical ideas. This is critical if the insight or breakthrough is going to be turned into reality and see the light of day. Assessing, analysing, planning, organising and selecting are equally critical and call for a very different behaviour from that of the earlier subconscious phase. In effect, the conscious, thinking mind hands the challenge or situation or reality over to the subconscious for it to work on and then takes it back again to complete it at a later stage.

One of the reasons we find this difficult is because of our ego. *We* want to do it and we believe that we can do it alone. We focus on ourselves and on our own resources and become self-conscious and wrapped up in ourselves. But self-consciousness is a disease. Consciousness is healthy as it gets us in contact and in touch with the rest of the world. Self-consciousness blocks this awareness because it focuses on oneself, on the ego.

Consciousness has no idea of 'I', of ego. It has no idea of one's separation from existence. It knows no boundaries. There is no conflict between the individual and the whole. You are simply flowing into the whole, and the whole is flowing into you. The whole goes on giving to you and you go on giving to the whole, and so connections are made and ideas arise.

When we focus on ourselves and become self-conscious we create boundaries around ourselves and so cut ourselves off from the rest of the world. We become isolated and unable to see connections. To be self-conscious is to be unconscious. Self-consciousness is a non-surrendering attitude – it is the attitude of conflict with life.

Osho likens this attitude to that of a wave of water that thinks it is independent of the ocean. It fails to see that it is the product of the ocean and its strength comes from the ocean of which it is a part and to which it contributes. Separation is meaningless. It is for this reason that healthy working in groups and teams is conducive to creativity. We will return to this.

This is in line with what Robert Woodroof said: 'There is no limit to what a person can achieve once they don't mind who gets the credit for it.'

Relax and trust life and yourself.

6. Working in infertile dead environments

In Ireland we have a game called hurling which is played with ash sticks and a tough leather ball. It is a bit like hockey but, among other differences, in hurling one can catch the ball. It is a very skilful game and takes some time to learn and generations to master. While it is played throughout the country, the really good teams all belong to certain regions of the country or counties. Some neighbouring counties also have pockets of very skilled players in the areas adjoining the strong counties. It is almost as if there is something in the air or atmosphere in these locations. But of course it is not as mysterious as that. The reason is that, in these areas, the hurling milieu is strong and so those who belong to and live in these milieus enjoy high levels of skill. They actually benefit from comparing and competing with equally or more skilled players around them. It is virtually impossible for someone who does not belong to these environments to become a really good hurler.

This 'law' also holds true for creativity. Unless we are operating in a 'field' with like-minded people who are also engaged in the same area and with similar interests and 'hunger', it will be extremely difficult to really excel and come up with creative answers. Others bring out the best in us. Silicon Valley is one good example of this; it seems that breakthroughs are native to this environment.

What does this mean in practice? It means that if we want to improve the chances of getting creative breakthroughs we do need to surround ourselves with like-minded people or belong to groups where similar endeavours are taking place. In this way we can build on the achievements of others and be pushed and supported in going after breakthroughs of our own.

It is quite possible to create such milieus within the workforce by establishing special kinds of meetings or sessions specifically dedicated to coming up with new and fresh ideas. Often it is better to hold these in a different location or special place so that all know and feel the environment to be a special one.

7. No space or room for reflection

This happens because efficiency and money and the short term come to dominate and take over everything else. This in turn is driven by stock markets, share prices, and exclusively bottom-line management. While all of these are, of course, important, they are not the only important goals or measures for the performance of a company and they suffer from a short-term bias. They are very much about getting as many golden eggs as possible from the goose without adequate regard for the health of the goose or its long-term ability to keep laying golden eggs.

So the argument is often made and heard that, while it would be great to take time out to look at alternative ideas, businesses, products, approaches and so on, there just isn't the time or resources for that. In budgets, estimates get trimmed to produce acceptable forecasts and 'unimportant' or less important items like creative reflection and searching get dropped.

Part of the reason for this is that we don't see the need for such time out because of an over-reliance on expertise in our organisations. We depend too much on our expertise and intellects and not enough on intelligence and insights. Intelligence is a totally different from intellect. Intellect is in the head; intelligence is a state of heart wakefulness. It means that when we are being creative, our whole being is at work – head, heart, body and all our senses.

This is why expertise and creativity do not necessarily go hand in hand. The expert carries libraries in his head but may have no vision. And because life does not stay the same, ever – it is constantly changing – the expert always lags behind. His response is always inadequate.

If you cling too much to logic you will never be able to be part of the living process that this existence is. The map is not the territory and no amount of time spent on the map will give real, accurate and rich information about the actual territory to be traversed.

For this reason, creativity is given only token support in organisations and people get this message very clearly. As a result, plans are made, organisations are designed and structures are installed that do not include any space for creative work. This only happens as an exception or when there is some kind of crisis. It gets used until the crisis has passed and then things return to normal. And the so-called 'normal' is far from what really is normal, in the sense that it is not aligned with how our delightful, and ever-changing, chaotic world really is.

Why not budget time out for thinking, exploring, questioning and standing back, in other words, for creativity? The welfare of your organisation rests on it and it will not happen by itself.

Make space for people to be creative.

Chapter 8

Growing the Creative Organisation

'As long as you are green you grow but the minute
you think you're ripe you begin to rot.'

– John Naisbitt

We have looked at the many killers of creativity that exist in organisations. And we have said over and over that our organisations
will only be successful to the extent that they are creative. So
what can we do to overcome these blocks and establish vibrant,
creative organisations?

I am going to go through some concrete approaches and
initiatives which, if followed, will at least help to ensure your
organisation becomes alive with creativity.

I am dividing these into four parts:

Part 1: Observing the golden rules of creative working
Part 2: The recipe and ingredients for a creative culture
Part 3: The seven steps in the creative process
Part 4: The alarm clock – getting off to a good, creative start

Part 1: Observing the golden rules of creative working

While it is fine to say how easy or difficult it is to be creative and
to point out how critical it is to everything we do in work and in
life, the question remains: What do we actually need to *do* to be
creative and to respond and work in a creative way?

To recover and develop our innate creativity, we need to follow
twelve commandments or golden rules.

i. Be courageous

One day in 1903, a man walked into a restaurant in Norfolk,
Virginia and asked for a barrel of oysters.

'What for?' the restaurant manager asked.
'There are two loony Yankees down at Kitty Hawk trying to learn to fly,' the man replied. 'And they want to eat some Lynnhaven Oysters before they try this daredevil stunt.'

The Wright brothers, two of America's most celebrated inventors, survived that flight, and many others. On 17 December 1903, Orville and Wilbur Wright announced that they would attempt to fly the world's first airplane: The Wright Flyer. The public and the news media, however, were sceptical. That day, only five people braved the sandy winds of Kitty Hawk, North Carolina, to witness history.

Creativity demands courage. Often it is the courage to be alone, to go it alone, and to expose ourselves and our hopes to harsh criticism or even ridicule. If you bring your goods to the marketplace, you should expect to have them criticised. Like everything in life, greatness does not come without effort.

Nor does it come easily and without pain. Few of the great works of art in any genre were created in an environment of relaxation and effortless work. In all creativity there will be some painful, risky and difficult activities. It involves a stretch for us. Our very capacities are stretched. We are in unknown territory where we are discovering new things and entering new places and uncharted waters. It requires from us that we be at our peak. It invites us to be great and to find the greatness within ourselves that is always there to be found. There is no avoiding this requirement.

For these reasons creativity calls for courage. It will take courage for you to take on the big issues, the major changes that are needed and the great opportunities that are there to be grasped in your world, in your environment. If you have an idea for a new idea for a new product or service or way of doing things, you know that your idea will have resistors. It can be easier to give up and slip back into the herd. You need not even feel too bad about this: 'Ah, sure, maybe it wasn't such a good idea anyway and it might not have worked.' Comfort. Peace. Creative death.

Be courageous.

ii. Be rebellious

When we think of the song 'Do they know it's Christmas?' and when we think of the Live Aid concerts in London and Philadelphia in 1985, we probably forget that all of this did not happen easily. Band Aid only happened and was a success because one person in particular made it happen and that person was a rebel

– Boomtown Rats founder Bob Geldof. Geldof continues to make great things happen because he continues to be a rebel, refusing to accept the status quo.

Creativity is in a sense a kind of rebellion. It is a rebellion against what is currently accepted and what currently *is*; it is a rebellion in favour of a better version of reality. It challenges what exists in favour of what does not. In so doing, it often has to step on the toes of those who belong to and uphold the existing state of affairs.

Because of this we should expect opposition of all kinds to creativity, and from many sides. People will cling to their existing state, defend what they have themselves created and resist alternatives as challenges to themselves and their creations. It is important to be ready for this and to identify who may be most challenged by our creativity or venture. It is important, too, to identify the forms opposition will take.

Don't expect a smooth journey if you want to make a difference and want your company to be special. Not everyone will agree with you or give you their support. It is virtually certain that they will find your ideas and behaviour strange. They will much prefer that you toe the line, be a nice friend and conform. But they will join you if you can stick with your dream, so don't lose heart. Be rebellious.

iii. Be a listener

The number of plane accidents caused by poor decision making and human error on the part of pilots has been reduced by a staggering 71 per cent in the past twenty years, making flying safer than ever and the least dangerous form of travel by far.

One of the reasons for this is better listening. In the business it is called Cockpit Resource Management (CRM) and it means that, instead of the pilot being the sole authority, the whole flight crew work together and communicate with one another. As a result, because the pilot or captain is listening, better decisions emerge when a multiplicity of viewpoints is brought to bear on real situations where a real need or breakthrough is badly required. This means that we listen to those whose thinking we admire and possibly share but we also listen to those who oppose us. We listen to them so that we ensure we understand what they are saying. Doing so will either confirm us in our position or idea, help us to develop and enrich it, or move us to change or dump it. Listening tests our thinking and stretches our creativity as we hear more options and get different perspectives. Equally, we should listen to and not ignore or dismiss the rebels around us. They, too, may represent insights and new ideas that we have never been able to hear or accept. Look for them. Find them. Listen to them. Be a good listener.

iv. Be persistent

We all associate Thomas Edison with the discovery and development of the light bulb and, even though he really only improved on an already fifty-year-old idea, he was the one who found a way of producing a reliable and long-lasting source of light. This was one of several major successful results Edison enjoyed as an inventor. However, it was one of literally thousands of failed results that Edison 'enjoyed'. 'Results! Why, man, I have gotten a lot of results. I know several thousand things that won't work,' he was reputed to have said.

To succeed in bringing about something new and worthwhile you must be persistent and stick with what you want and believe in; you must be willing to take a stand against perceived wisdom if

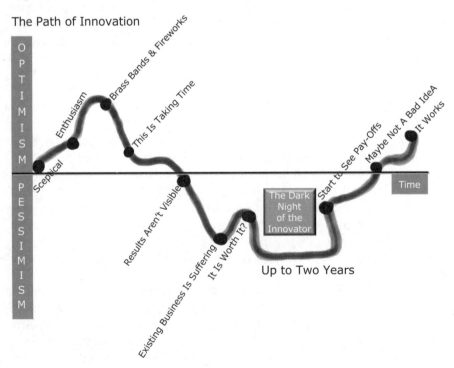

8.1. Dark night of the innovator or change agent.

the conditions warrant it. Creativity involves and creates tension. Creative thoughts evolve in a gap filled with tension – a tension between holding on to what is known and accepted while tending towards a still ill-defined truth that is barely glimpsed on the other side of the chasm. It is easy to give up.

At first there may be some enthusiasm for a new idea or proposal but, as time goes on, people can lose faith in it as things get more difficult and there is no real sign of any great improvement. This is often irreligiously called 'The Dark Night of the Innovator' (see figure 8.1).

So, if the going gets tough, don't give up. Be persistent.

v. Love what you do

Creativity is about loving what you do. You will not be creative if you do not love what you are doing. Loving what you do will lead you to be creative. Every creative person is to some extent in love with their field.

The Irish entrepreneur Paddy Campbell who, with his wife Veronica, founded and grew the large catering company Campbell Catering and subsequently rescued the ailing Bewley's Café group, told me recently how bored he was with it all. And he was not only bored with business but with other things, like golf. Now, Paddy spends every day painting and sculpting. day is just not long enough for him to do what he loves doing and which absorbs him completely.

It is the love of something that leads to creativity. 'If you are looking for fame or fortune, you will cease to be creative,' Osho says.

One can be creative in any field by doing what they do with love and delight. The smallest things become great if handled with love and delight.

This means again that we do not have to limit creativity to special moments or special areas. We can be creative in anything if we handle it with real respect and love. The first key to being creative is to simply love what you do. Be meditative and focused while you are doing it. Then apparently boring activities like cleaning can become creative. If you clean the floor with love, you have done an invisible painting. You can make every day a great and enjoyable day by loving what you do as you do it and losing yourself in it, falling in love with it no matter how simple it may be. Love what you do and do what you love.

vi. Become a child again

Creativity needs freedom – freedom from the mind, freedom from knowledge, freedom from prejudices. A creative person is one who can try the new. Like children who are free to love and explore everything new.

'Daddy, is that white, wet noise?' the young kid asks his dad walking along the beach.

'No, son', the father says, 'that's the sea!'

As we grow older we learn to adjust to the world around us and, while this is very important, it also builds walls and barriers of fear around us. We daren't appear foolish. As a result, we lose our freedom to think and explore.

'Grown-ups love figures,' Antoine de Saint-Exupéry's Little Prince says:

> When you tell them that you have made a new friend, they never ask you any questions about essential matters. They never say to you, 'What does his voice sound like? What game does he love best? Does he collect butterflies?' Instead, they demand: 'How old is he? How many brothers has he? How much does he weigh? How much money does his father make?' Only from these figures do they think they have learned anything about him. If you were to say to the grown-ups: 'I saw a beautiful house made of rosy brick, with geraniums in the windows and doves on the roof,' they would not be able to get any idea of that house at all. You would have to say to them: 'I saw a house that cost £4,000.' Then they would exclaim: 'O, what a pretty house that is!'[28]

We need to re-learn in order to see the world in new ways, the way children can see it, the way it actually is.

We often crush the creativity in others by teaching them the 'right way' to do things. If you always follow the right way to do a thing, you will never be creative because the right way means the way already discovered by others.

A creator has to be able to look foolish. A creator has to risk his or her so-called respectability. By definition, anything truly new will at first seem strange. People will not recognise or appreciate it. For this reason many great works of art were not appreciated or recognised during the life of the person who created them. To create something we have to stray outside what everyone else sees as normal and good and often be seen as naïve or silly. They will not see *us* as normal! This is a lonely place to be. We can only be in it if we truly love and are convinced about our idea or work. It is this that will keep us able to hold on to our idea or creation. At times we too will doubt ourselves and wonder if in fact we *are* mad and if we are just being childish and unreal! Be fresh. Be new. Be like children.

vii. Be attentive and make the effort

Creative work always requires effort. It is easy to admire a beautiful work of art and forget or ignore the hard work that went into it. People are constantly on the look out for the magic formula, the trick, the silver bullet that will turn on creativity and turn out the wonderful solution. Some of this thinking comes from our laziness but some of it is due to a misunderstanding about what creativity is. Because the final piece is often so quick and so magical, it can appear that the whole process is equally quick and magical. The field of the visual arts is a good example of this where the final painting may look straightforward but the work that has gone into it prior to its final stage is enormous. The effort can be exhausting and the temptation exists to try to side-step and avoid the necessary effort. The beauty lies in not doing so and in persisting with the challenge until the breakthrough emerges. Be attentive to the beauty in all the details around you. It is always there.

viii. Question everything

I worked for a number of years for General Motors (GM) in its days of greatest success. Much of the success of GM came from its great systems and some powerful leadership. One such powerful leader was Alfred P. Sloan. Earlier I told how one day he adjourned a board meeting soon after it had begun, saying, 'Gentlemen, I take it we are all in complete agreement on the decision here. Then I propose we postpone further discussion of this matter until our next meeting to give ourselves time to develop disagreement and perhaps gain some understanding of what the decision is about.' He believed that everything needed to be questioned, especially when it appeared there was little need to question.

We have to question everything and not take anything for granted. We do this as children and we need to continue to do it in our working environments so that we learn and grow and change and find new and better ways and worlds. This is a challenge. We can take things for granted. We accept what *is* and believe that the current way of living and being is the only way. We get comfortable with what we have and with how things are. But, more dangerously, we cease seeing alternatives because we cease looking for them. We can't imagine any other way of being or doing things or any other state of affairs.

Questioning everything is not always welcomed by those around us either. People like to settle for what is and enjoy some so-called peace. When questioned, we can feel we are being blamed for how things are. We become attached to our plans, our lifestyles, the decisions we took, the strategies we formed, the way of life we followed, the systems we designed and operate. Challenges to all of this are unsettling for us. And, yet, we know that every time we question we learn and gain. It happens to be true that we are always really wrong about everything in the sense that there is always more to be learned. This is the heart of the scientific process, which endlessly questions, knowing that all it will ever reach is the best theory *to-date*. We need to practise this process all our life and in every area of our work and organisations. If we don't ask the questions, life or reality will. The world may not have time to wait for our answers. Be questioning.

ix. Be humble

In 1989 a United Airlines flight experienced a major explosion and ended up losing all its hydraulic power, essentially the systems that control the plane. There was no known way to rescue the situation but the captain and his crew did manage to land the plane. However, in the process 112 passengers died. But, against all the odds, 184 passengers survived. This achievement, which was then seen as impossible, only happened because of the genius of the pilot, Captain Haynes. But he does not take the credit. 'For most of my career', he said, 'we kind of worked on the concept that the captain was *the* authority on the aircraft. And we lost a few airplanes because of that. Sometimes the captain isn't as smart as we thought he was.' Haynes is very clear that he could not have saved the plane by himself on that day. He says that if he hadn't used the experience of the others, he is certain he would not have made it. 'We had 103 years of flying experience in the cockpit trying to get that plane down.'[29]

As leaders we often know what we think is right and best, but this does not mean that we go it alone. In other words, we need constant feedback to check and test our insights. We must, therefore, seek, receive and accept feedback all the time from our environment. This calls for humility on our part – are you prepared to listen to feedback rather than impose your views and plans on the world? Our decision making is only valid and responsible if we have the humility to accept 'executive' feedback from the universe, from what is. This is a central learning moment in the self-correcting process. If we do this and learn, then we will have more data for the next time we make decisions, and we will get things even more right.

We need to establish systems, forums and meetings by which to pursue this feedback and seek it out. Such openness to feedback will not happen by default. We have to set up the mechanisms that will seek it out and protect it against assault from all sides. The great opponent of feedback is pride and the ego. We don't like to be wrong and we forget that we are always wrong. Feedback will allow us to get closer to being right more often.

Such an approach and attitude is contrary to the version of managing that we normally have, which is built around certainty and being right. This is the paradox –the more we recognise and accept our inability to be absolutely right in our positions and decisions the closer to right we will be! So, in fact, humility, learning and being right all belong to the same stable. Be humble.

x. Be positive

I find drilling and soldering quite challenging. Ellen McArthur did too, but then she was talking of doing it 90 feet, or 27 metres, up a mast of a boat in the South Seas. In February 2001, Ellen at the young age of twenty-four, completed the Vendèe Globe, the world's toughest yacht race. She was the youngest Briton ever to circumnavigate the globe and the fastest woman ever to have done so. Up the mast she went in the South Seas:

> As usual a beautiful calm sunrise turned into a gusty bit of sea once I'd reached half way. I must have looked fairly silly as I had a long wand strapped to my back, and a massive bag of tools... (it's a bit far to come down if you've forgotten something!). It went off ok other than the violent motion, and the amount of sanding needed to fit the wand....Once fitted I had to drill out for the retaining pin – quite a task juggling drill bits and drills at 27 meters! The painful part was the slamming in the waves, causing the bag with drill bits in it to poke into my leg....the beautiful part was taking just a second to glance out over that

orange sea scape as the sun rose.... The waters surface so deli-
cate as the waves texture it.... Just stunning....[30]

Ellen had to be positive and to believe in herself and in the power
and strength all of us have available to us.

'I reflected on how much people are capable of. But while it's
tough, it's still our choice, and in that way we are very, very lucky,'
she writes.[31]

Negative impulses will not work in terms of bringing about creativity. Psychologist Mihaly Csikszentmihalyi says that no creative
thought or created thing grows out of a negative impulse.[32] The
negative may be an initial driver to go and seek a solution but it
is only a driver. Being negative is easy. It requires no effort and
makes no demands on courage or calls for action based on hope.
Nor will it ever give birth to anything new. Being positive leads to
the birth of ideas and breakthroughs built on attitudes of hope.
Canadian writer Robertson Davies says he has known people to
embrace the tragic view of life, and it is a cop-out. They simply feel
rotten about everything and that is terribly easy.

Being optimistic and hopeful requires taking a different view
of a situation or reality. It can mean standing back and seeing
it in its broader context. This means that the situation becomes
entirely different. It becomes part of a greater whole and, as a
result, all kinds of meanings break through and new possibilities emerge. Nothing is meaningful on its own. Everything and
everyone is part of a larger context and totality. We can only really
make sense of things in their larger contexts.

This may require taking a longer-term view as well as a more
distanced view of a situation or problem. Little real meaning or
sense is to be found in the short term; everything eventually will
make sense in the long term. Again, as Robertson Davies said:
'If you take a long view, I do not see how you can be pessimistic
about the future of man or the future of the world. You can take a
short view and think that everything is a mess, that life is a cheat
and a deceit, and of course you feel miserable.'[33]

Every company and organisation will be somewhere on the
positive–negative spectrum. The dynamic within the organisation
will be critical to how creative it is and on this rests the future of the
organisation. For this reason, the level of positivity in a company
is a critical element in how creative it will be and ultimately how
successful it will be. Management systems are composed of so
many mechanisms and measurements and controls to spot what

might be wrong, that it is easy for negativity and negative mindsets to develop. Controls and fear of mistakes and things going wrong, while understandable and healthy, can dominate in organisations and create an atmosphere of fear and caution and negativity. Equally strong positive mechanisms need to be introduced that celebrate successes, that pursue opportunities, that recognise achievements, that look for new possibilities, and that set high goals and targets. Above all, organisations need people of hope and positive and visionary leaders. New ideas will not progress unless this kind of positive environment exists and creating such an environment is a key role for a leader. Be positive.

xi. Treat nothing as ordinary and everything as extraordinary

One of the clues to becoming more creative and one of the great rewards for being so is the discovery that nothing is ordinary and everything is extraordinary. This is a beautiful discovery. It enriches our lives and opens the doors to great discoveries and breakthroughs. Maybe you don't know what I mean by this.

Take a look at your desk and at what is on it. I bet you will not find one thing that is 'ordinary' in any sense of that word. On my desk I see many things – far too many, in fact. But among them are papers, of course – ordinary A4-size pages. But, if I trace the origins of these, I find that they are really quite extraordinary. I bought them in a local stationery shop, which got them from some distribution company who got them from some manufacturing company that made them. I think of the people who made them, of the equipment they used, of the deadlines they met, of the quality they achieved, of the satisfaction of getting them finished and packed. And of course if I go back any further, I end up in some jungle that someone planted a long time ago. Anything but ordinary.

Then I think of what I could use one of these pages for. How it could be used to capture one great idea, do a wonderful drawing, share a powerful secret, house a beautiful poem, declare love to someone, be the basis of a major contract, etc. The page is full of possibilities and is anything but ordinary. And the clutter on my desk also includes a stapler, a toothpick, a CD and many other wonderful and extraordinary *ordinary* things. Try it. Have a look around you.

This is not an exercise. It is reality. And all of our reality is equally full of wonder.

Part of being creative is the ability to see things in this way, to refuse to see anything as ordinary. Why? Because it is not ordinary. Everything is full of magic because of its link to every-thing else and because of the enormous possibilities it contains. This does require some work to ensure that each day is treated as not just another day and that each situation is seen and under-stood with all the richness of potential it contains.

Our big allies in being able to bring this off are problems and surprises. These are messages for us to see what actually is and they attempt to rid us of our sleepy state of not seeing what is really going on. To hear the message that surprises us and to face up to problems, we have to do two things:

a. See and feel what is going on and to do so in an incredibly honest and courageous way.

b. Open our mind to and explore all the possibilities the situation offers us.

The thing is to see the possibilities the situation or problem gives rise to. This calls for more hard work built on a conviction that there is more there, that more is possible. This calls for some practice and some re-learning. Practice is necessary because we have got into bad and lazy habits of only seeing things in line with our own views and expectations, 'as they are' we say even though it is not as they really are at all, only as we see them to be in a very narrow and boring way. It takes practice to get to the infinite possibilities in things. We can do this by re-learning skills we had when we were children where we made all kinds of things into all kinds of other things to suit our imagination and needs. In my childhood days hurley sticks became rifles, rafters became horses, horse shoes became horses, hills became battle-fields, trees became armies.

To practise this just a little, take any object on your desk right now and find ten alternative uses for it. On my desk I see a four-coloured pen which I could use as:

a. A weapon

b. A nail

c. A digger

d. A back scratcher

e. A secret

f. A juggling tool

g. A pointer

h. A toy

i. A spinning top

j. A paint brush

Then we can progress to 'ordinary' situations like meeting a colleague at work and change or imagine it as:

a. A debate

b. A duel

c. A romance

d. A tutorial

e. A game of verbal table-tennis

f. An exercise in language study

g. A lesson in body language

h. A listening exercise

i. An opportunity to discover and get a breakthrough

j. An exercise in concentration

Suddenly the world becomes a place of great fascination and richness. The ordinary becomes quite extraordinary. We enter a world of possibilities. We cease to be passive victims and become active creators. Be extraordinary.

xii. Live with wonder and curiosity

Doing all of this involves a special kind of state called wonder. Wondering is about curiosity and speculation and is based on an attitude towards everything in the world as being interesting, and deserving of exploration and attention. This again is something we need to practise and something we need to re-learn. We need to practise it as we grow out of the habit of wondering and begin taking things for granted, naming them, limiting them and taking them into our world where we choke the wonder out of them. We make them ours and they cease to exist in themselves. We become very good at this and very fast at doing it so that we spend less and less time exploring the magic and wonder and depths in things.

Of course, as children we did this endlessly to the great annoyance of our parents and adults around us. Then we did it less and less and now we hardly do it at all. We need new stimuli to arouse us to any level of interest or wonder.

Let's do another simple exercise to explain what I mean. Take some object in your vicinity and do some wondering about it.

I have a pencil...

a. I wonder how old it is.

b. I wonder when pencils were first invented.

c. I wonder how much I could write with it if I kept using it; could I write a book?

d. I wonder who made it.

e. I wonder what happened to its sister or brother pencils that were made on the same day?

f. I wonder what will happen to it.

g. I wonder how I got it.

h. I wonder what is the greatest use I could put it to?

i. I wonder at its simplicity and its power.

j. I wonder at its beauty.

A good dose of wonder, curiosity and interest in what things are like and how they work will enrich our lives and all we do. It is simply another example of what we have said all along – that creativity and being human are virtually synonymous. Working in this way will also broaden the range of responses we give to various situations. Be wonder-full.

Some of these golden rules are or appear to refer to the individual. But the individual is always part of and affected by the culture in which they operate. So it is important to get this culture right too and fashion it so that it supports and promotes creativity in every part of the organisation.

Part 2: The recipe and ingredients for a creative culture
While it is always possible to be creative, it is so much easier to be creative if the culture in which you live and work is a creative

one. This is why we have Silicon Valley as an environment for computer technology, Florence for painting, Vienna for music, and other centres of excellence all of which encourage a particular specialty. So, in a company or any organisation, it would be enormously helpful to people if we could provide a creative culture for them to work within.

How do we do that? Here are eight things you can do to develop a creative culture in your company.

i. Create a sense of purpose and make sure all understand it and buy into it

This is easily done. It is what initially formed or drove someone to start a company in the first place on the basis of an unmet need or unsatisfactorily met need. A sense of purpose is found by asking simple questions about what the company or organisation is about, its *raison d'être*. If everyone understands the meaning and purpose behind the organisation, this will provide the energy for all creative efforts and will underpin searches for new and better ways of working and new and better products or services.

Think of your own company or organisation. Forget the accountants and the bottom line for a minute.

- What is the whole thing about?
- What difference is the company making or what difference does it want to make?
- What did the founders or originators see as its purpose?
- Why is working in this company a good way to spend your time, your days, your life?
- How would you invite or persuade someone to join the company?

ii. Ask lots of good questions and encourage questions

Doing this and doing it consistently will help discover needs, issues, problems and weaknesses within the company. It will also uncover weaknesses as well as opportunities. Questions will keep minds active and alert and awake. We all slip into routines and continue to do things that have little or no value. We take things for granted and stop checking the reasons why we do certain things. We need to question everything and welcome those *awkward* people who love challenging and asking questions.

Equally we want to hear questions. We want to welcome them. They will make us think. They will make us wisely and prudently doubt our dangerous certainties.

- What do you want and need to question about your organisation?
- What are you not questioning? What are you taking for granted?
- Who are the good questioners in the organisation – the people we often avoid?
- When you ask 'Any questions?' do you really want them?
- Do you ever hold forums just for people to ask questions about what is happening and why things are being done the way they are?

iii. Engage and involve

Every time we get people involved in an issue of substance we are opening up possibilities for new ideas and perspectives. The practice of doing this and of soliciting different viewpoints will act as a continuous well of rich ideas and contributions to improving the organisation and keeping it alive and vibrant. This is easy to do. It is only difficult because of our mindsets about management and the role of the manager. We think we should know it all. What is worse, we sometimes *think* we do know it all, at least about our own organisations and what needs to be done. Remember, 'None of us is as clever as all of us.'

- How well do you run your meetings? What would others say about that?
- Do people really feel involved, engaged and listened to? What would they say if you asked them?
- Do you ask them?
- How often do you change your mind as a result of listening to people?
- Is involving others part and parcel of how you work or do you only do it occasionally and even then with only certain people?
- How familiar are your own managers in facilitating and involving their people?
- Is it a core part of their jobs? And of yours?

iv. Manage and control less

This can sound contradictory, as management is often seen to be all about control. While this is true to an extent, we do have to learn to control the right things. We can never really be in control of everything and our best way of dealing with the controllable is to trust people to each look after their particular piece of the wider picture. In that way we have a network of management which has a far greater capacity to control and we have to trust them and to let go. It is a vicious circle in the sense that the less we trust people, the less trustworthy people will be and the more we will be confirmed in our stance not to trust. We all know that risk and reward ride side by side. And if you avoid one the other will also pass you by. How easy is it for you to trust people?

- Have people disappointed you or let you down in the past?
- Do you believe in taking risks with people?
- How trusted do your people feel?
- Are they trustworthy?
- How and in what areas could you take more risks with people and control less?
- Do you really believe that the greatest gift you can give your people is to trust them?

v. Create teams and people networks

This follows from the previous point. Groups of people will have enormous power to make things happen if they are organised into teams and networks. In this way things get done naturally with little need for management or control. New York or any major city only has food for about two days! The miracle of the supply of food is not managed by an overseer but happens through the myriad of networks that make up the life of the city.

- Are teams and team working seen as something nice to have or as something critical to your organisation?
- What experiences have you had of the power of teams and team-working?
- How supportive are people in general?

- How much are people driven by their peers and by the will to not let their teammates down more than by pleasing their manager?
- How much pride is there in the organisation and in individual areas?
- Do people have real and shared goals?

vi. Pay a visit to all the sacred cows

Anyone new to any organisation quickly comes to meet the various sacred cows around the place. 'We have always done it like that!' they hear. Those within the organisation know better than to even whisper that the king may have no clothes. We need to get to know all the sacred cows and then have the courage to challenge them and kill them off if necessary. While it does require courage, doing this will have enormous benefits and bring great freedom to the company. Many will wonder why they had not done it a long time ago.

- How could you find the sacred cows in your organisation?
- Have you yourself reared any sacred cows?
- How would you know? Who could you ask?
- Are there some things you could stop doing in the morning without jeopardising the operation?
- Who could you invite in to help you see and find the sacred cows and the things that are serving no real purpose any longer?
- How about a regular sacred cows slot in your meetings (where you talk about why they exist and getting rid of them) at least once a month or quarter?

vii. Question your beliefs

We all have beliefs about ourselves and the world and about what is possible. We operate to these beliefs. They empower us and they limit us depending on how good and accurate they are. We think they are real even though we have made them up. For that reason it is good to look at what we have made up and check if it is good and accurate and healthy. We have to work at this because we do not see them as beliefs at all but as reality. It requires conscious work to find the important beliefs, challenge them and replace the bad ones with better and more helpful ones. Each time we do this we are opening up a whole new field of power for ourselves. And this is achieved by a small bit of mental work. What a prize!

- What are three beliefs you have about yourself that might be holding you back and which may not be true at all?

- Find one or two negative beliefs you have about yourself and turn them into positives, not by denying them, but by using them to develop a strength.

- What beliefs about the organisation or your world should you take a look at?

- What is a belief commonly held in your company which, if you were wrong about it, would make a great difference to your performance and results?

- Do you know of many people who are far better than they think they are but whose beliefs are proving them right?

- How could you help them change these beliefs?

- Who could help you change your own?

viii. Set yourself up to be creative

Creativity will not happen unless the company is structured to facilitate it happening. As I have said, many of our meetings and systems look to the past, reviewing, looking at reports and analysing results. Important as these activities may be, they will not create a future for us. People who live and work under these systems get conditioned by them. Surprises, risks, possibilities and what we want are all left for the greater part to chance. They are seen as exceptional. Or they are left to certain parts or areas of the business to whom they are seen to belong – Marketing and Research & Development, for instance. We need different meetings, job titles, behaviours and structures that promote and support really good creative thinking.

- Are your systems and ways of working based more or less on a stable and, to a great extent, unchanging world?

- How many creative meetings or sessions are held per week?

- If the future is unknown and uncertain, is the organisation designed to cope with and be ready for this kind of world?

- Are managers seen as being change agents or are they there to simply manage what exists?

- How are problems and surprises viewed? As exceptions? As bad news? Or as reality and opportunities for change and betterment?

Part 3: The seven steps in the creative process

Many creative people appear not to follow any clear process in being creative. This may *appear* to be the case but there is virtually always a process at work, however fast and invisible that process may be.

There are many processes that people can and do follow. Notwithstanding this, there is a pattern that most creative processes follow. Here I will talk about a group creative process as part of that creative way of working that I have spoken about. What follows are well tried steps that I have been using and have seen to work and work well.

i. Setting up and getting going

This is about calling a meeting, getting it started, and getting people on board, interested in and decided on tackling or exploring a situation. It creates the motivation to tackle an issue and to stick at it.

Take a very simple work issue like a persistent problem with a customer. When the decision is made to tackle this issue and to do so in a creative way, something new happens. A commitment is made to go after something in the belief that there is a better way. Nobody actually *knows* that there is a better way. The risk of it being a blind alley always exists. So the decision to call a meeting or to sit down and work on it in a new way is a brave one and involves an act of faith. It also releases or generates energy in oneself or in those with whom one is going to work.

A good way to tackle such an issue is to begin with the words: 'How can we...' This injects energy into the issue. For example, 'We have very low sales for this year' is not a very energising statement. Change it to something like: 'How can we increase our sales for this year?' or 'How can we make this year a really successful sales year?' or 'How can we make customer X our most satisfied customer and our biggest ally?' puts a very different angle on it and invites a response and a search for ways to make it happen. Suddenly we have a world with a challenge in it, even if we have no idea as yet what to do about it. We are off. Things will never be the same again. A step has been taken.

If this seems a fairly innocuous step, try it on some problems you have now.

a. Think of some problems you have at present

Maybe some come immediately to mind or maybe you have to dig around to find one. Either way, something has happened. You have brought to your attention a situation in your life that is not as you would like it to be. This is what 'problem' really means. It could be that becoming more aware of it will mean that you will want to do something about it and you may decide to do something about it.

b. Now take any one of those 'problems' – perhaps the most important one – and think of it in terms of 'How can I...?' or 'I wish....'

What does this do to the problem? Does it not feel a bit different now? 'I am overweight' becomes 'How can I lose weight?' or 'How can I be in better shape?' 'I have a problem with a family relationship' changes into a challenge – 'How can I improve the relationship with X in my family?' By doing this, you are making at least the beginnings of a decision to do something or to think about doing something about the problem. You have changed from being passive to being active, from seeing a situation as a given reality to seeing it as something that can be changed and that you would like to try to change.

A lot has happened in this first step. If that is so when working on individual problems, it is many times more so when it is done in a group or team setting. Already we have made progress.

ii. Exploration – analysis and immersion

This step is normally called 'analysis' as this is when an issue gets tossed about and explained, questions are asked, and background is given and 'analysed'. 'Analysis' is a poor and deceptive word to use for what is needed at this stage. It gives the impression that all problems can be broken into their respective parts, everything understood, the causes found, solutions identified and the problem 'fixed'. This is true for some problems of a purely technical nature, though, even here, this approach will very often be found wanting. This step is really about getting a feel for the problem that will open it up and open up minds and hearts to get creative breakthroughs. It is not just about getting an intellectual understanding of the problem but a feel for it in its totality. This stage involves:

a. A brief explanation of the issue and the background to it.

b. Why it is a serious or worthwhile issue and why it is important to resolve it or find a way forward.

c. A look at what current or previous thinking or efforts have led to

d. What a really good solution or outcome would deliver and why it would be so great.

It may seem strange that we do not demand more information and analysis at this stage, but, when we are looking for a creative solution, too much information can get in the way; it can block us from being able to think of and imagine alternative solutions. We can end up being so expert in the problem that we are unable to think of ways out of it. Having a problem can be a bit like being trapped down a hole. The only people who are any good to us, as we saw earlier (see page 79), are those who are *not* down the hole.

If we all end up thinking in the same way as the person with the problem, then we will be of little use. For that reason we have to curtail the natural desire to know all there is to know about the problem. Getting things 'wrong' can often lead to surprising and good results, as Christopher Columbus, who set off to find the Indies and instead found America, could testify.

While all of this is happening people will be listening. But the kind of listening they are doing is important. They can be listening to:

• Learn about the problem or challenge

• Be entertained

• Understand and get to the bottom of the issue

• Show an interest in the issue and in the person who has it

These are all fine things to do but we want more! We want people to listen actively.

What does 'listening actively' mean?

It means that we listen, not only to understand, but also to get ideas and perspectives in order to help. So, during this important step, we need people to listen to the person talking in order to understand but also to listen to what is going on in their own heads in order to find perspectives and ideas to help. So, in a sense, they are listening to two 'conversations' or events – the one in the room and the one inside themselves. This we call In-Out listening – being in the room, in the meeting and also being outside in the sense of paying attention to what you are thinking and feeling.

This might seem a lot to do but it is very feasible and we actually do it all the time, We call it 'being distracted'! Rarely do we give 100 per cent of our attention to what another person is saying. This might not be a very good thing to do in school or even when listening to a friend, but when we want new and fresh ideas it is a good thing to do. And we can do it because people speak at a rate of about 150 words per minute and we listen and think at around 900 words per minute. So we have six times spare capacity to think and be active while listening.

What do we listen for?

All kinds of things:

- Concrete ideas or suggestions to resolve the issue
- Feelings about the particular item
- Connections we make to other situations
- Distractions completely removed from the actual topic – things we have to do, things that pop into our heads, associations we make based on some words the person speaking used, etc.

One way of doing this is to separate a page in two and use one side for noting the points the person is making and the other side for what is occurring to yourself at the same time. Then, by the time the person is finished explaining the topic and going through the four questions mentioned above, you already have lots of ideas. And they will be new and fresh ideas, different from the ideas the person explaining the issue might have because you are different and think differently and are not 'down the hole' with them. In fact, working in this way will actually prevent you falling into the hole.

This works so well that, even at this step, you will be well on the way to gaining new perspectives and contributions to the topic being discussed.

iii. Get ideas, perspectives and contributions for the creative insight

At this stage, ideas, views, suggestions, perspectives and recommendations are sought and collected as raw material for a possible breakthrough and for a new insight into the issue. There are many approaches to doing this but it is important that these not be limited to ideas or so-called solutions as in traditional brainstorming exercises. They need to be much broader and deeper than this, so anything goes once it is a reaction or response to the issue or challenge. It is important, too, that all are 'collected' and noted and none lost. We are not looking for the bull's eye or silver bullet here but for a rich combination of various viewpoints that together can lead to a completely new and different outcome or breakthrough. The truth and richness will not be in any one idea or viewpoint but in the combination of some of them, in the mix of them and in the rich interplay between them.

The importance of handling it in this way, as distinct from traditional brainstorming, is that it is a process we are talking about and not just collecting ideas. We are setting something in motion that takes on a life of its own and that creates and builds momentum in a group of people about a particular issue. This is not about collecting ideas as if they were things, bits and pieces, items of different kinds that may serve to crack the problem. It is about getting a process of thinking and searching going in a group that will work on the issue which itself is something dynamic that requires a total solution. This dynamic is something live that goes in all sorts of directions in pursuit of the solution. A new process of thinking is created in which a 'group mind' gets formed, which is far more powerful than any one mind or even a collection of individual minds. This in turn leads to the issue or situation being seen in a more holistic and integrated way which may not only resolve the issue but will take it and the group to a different place. Not only does the problem change but the group changes and becomes something else – new and powerful.

This part of the process needs to be well led so that this coalescence of the group happens. The coalescing happens by a continued contribution of points of view, each building on previous ones, linking to each other and triggering each other so that a flow happens which takes on a life of its own. The leader or facilitator keeps this flow going, reminding the group, if necessary, of the original challenge and of its importance, ensuring all ideas are heard and recorded, and inviting all to contribute, especially those who may need to be invited and who may feel they have not as much to contribute as others. The leader looks after the group, the person who 'owns' the problem and the problem or challenge itself (see the idea of *clientship* in Chapter 20). The leader also decides with the client or main owner of the problem when they feel a solution has been reached or when enough material is available to work towards a solution. If the latter is the case then it is time to evaluate and select the most promising ideas for a solution. But very often the problem will have been cracked already.

iv. Evaluation – identification of the most likely contributions towards a breakthrough insight

This stage is straightforward – it is about selection. But it is not – except in very exceptional circumstances – about the selection of the one brilliant idea that will solve or resolve everything. It is more about selecting themes, looking for combinations of ideas and inputs, searching for hypothetical solutions or even identifying some major 'wonder-full' and way-out proposal that could begin a whole new way of seeing the situation.

There is a danger at this point in being too 'realistic'. What is meant by this is the tendency we have to go too early for what is most feasible and practical. While this is important, if we try to get there too early in the process we will fail to be sufficiently new, exciting and ultimately successful in getting a really good outcome.

In my Synectics days, we had a way of checking the real value of potential solutions to problems or issues. We called it a NAF rating:

- **N** – How **N**ew is the idea?
- **A** – How **A**ttractive or **A**ppealing is it?
- **F** - How **F**easible is it?

Feasibility is important but only after we are happy that the idea is New and Attractive. It is easier to build feasibility into a new idea than to try to breathe newness into a feasible but small or poor idea.

We can plot the various contributions received on a matrix which has the Value of the contribution on one axis, i.e. how valuable is it in terms of really offering a major breakthrough. On the other axis we rate the Feasibility of the contribution.

```
V ┌─────────────┬─────────────┐
a │             │             │
l │             │             │
u │      1      │      2      │
e │             │             │
  │             │             │
  ├─────────────┼─────────────┤
  │             │             │
  │      4      │      3      │
  │             │             │
  │             │             │
  └─────────────┴─────────────┘
                          Feasibility
```

8.2. Evaluating ideas.

So we can see the various boxes 1–4 into which contributions might fall.

Box 4: There might be some ideas or suggestions in this box that people – even their owners – might regard as not being worth consideration as they lack both Value and Feasibility, or don't have enough of both of them.

Box 3. This box can get crammed. This happens because people like ideas that are practical and comfortable. This is fine and works well for straightforward and relatively easy situations but be careful. Ideas from Box 3 will not change the world or lead us to any great breakthroughs. Watch just how many ideas and contributions fall in here. By all means, use them. Don't neglect them or ignore them. Use them because:

a. They might lead on to other things and to a breakthrough.

b. They get things going.

c. They create momentum.

But don't settle for them. Look for more and better contributions.

Box 2: This is where you will find those better contributions. Anything in this box is great! They are of high value and also

124

very feasible. Enough contributions or even one or two really good ones in here and you have your breakthrough. You're away.

Box 1: This is the tricky one. What we have here, as you can see, are ideas that seem valuable and interesting but are not feasible or practical. The problem is that these often get dumped for being good but unrealistic, pie-in-the-sky notions. What they are in reality is a collection of contributions with great value in them that need more work to turn them into being feasible. This is the easier part. Remember – it is easier to build feasibility into a creative, if wild, idea than to build creativity into a very practical but non-creative idea. If ideas in Box 3 are gold dust and ideas in Box 2 gold nuggets, here we have huge rocks, boulders, with glimpses of gold in them. It would be worthwhile to explore them some more and very foolish to ignore or abandon them.

Going too early for the feasible and practical options is the single biggest mistake made in sessions where creative or breakthrough ideas are needed and sought. A different kind of attitude is needed, one that is open to hearing and holding on to way-out ideas. There is the principle that 'If at first an idea is not absurd, there is no hope for it.' This also calls for a process to take these ideas and work and refine them into a new and powerful way forward. This takes us to Step v.

v. Emergence and decision making

This is the hardest step and the one that can take most time. There are two aspects to this step – one is ours and one is not ours. Emergence is not really within our control. I use 'emergence' because often we have to wait for the breakthrough idea to emerge. This is not a passive waiting but a very busy one. We examine, tease out and look into the contributions that hold most promise. We reflect, go silent and wait for the breakthrough to come, to emerge. We are desperate for a breakthrough and patient waiting for it. We look for it and know we may not find it, but *it* may find *us*.

Like for the other steps there are some guidelines to help make this step successful. Most of these revolve around building a tolerance and, indeed, a welcome for strange or crazy ideas. This is not easy. Such ideas are normally called 'bad ideas'. So, in effect, we have to help people to accept, for the moment, bad ideas. In fact, there is no such thing as bad ideas or good ideas either for that matter, if by 'good' we mean perfect. Every idea will have some good in it and some flaws or weaknesses. It looks a bit like this:

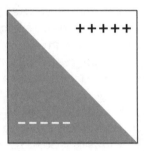

8.3. Ideas.

The trouble is, when we hear an idea we immediately zone in on the negative side in it. We do this for very good reasons. It is not that we are negative by nature. Imagine if, for example, you wanted to have more free or disposable time and I suggested to you that you do everything a bit slower. I bet you would immediately see a lot of problems with my hot idea! If I insisted that my idea had value you might even get irritated with me. This, I repeat, is not because you are a negative or bad person. It is because you naturally focused on the negative in the idea and, taken at face value, doing things more slowly would seem to have some downsides to it in terms of saving you time. No argument.

But it also has some good points. The trouble is that we can't get at these because we are blinded or blocked by the negative aspects. But if I persisted, I bet we could come up with a few good things about this idea that would actually help with your need to have more time. We might say that at least you would be doing everything with greater comfort and less stress. It might mean you do more planning. It might mean that some things just will not get done and will have to be dropped. It might mean being more relaxed. It might lead to things getting done really well and done once and for all. So, in summary, out of this 'bad idea' we now have the following strategies:

- Only do the things that are really important and have to be done and get rid of all the others.
- Plan more and better.

- Do everything well so that it gets done once and for all.
- Practise doing everything in a relaxed and cool way and find a way to de-stress yourself or to reduce the stress in your life and work.

Not bad for a 'bad idea'!

For this emergence step we need to get good at, practise and use this simple process as demonstrated above.

a.   Hold on to the strange or bad idea.

b.   Get behind the negative bit to the value that is there.

c.   Find ways to use this value without involving the negative parts.

d.   Prepare a new plan based on the combination of all the value in the idea.

This step is difficult because we are in a completely new territory or ocean, far away from the dry, firm land of the logical, practical and real. But this is the voyage to a new reality if we have the faith to play our part and trust the winds and currents to take us there. They always will.

vi. Decision making and action

This step follows or flows from Step v but it does have to be taken. It is important that it be taken for a few reasons:

a.   Naturally it is important so that something actually happens and gets done. Strange and silly as it may seem, having had a 'good meeting' can satisfy some people and can be enough. Apportioning or agreeing responsibilities can be a less attractive exercise.

b.   It is important as an encouragement to continue this way of working as results and visible outcomes give encouragement.

c.   It is also important for learning as we only know what works from *doing* things and so the process of taking action will give us invaluable and irreplaceable knowledge of what works so that we can get it more right next time. In this way, the whole process will be truly a learning one.

This step is straightforward and consists of agreeing:

a.   What needs to be done.

b. Who will do it.

c. When it will be done.

Who does it can, of course, be an individual or a small group who champion the action.

vii. Review

This step is one that rarely happens and, as a result, invaluable learning opportunities are lost. The review here is of the meeting itself and of the process that was followed. This need not take time but great lessons for the next time can be learned.

There are many ways to review a meeting but one way that I favour is to simply ask how we did things under three headings:

- The task.
- The group.
- The individual.

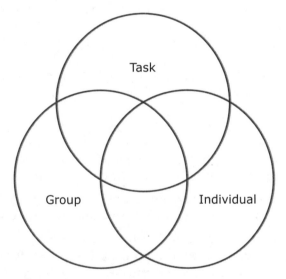

8.4. Reviewing meetings.

By 'task' I mean simply the challenge, the problem or the issue that was being worked on. How did we do in terms of solving it or getting a good result or outcome for it?

By 'group' I mean how we worked as a group of people, as a team, how cooperative were we, how united were we, how well did we listen to each other, respect each other?

By 'individual' I mean how was the meeting or session for me? How did I feel? How did I perform, not only in how big a part did I play but how respectful I was, how open I was and how 'un-needy' I was?

A way to do this is to get each person to score themselves out of ten under each heading and then hear and note all of these on a flipchart and find out a bit about why people rated themselves as such.

Spend some more time going over the low scores with the group, not to be negative or critical but to learn and improve. This needs to be handled in a way that does not create over-defensiveness on your own or anyone else's part, so it is good to note the various comments so that people feel heard without necessarily implying that they are right in what they are saying.

Doing this can mean that every session, every meeting, is a learning experience and that every single person present is given the opportunity to learn and improve.

These seven steps need a lot more elaboration and need lots of practice. For now they will suffice as descriptors of the broad lines that a good formal creative process can follow.

Part 4: The alarm clock – getting off to a good, creative start

Creativity and thinking and working in creative ways are not things we can just turn on and off. It is an attitude to life and to the world. It is about trying to live each day as creatively – in the full sense of that word, as already mentioned – as possible. Doing this is the work of a lifetime and making this happen and making it part of our lives will not happen by default. One way that I find helpful is to try to make the most of each day and treat it as a gift. This needs to begin early. If you don't catch the day early on, you may find yourself in the middle of it...and lost in it. For that reason it is a good practice to get the day off to a positive start. One way to do this is to use a process similar to one that author Anthony Robbins recommends. So, every morning when you wake up, instead of letting a flood of worries and anxieties or the morning radio good-mood assassination show take you over, why don't *you* decide what you think and take control of your brain.

You can do this by deliberately asking yourself some questions:

- What am I happy about in my life at present? How does that make me feel?

- What am I excited about in my life? How does that make me feel?

- What am I proud of in my life at the moment? How does that make me feel?

- What am I grateful for in my life at present? How does that make me feel?

- What am I committed to in my life at present? How does that make me feel?

- Who loves me and who do I love? How does that make me feel?

Sometimes this exercise takes effort but it is always valuable.

I mentioned this process to a friend I meet for an annual Christmas party some years back and he liked the idea and noted the questions. A year later he told me a story. He had told a friend about this process I had mentioned to him and he too liked it and noted the questions. As it happened, this person had a friend in Australia suffering from depression and he shared the process and the questions with him. It changed his life. For some reason this simple process worked for this person. How many behaviours and people have been changed as a result of such a little action as sharing something with a friend? One small action can make a huge difference and trigger positive actions in other people, helping them to face and address their lives in better ways and play a bigger part in the situations and worlds in which they live.

If this seems too grandiose I ask you again to recall Marianne Williamson and her mantra: 'Your playing small does not serve the world.' Let us not play small. Let us take ourselves seriously and be aware of how we can and do shape our worlds by the quality of our responses to our given situations and realities. We can do it every day and make every day an adventure in living. So begin early. Catch the day at the outset and make today a creative day, a day spent bringing forth the truth and beauty of your particular situation. Try to manage to be really human...every day.

Section III – Real Power

Chapter 9

You Are More Powerful than You Think

'A teacher affects eternity; he can never tell where
his influence stops.'

– Henry Brooks Adams

Nor can you.

Your circle of influence

On reading the chapter title above, two thoughts might cross your mind:

1. Yes, I might be more powerful than I think, but if so, not much.

2. My influence is relatively small and limited.

Let's see!

Changing the world

How difficult do you think it would be for you to change the world and how much effort would it take? How about just changing your whole company or the organisation you belong to? How difficult would that be? How about your particular area or department within your organisation? And what about changing yourself?

None of these are easy. Not even the last one. They look a bit like figure 9.1, where:

- Box 1 is difficult but not too risky, like learning Chinese.
- Box 2 is both difficult and risky, like cycling along the Great Wall of China.
- Box 3 is risky but not too difficult, like unfurling a Taiwanese flag in Tiananmen Square.

9.1. Changing the world.

- Box 4 is not very difficult and not very risky like eating a Chinese meal with chopsticks.

If we take four campaigns you might undertake:

1. Changing the world.
2. Changing your company or organisation.
3. Changing your own area or department.
4. Changing yourself.

They will probably go into different boxes on our matrix.

So, we see that, while it is not easy to change myself or my department, it is easier than changing the whole world!

The place to start, then, is with ourselves and to work our way across. We will only change the world by first of all changing ourselves and then those we immediately relate to and influence. We are first working in an area where we do have *some* control and power to influence.

Who? Me? Poor little me!

Bringing about a change or improvement in things around us is still a massive task and we could justifiably ask ourselves: 'Who am I to take on this responsibility and burden of changing any of these? How could I possibly set out on such a journey with the limited resources I have? Me?'

First of all, we have to give some real attention to 'little me' and realise the full truth of who we really are.

Oftentimes we see ourselves as being on our own. We feel it's entirely up to us and that we are fighting a lone battle to make things happen.

The good news is that this image is a lie. It does not look at all like that. *You* do not look at all like that. Here's how you look and how you are:

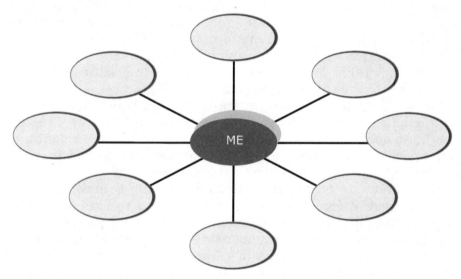

9.2. Circle of relationships.

In other words, you are the centre of a set of relationships.

I say you *'are* the centre of a set of relationships' and not 'you are *at* the centre of a set of relationships', which also happens to be true.

This is because you are who you are because of people around you. You have been 'made' the person you are by the people who reared and formed you and shaped you along the way. You are only human by having been humanised. You are not a human being because of having eyes and a nose and a brain. You are human because you *learned* to be human and you learned this from other people – parents, brothers and sisters, friends, teachers and many others along the way. People who were reared away from contact with other human beings are great examples: they failed to turn out to be true human beings despite looking exactly like any other human being and possessing all the organs and faculties of every other human being. Forms of isolation of children from adults and other children lead to various forms of psychosocial dwarfism. While no more than one hundred cases have ever been described, the key features include, first, a very slow rate of linear growth, with height for age among the lowest 1 per cent of the population; remarkable features of behaviour, including a disrupted sleep pattern with wandering at night in search of food a usual symptom; hyperphagia (an insatiable appetite); polydipsia (an insatiable thirst); and pain agnosia (an insensibility to physical discomfort). Social relationships with both peers and adults are characterised by a lack of any affection and the children are usually miserable and hyperactive, have a low self-esteem and display moderate to severe learning difficulties.

So we have been made human and this process continues throughout our lives. We make each other by who we are. We condition each other. We adjust and behave always in relation to other people, to how they are, to how we see them, to how they see us and to what we believe their expectations of us are.

So, for now, to make sure what I am saying is making sense, why not take a few minutes to think of who the key people in your working life are. We will confine it to working life for now, as this is what we are currently focusing on. Your boss or manager will feature as well as those to whom you are manager and, of course colleagues and others with whom you have to deal and relate. In some cases you may need to take account of people in terms of groups to avoid cluttering up the whole image. Take a few minutes for it.

So, you are the centre of all these relationships. How you see these people, treat them, talk to them, relate to them and so on will greatly affect how *they* are, especially if you are a manager to some of them.

In turn, of course, these people are centres of other circles of relationships and so they too will have great effects on these people, depending on how they are with those people...and so on it goes.

So, it is not just the people in direct contact with you that you influence but all the people with whom *they* are in contact too. This is not a mechanistic model, but an organic or quantum one. It will not come about in a cause-and-effect way but in a chaotic

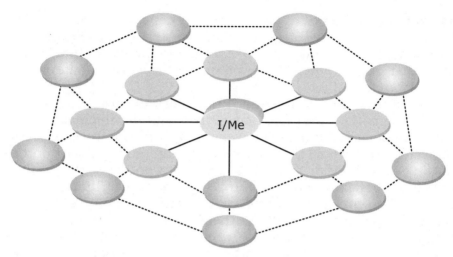

9.3. Circle of relationships.

and uncontrolled way. We just do not know the extent of the effects we have on people and how powerful these will be. So, in terms of changing things around you, a lot is possible and you have a lot of influence, a lot of power – a lot more than you probably think.

Humanising and making each other human

When driving to Dublin in heavy morning traffic, I frequently come to a major road with an endless line of cars and no way to get on to the road. Eventually, and usually fairly promptly, someone on the major road will stop and let me into the traffic in front of them. I wave and turn on various kinds of lights to show my appreciation. What interests me is that I find myself subsequently doing the very same thing, that is, letting others in in front of me. I have been 'changed' by the person who first let me into the stream of cars. In a quiet and subtle way their behaviour has made me that bit more human – at least for that journey.

See how powerful you are, then, and the enormous effects you can have and are having on the people around you? While this is a small example, I bet you can think of people who had great influences on you in your life – people who believed in you, who gave you a chance, who cared for you and gave you attention. So, in terms of changing anything, you are immensely more powerful than you might have thought you were. You can have enormous effects on people all around you. You have enormous power through your relationships and it is a great responsibility to be in a position of influence at the centre of a network of relationships. So, as managers, we have to take ourselves very seriously, in terms of how truly important we are to others and in how powerful we can be in influencing or changing the world, whatever that means for each of us.

Why is this important? Well it is important, of course, for the people themselves and for their welfare and development. But it is also important for the effectiveness of your own work or overall project. These people that you influence are, in fact, your portals to the outside world. You touch, influence and impact the world through other people in your circle of influence. Ultimately, how effective you are in the world will depend on the quality of the relationships you have with all these people. It is absolutely true that you are only as good as your relationships. It is an enormous responsibility and privilege to be in such a position and one we should not take lightly. However, it is one we should welcome and feel immensely grateful for.

Taking ourselves for granted

I stress this because we can forget how important we really are and we take ourselves for granted. This may seem strange but if you look around you, you will see it all the time. I see it when I visit hospitals. Some doctors and consultants (not nurses usually) forget the importance they have for patients who hang on their every word. They get accustomed to seeing people anxious and unwell. They stop realising the difference they can make to how people feel. Worried patients sit for hours waiting for appointments to get a diagnosis or a result of a test. Their whole lives hang in the balance. But for the doctors or consultants, it is just another day, another patient. A nurse friend of mine told me how she got a phone call to her ward one night and the caller said: 'I am just calling to see how Daddy is.' My nurse friend, who was under some pressure, replied: 'But who is "Daddy"? I've got thirty-five patients in this ward! How am I supposed to know who your daddy is?' The caller gave her father's name and added: 'Would you make sure not to put too much milk in his tea. He likes only a small drop.' My nurse friend told me that it was the first time she actually saw that patient as a person.

Lest you think I am being over-critical of others, I remember many years ago being involved in a very heavy recruitment programme in General Motors. We had to hire 150 people over 3 months so we had days of endless interviews. I can remember one morning coming out after two hours of interviewing to a very welcome cup of coffee. I was about to take my first sip when another candidate for interview walked in. I felt so annoyed and pressurised. 'Can I not even have my coffee break in peace?' I thought. For me that arrival was an interruption to my coffee break. For the interviewee, it was one of the most important days of their year or lives. They had got telephone calls wishing them well the night before and kisses of good luck as they left the house that morning. But for me they were an interruption to my coffee break.

For these reasons it is important to regularly take stock and pay attention to the key part you play in people's lives. Because we have so many other things to get done as part of our jobs we can forget the people around us on whom we depend to get most things done, and who are important people in their own right with rich and deep lives to be lived like ourselves. We must not take ourselves or those around us for granted.

Who are you? Being who you really are

To play this part well you have to be aware of your importance and you also have to just *be*. While your behaviour and communication are, of course, important, and how you handle others is critical, how you actually *are* is the most important factor. So, it is important to pay attention to yourself, to who you are being, to the kind of person and presence you are to the people around you. Remember again Marianne Williamson's words about not playing small.

People see you as you *are* and not just as you say you are or as you behave. This is about your values, what you represent, what you believe in, what is important to you, your beliefs and principles and, above all, your hopes and what you want. It is about your integrity and your credibility. It is about your deepest meaning as a person, your vocation, your role in life and the part you want to play in the world.

Getting clear about all of this involves spending time with yourself alone or with a good friend or good coach to get to the deepest parts in you that make you who you really are and want to be. This is a dangerous area for me to comment on as it can impinge on the most intimate and deepest part of a person's life so take it for what it is worth and ignore or skip it if it is troublesome or not helpful.

Some useful questions that I believe are valuable in helping us get to our true selves are:

1. Imagine yourself when you were very young (whatever age you like) – what do you think your wishes or dreams for yourself were then?

2. How might those dreams translate into meaningful terms and a meaningful role for you now?

3. What are some things you have done that made you really proud of yourself?

4. What do you think it is that makes you most *you*?

5. What are the three fundamental principles you have as a person?

6. What do people most require or need from you, even though they cannot say it?

7. When and how do you let yourself down? How would you feel if you were always faithful to your true self and never let yourself down?

8. What is the unique contribution you can make to the world from where you are now? For what were you born?

9. What do you most love about yourself that is key to you? Your core?

10. If there was nothing holding you back, no fears, nobody, no low opinions, what would you do that would really fulfil you and your dreams?

Using these questions, spend some time answering the following:

1. What do I really want to achieve in my present role that would be true to who I am, based on the above questions?

2. Who and how do I want to be in relation to the people around me, based on what I want to achieve and make happen for myself and for others?

3. How will I know that I am being the kind of person I want and need to be?

Press-ups and sit-ups

The Circle of Influence exercise, like all exercises, has to be carried out on a frequent basis because, as we have said, we forget and take ourselves for granted and stop realising how important we are to the people around us. This, in fact, is our key role as managers, as we will see later – to impact and empower all those around us and who work with us. We can help to make them more human and, in the process, manage to be more human ourselves.

Also, in the process, we will achieve a lot more and our areas will perform a lot better. Don't forget that the people in your circle of influence are your points of contact with the outside world, your gateways to your work environment, the means by which you change and make things happen. The better your relationship with and influence on the people around you, the more successful you will be. You will have the great satisfaction of enjoying good, healthy, wholesome relations with people around you and the satisfaction of achieving more and being more successful as a manager or professional.

I am saying that the quality of your relationships with your people will have a great influence on your people and on their performance. It is to this that I will now turn in Chapter 10. How important or impactful might it be to have good relationships with people who work with us or 'for' us?

Chapter 10

Exploring and Releasing the Infinite Potential of People

In managing to be human we have to aim high. What I mean is that we are not after being human in the sense of understanding, accepting and living with the weaknesses and limitations of people – ourselves included. We want to be – and to help people to be – truly human, which means being the most that we can be. Our great responsibility and great privilege as managers, leaders and, indeed, as people is to influence and impact on those around us so that they are or become the most that they can be. A great part of *how* impactful we can be and how much difference we can make is down to us and to how we are and how we behave. But not all of it. The other part of it rests with how much potential there is in the people we work with to perform better and make a difference.

Sometimes when I work with sportspeople, at a very early stage in our work together, I tell them in a feigned tone of arrogance: 'I will want to *re-make you* as a footballer, tennis player, etc.' They look at me with a mixture of fear and disbelief. Then I say, 'Well, let me correct that. I want to make you who you really *are*. I want to work with you to help you become the great player you *really* are. I want to work with you to bring out the *real* you – the you that is hidden behind the fears, false beliefs and low impressions of yourself that are holding you back from being who you really are.'

Then we're off.

The two Ps

I say all this to them because I know it is true. We are all only realising a percentage – and a small one – of our real potential.

I draw it like figure 10.1.

POTENTIAL
PERFORMANCE

10.1. Two Ps: Performance and Potential.

We all know this is true. There are days when we can do no wrong – days when every ball goes in the hole, when the words flow from our lips, when everything turns to gold. And there are other days – Monday-like days – when no words come, putts don't fall, ideas don't come; we stumble along through the day or job. The difference can be enormous.

We all know, as well, the frogs who turned into princes – the people who in school weren't up to much but who later turned into very successful and brilliant people. Or the mediocre ones who left the company and started up their own businesses, display-ing talents and abilities that were not apparent while in the old company. They were simply not realising much of their real ability or potential in that particular environment. But the potential was there, as always.

How do we know our real potential? Or that of others?
We don't. We can't. But we do get glimpses of it and we know it is a lot, a lot more than we are currently realising.

I often ask this question of companies I work with: 'Where would you put the level of performance of people in your company

144

against their potential?' This doesn't ask how well people are doing but how well they are doing compared to how they *might* do or *could* be doing.

Take a second to answer this for your company or organisation.

The answers I get from the companies I work with vary. Some say that their people are working to 70 per cent of their potential. Some say 30 per cent. Many go for 40 or 50 per cent. Invariably the answers I get are on average around 50 per cent. And I am talking of big successful corporations – Coca Cola, Kraft, Unilever, etc.

Before they get downhearted or annoyed with me for asking them questions that lead to answers that might make them feel bad about themselves, I point out to them that it is really good news, that they have so much more potential in the company for the finding and taking. Even a 10 per cent improvement would be enormous. And it is free! All they have to do is to find out what is holding people back or getting in their way and remove it and the improvement happens – just like my footballers and sportspeople.

What has this to do with managing or managers?

Everything! This is the great privilege and vocation of being a manager – to help people realise their full potential; to help them be the most they can be and be who they really are.

There are two reasons for doing this:

1. It is good for them and helps them be the most they can be and so fulfilled and happy.

2. It is good for the company or business because it leads to improved performance – often dramatically improved performance.

To make this discovery of potential happen, you first of all have to believe it, of course. That is the first step and we will come back to that later. For now, let's indulge ourselves in the glorious task we have of releasing the greatness, beauty and truth in the people we manage.

How do we release people's potential?

Well, as was already said, you first have to believe it. But what happens if you don't believe that the people in question are so great?

Well, first of all you may be wrong (in fact you *are* wrong) and secondly it may be a self-fulfilling prophecy. Your beliefs may be part of the problem. How *you* view people is not incidental to how *they* view themselves. Did you ever come across someone who believed in you? Who even believed more in you than you did in yourself? I have. And I am so happy they were right. I could tell many stories of people who believed in me along the way to whom I am very grateful, but to avoid embarrassing them let me give an even simpler example.

I was playing golf in Chiang Mai in Thailand some years back. I had a female caddy who had little English but a good awareness about golf. She was very helpful and attentive and interested in me, and I felt good. I even began to play fairly well. Then an interesting thing happened. She began to think I *was* good, or at least better than I am. And so she would hand me clubs for certain shots that I felt were well out of my range. When I protested or looked at her in doubt she would have none of it. She thought I could hit the ball with a five iron over a tree to a green 160 yards away. I knew I couldn't. But I tried it. And, yes, I did it. And on it went. Very simply, that girl believed I was a better golfer than I actually was, or thought I was. And I played better than 'I really was'. Or maybe, in fact, I played as I really was and not as I had believed I was. That was the real me. My caddy had discovered gold I never believed was there.

The rector of a university in California called in five of his professors and told them that, because they were the top five lecturers in the university, he was apportioning them the 120 top students because he believed these students achieving very high results would enhance the image and standing of the university. The professors were delighted and went off to get going with their brilliant students.

Sure enough, the students achieved unprecedented results. The rector called in the five professors to congratulate them. They were pleased and accepted the praise but, in the interests of honesty, reminded the rector that he had given them the 120 top students.

'No,' the rector told them. 'I picked the students at random.'

They laughed at being tricked and felt even more proud of their achievement.

'How wise of you,' they told the rector, 'to select us, the top five professors, to achieve such great results.'

'But I didn't' the rector told them, `I picked you at random too'.

The power of belief.

We will come back to this later and to the theory of it and why and how it works. For now, if we want to settle the argument between us about those people in your company who you really believe are not up to it, why don't we do a little experiment, even if it will not resolve our disagreement overnight?

1. Identify or choose a few of these people.

2. Now imagine how they would be if they upped their performance by only 10 or 15 per cent. No miracles yet. Yes, I bet this is hard to do! But you have to do it. Just make the effort. Right now. To do it you have to form pictures of these people performing really well. You have to make up these pictures or images, create them. Make the pictures big and clear and very positive. See the person doing really well.

3. Do this a few times and then do it every day for a week.

4. Live out this new image of the person.

5. Relate to them in this way.

6. Talk to them along these lines, even about the areas where they could improve if appropriate.

7. Act out this new image of the person.

8. Believe it.

Then see what happens. There is no need to say any more. We will only know if it works after you actually live and work in this way, at least for this little exercise.

Our allies: Forces on our side

One of the reasons why this exercise will work is because we are working on or playing with one of the most fundamental traits in us as human beings – the desire to improve and to be better. So, when we touch on this hidden and possibly forgotten gold in people, we are on to a winner. We have got great forces working with us that we can tap into and release. It is our task to release these forces – for the good and welfare of the person and for the good and welfare of the organisation.

Part of doing so involves us removing what may be blocking this happening; often these blocks are multiple ones. It is to these that we will turn in Chapter 12.

But before we go there, it is important that we do not forget ourselves in all of this. How much of our own potential are we realising? Probably not much more than other people around us. For this reason we need to do the same exercise on ourselves and find out how we are going to get in touch with our own hidden richness. While we can do this on our own, it will be far better if we can find someone good with whom to do it, perhaps a coach. They will help us by being with us, being interested in us, asking us the questions we may not want to ask ourselves, believing in us more than we may believe in ourselves, just like my Thai caddy. A coach will make a great difference to your performance if you find and use one.

A whole new adventure can begin for you and for so many around you if you simply believe in the real greatness and humanity in people.

Chapter 11

Transforming People

'The transformation must occur in business if the requiem scenario is to be averted.'

– John Milton (businessman)

Have you ever been in the company of someone 'special'? Someone out of the ordinary? Someone that seemed to fill a room or from whom you felt something really special? Or maybe you can think of someone with whom you are perfectly relaxed? Who makes you feel really comfortable, at ease?

I went to see Eckhart Tolle, the author of *The Power of Now,* some time ago. I, like others, listened to him for around two hours. But it was not just about listening to him. We were *with* him. For two hours he spoke to us but, more than that, he was *with* us. There were no visuals, no sideshows, no flashing lights or power-packed videos. Nothing. There was just Eckhart Tolle talking to us, and no one moved a muscle for two hours. I felt different. I felt I could have stayed there forever. It was not a projection of mine. I was not expecting too much. I arrived quite late to the venue and was quite frazzled. I was anxious and a bit uptight. Inside five minutes I and the 500 other people in the room were transformed into being at peace with the world and ourselves.

Here's a quite different example: A good friend of mine wanted to buy a car recently. She described what she was looking for as 'sexy'. She spoke to a car salesman she knew and asked him to look out for such a car for her. After some time he came back to her and told her he had a nice second-hand car for her. Negotiations had begun. A deal was in the making. The car new cost around €33,000 and it was less than three years old with a very low mileage. She asked me about how to handle the negotiations with the car salesman and I coached her through a process which essentially consisted of her being honest with him. We will never really find out if the deal she got was the very best one. It certainly pleased her. I was around when she finalised the deal on the phone. The conversation went something like:

My Friend: So what about the price then?
Car Salesman: Well, what figure did I mention to you originally – was it €15,000 as well as your old car?
My Friend: No, you actually said €16,000. [she was being very honest here!]
Car Salesman: Oh. And we did put in the Blue Tooth device and connected it to your own phone and a few other additional things.
My Friend: Yes, I was delighted with that. Many thanks.
Car Salesman: So, how would €15,500 be for you?
My Friend: Yes, that would be great. Thank you very much.
Car Salesman: Not at all and you know that if you have any problem at all to come back to me.

This was the final conversation of a longer communication over a few days. My friend was very happy with the price she got. She had told the salesman what her resources and expectations were and the price more than met these. She feared he might have asked for €20,000. We will never know if this was the best price that she could have got. Not even the car salesman could tell us that. Both of them ended up pleased with the transaction.

I happen to believe that my friend, by her open approach based on a real human relationship, helped him to be more honest, more generous and more human. I also believe that, had she tried various tactics with him and played games like threatening to go to other car sales people or exaggerating how little she was prepared to pay, she would have put him on his guard and he would have dug out and put to good use all his sales skills which were far greater than hers. Given that she was probably willing to go for something less than €20,000, I think he might have got around €18,000 had she tried to win a negotiating battle with him. The point I am trying to make, whether you agree with my suppositions or not, is that, by her behaviour, she transformed him from being a hard-nosed, clever salesman into being a friendly, fair and generous human being, or even friend. She transformed him by her attitude, honesty, openness and maybe some real charm too. (And he will have won too. Not only will she go back to him in future but she will probably recommend him to about ten other people and tell her story to them. So he will have fulfilled all the criteria for what makes a good negotiation:

- Best price.
- That the other person can afford.
- That the other person is happy with.
- Done in a way that protects and enriches the relationship.

The transformation – bringing out the goodness or the best in people

Yes, that is what we actually do when we bring about a change like the one I just described. We make the person a different person, or we evoke a different version of them. Oh yes, I know that they look the same with the same eyes and arms and legs but underneath very different things are happening. Even biologically very different things happen when a person is in a relaxed and confident mood compared to when they are anxious, fearful and nervous. Cells depend almost completely for their welfare and development on their environment. Two identical cells put in two separate Petri dishes will fare completely differently. The one in the healthy environment will thrive and the one in the unhealthy environment will fail and eventually fade away, even though they are identical at the outset.

Our genes are like a blueprint but it is the environment that makes the difference. The environment reads and engages those genetic blueprints and is ultimately responsible for the character of a cell's life. So, even at the most basic, biological level, we are affected by our environment.

More and more we are understanding that what matters is not so much our genes but how we respond to our environment. Our life is not determined by our genes but by our responses to the environmental signals that propel life. And we are constantly changing and establishing that environment. We can transform an environment and so a person.

As Goethe said: 'Treat people as they are and they will remain as they are. Treat people as they can and should be and they will become as they can and should be.'

I have had a long-term involvement in sport and it has puzzled me for a long time how a football team could be so good one day and so poor the next. It looked as if it was a completely different team. (In fact it was.)

What also intrigued me was that, during a game, losing teams were much more tired than winning ones.

I have been a follower of Meath County Gaelic football in Ireland for many years. I first became fully involved in 1996. The previous year a good Meath team had been badly beaten by Dublin in the Leinster provincial final. They were beaten by ten points. I remember after the game talking to some of the players who spoke of how tired they were. They knew it was not because they were unfit, as they had trained well and had beaten several teams with ease on the way to the provincial final. Yet, on the day: 'We were out on our feet,' they told me. 'Even the fittest of us!' They spoke of it as if something had happened to them on the day. The following year when I was involved – and not necessarily *because* I was involved – Meath won back the provincial title and went on to win the All-Ireland Final. What was a bit unusual was that the team did this with the bare minimum of players. There were virtually no injuries and the team ended each game with lots of energy. Some of the players were not the same ones who lost the previous year, but many were. And yet there was a transformation in how they performed and, more interestingly, in how they felt. There were no injuries, no tiredness.

Put fairly simplistically, what happens is this. We have in our cellular structure two fundamentally different mechanisms. One, the adrenalin system, moves us towards things that are good for us and the other one, the immune system, moves us away from things that are bad for us. These are two opposite movements. So if there is something that is good for the cell and the body, then the body moves towards that to assimilate it and engage with it. The mechanism opens up to the good and healthy factor or ingredient. Food and air are obvious examples of things the body will move towards. When there is a threat to the system, then the cells and the body move away from the threat. They close down. The body has to be in one or other of these two positions – opening up or closing down. Here I want to concentrate on the immune system and what can happen to it under pressure or stress.

There are two protection systems, one against external threats – the Hypothalamic-Pituitary-Adrenal (HPA) system – and one against internal threats. When the brain's hypothalamus perceives an environmental threat, it engages the HPA system by sending a signal to a gland called the pituitary gland, the master gland which is responsible for organising the 50 trillion cells of the body's community to deal with the impending threat. A signal is sent to the adrenal glands informing them of the need to coordinate the body's fight or flight response. Blood is taken from one place and sent to another and growth is inhibited. When faced with a threat, all the blood goes to the arms and legs to get away from or confront the threat, which is fine for short periods. But, while this is happening, the immune system closes down as all the body's energy goes to fighting or fleeing. And so, over the course of a football game, for instance, while all this is going on with high levels of anxiety, no energy is either being conserved or created. Anxious players not only feel tired, they *become* tired.

Activating the HPA axis through a threat or perceived danger also interferes with our ability to think clearly. Under stress, hormones constrict the blood vessels in the forebrain, which is the centre of executive reasoning and logic. Instead, the fear or stress causes the vascular flow and hormones to activate the hindbrain, the source of life-sustaining reflexes. The stress signals repress the slower processing conscious mind – the forebrain – to enhance survival but this comes at a cost: Diminished conscious awareness and reduced intelligence.

'When you're frightened you're dumber,' biologist Bruce Lipton says.

This is what I believe happened to the Meath team in those two years and is what happens to teams and athletes every day. Anxiety and fear of losing activated the HPA which actually weakened the team and drained their resources. This is common in all sport. It might seem extreme to talk of fear and damage in such strong terms when we are only talking of sport. But our emotions sometimes cannot distinguish what is really important from what is trivial. I once heard of a person playing golf with a well-known heart surgeon. He was shocked to see the shake in the surgeon's hand as he held the putter. He thought: 'My God, how can he hold a scalpel?' The scalpel was no problem to this surgeon, but his emotions and nervous system were getting messages that missing the putt was a serious business and so they kicked in with all their might.

How do we transform people or make them stronger and better?

I am using this example of sport to show just how different, physically or biologically, a person or a group of people (team) can be from one day to the next.

This is the power we have in every relationship we have with people around us – the power of transformation. If we can physically transform people –which looks impossible – surely, then, it is possible to transform the more malleable psychological part. We can open them up to being powerful people or close them down. We can 'make' them into different people by how we behave and how we are. So, my friend may actually have brought about all kinds of changes in the car salesman by her approach and behaviour, real physical changes which of course led to the change in his salesman behaviour. She managed to make him (more) human. Those of us who were with Eckhart Tolle that evening left feeling different to how we felt when we arrived, physically and psychologically.

You too have the power to do this, to transform people by how you are and by how you see them and relate to them. You also have the power to block growth and creativity in people as we will see in the next section.

Chapter 12

Blocks to Performance

'Think you can, think you can't, either way you will
be right.'

– Henry Ford

If it is in our nature to seek perfection and excellence, then why does it not happen as well or as often as we would want or expect it to? Why do we need so much management, training, support and help to achieve higher and better levels of performance if it is in our nature to want to improve anyway? It has to be because something is blocking this natural desire and drive in us. We need to find out what it is.

There are in fact two sets of blocks:

1. How we all block ourselves

2. How we block others and are blocked by others.

If we are going to discover ways of reaching new levels of satisfaction and achievement, then we will need to know and then deal with what is getting in our way, what is preventing us and others from being and doing what we want to be and do.

1. How we block ourselves

The most common ways I see that we block ourselves are:

i.   *Fear of making mistakes, of getting it wrong, of not making it, of not being accepted.*
     The need to get things right prevents us from taking necessary risks. Excessive caution limits us. We play it safe.

ii. *Fear of getting outside our comfort zone.*
We all establish boundaries of comfort behind which we feel safe and this prevents us from exploring what falls outside those boundaries. As a result, we cut ourselves off from large segments of life.

iii. *Our lack of self-belief and confidence in ourselves.*
We can only act in line with our beliefs and often we create a network of beliefs around ourselves and around the world we live in. Rarely are these beliefs really accurate. Most times they are inhibiting.

iv. *Our inadequate skills level and knowledge.*
If we lack and have not developed the necessary skills then we will not be able to do what we may want to and need to do.

v. *Lack of clarity and focus on what we really want; poor goals.*
If we settle for poor goals or have reneged on or never really respected our deep desires and needs, it is likely we will not realise our full potential.

vi. *Blaming others – the organisation, our manager, life.*
We can easily disempower and limit ourselves by blaming and handing over our power to others.

vii. *Not spotting or taking opportunities around us.*
There are always opportunities beckoning to us but so often we don't spot them or don't take them.

viii. *Poor relationships and turf wars that distract us and waste energy.*
There is nothing so engaging as a good battle and nothing so wasteful of energy that could be used for other and better things.

ix. *Failure to take responsibility for things.*
We can leave things to others and fail to see and play our unique part in shaping our situation or our world.

x. *Lack of persistence; giving up or settling for.*
If things do not work out great for us we can easily settle for the mediocre. Lots of people will feel very happy when we do that and settle into our comfort zone. It allows them to continue in theirs too.

So, here are two questions that are important for you to answer:

i. Which of the above points are you letting hold *you* back? There have to be at least three. Plan now what you will do about them.

If necessary or appropriate, identify who might help you with this – a friend or coach. Sometimes we just don't see some obvious things ourselves.

ii.   Which of these do you see holding back some key people around you? Spot them, name them and plan how you will help these key people to deal with them. There will be no shortage of these.

You owe it to yourself to do this exercise. It will make an enormous difference to how truly human and fulfilled you are and to how effective and successful you and your people are.

2. How we block others or how others block us

The second category of blocks is how we block others or are blocked by others.

This list is the fruit of asking people in organisations for many years in many companies in different countries what they feel is blocking them from performing as they would like to.

i.   *Goals and objectives*: Goals and objectives are not clear or exciting enough, nor is the overall purpose of the organisation clearly understood, meaningful or exciting enough.

ii.   *Attention and listening*: We don't listen enough to our people and take on board their ideas and contributions or probe and facilitate their thinking. We have no formal mechanisms for doing this so it only happens by chance.

iii. *Management style*: People spend more time following than leading because managers 'know what to do' and want things done their way. 'The right way is my way' and, as a result, people lose initiative, and interest.

iv.   *Trust*: We don't give people enough opportunity to perform well by standing back and letting them get on with it, trusting that they are wise enough and committed enough to do a good job. As a result, people don't take enough responsibility.

v.   *Recognition*: We don't recognise good performance often enough and don't make people feel good about themselves and about their contribution.

vi.   *Information and involvement*: We don't keep people sufficiently informed or involved. People often have to work in the dark and even when they do get information it is not given in the right way; people are not sufficiently involved in what is going on, nor are they in enough direct contact with the outside world – the customers.

vii. *Management over-control*: Managers want to hold on to things for insecurity reasons and are unable to let go. There is little real ownership of tasks as a result, and no creativity or innovation.

viii. *Too many rules*: We fail to bring out the flair in people and we manage more by rules and regulations.

ix. *Criticism*: We over-criticise and jump on mistakes and problems. We are hard on people or at least on some people and this damages their confidence. There is too much fear and people are very defensive, with the result that a blame–defend culture or war is raging. We do not forgive mistakes and people then play it safe all the time.

x. *Support and tools*: People are not given enough support in terms of the tools to do the job – training, back-up, resources.– and the structures are wrong as well. Hierarchy and layers and levels have a very negative effect on how people view themselves and their role in the organisation.

xi. *Respect*: There is not enough respect for and trust in senior management and in how things are run and handled. People go along with things but really don't have much confidence in the leadership or in the direction they are going – whatever it is. There is also a 'them and us' atmosphere which is energy sapping.

xii. *Trust and faith*: We don't really trust people and see the greatness in them. We treat them as people who need to be supervised or managed or they will not perform. A vicious circle develops from this whereby people treated in this way begin to behave accordingly. We don't expect too much and we get proved right!

There are two questions to ask yourself at this point:

i.   Which of the above blocks have you experienced from people who have managed you or in organisations where you have worked?

ii. How would you rank the blocks in terms of being most common or most serious, in your experience?

If you have any numbers noted from this, then it is very probably the case that you also block people or operate in ways that block people. This may be not so much about something specific you do but may be about your operation of an existing system, process or approach in your organisation.

Ask yourself – in what ways might you be or are you blocking people from performing as they can and want to perform?

If you can't find any ways, or even if you can, it might be prudent and beneficial to check this out with others, to ask some people how you actually block people, however inadvertently or unintentionally. There are always some good friends in our lives – people who can say things to us that we need to hear and from whom it is easy to hear them.

There may be ways to find this out without openly *asking* people – through observing how people relate to you, through subtle enquiries, through honest reflection and self-coaching.

It is really worthwhile to do this. Imagine if your managers did it and took it really seriously and the difference it would make.

The issue is a little more serious than just having two sets of blocks. The problem is that the blocks are not mutually exclusive. Many of them impact on and complement each other in a double-negative dynamic.

How We Block Ourselves	How We Block Others or How Others Block Us
1. Fear of making mistakes, of getting it wrong, of not making it.	1. Goals and objectives not clear enough.
2. Fear of getting outside our comfort zones.	2. Not enough attention and listening.
3. Our lack of self-belief and confidence in ourselves.	3. Poor management style.
4. Our inadequate skills level and knowledge.	4. Lack of trust.
5. Lack of clarity and focus on what we really want; poor goals.	5. Lack of recognition.
6. Blaming others, the organisation, our manager, life.	6. Insufficient information and involvement.
7. Not spotting or taking opportunities around us.	7. Management over-control.
8. Poor relationships and turf wars that distract us and waste energy.	8. Too many rules.
9. Failure to take responsibility for things.	9. Too much criticism.
10. Lack of persistence; giving up or settling for.	10. Lack of support and tools.
	11. Lack of respect.
	12. Lack of trust in people.

So, these two sets of blocks actually complement each other and one worsens the other. Human weaknesses and frailties in people are actually exacerbated by how we manage.

Be not downhearted

Very often when I do this exercise with people they feel a bit disappointed with themselves or a little offended by the thrust of the message. They take it personally. I hope you don't. For the greater part, the fact that we as managers block people from performing as they can and want to is not so much about us as people but a lot more about us *as managers*. As I mentioned, I have asked this same question about blocks in very many different companies and very many different cultures around the world and very many of the same blocks get named. This always amazes me. How could the same issues occur in so many different companies and across so many entirely different cultures with very different histories? What is the common denominator or fundamental cause that leads to such similarity in how we get in people's way in terms of their performance?

I once came across a quote from Ray Stata. Ray Stata was the CEO of Analog Devices when he said: 'People want to be great. If they aren't it's because we as managers won't let them be!' I was struck by this honest, hard-hitting, self-accusatory statement from a very successful manager.

Ray Stata is not actually criticising individual managers so much as raising questions about managing and managers in general. In effect, he is saying that managers prevent people from being great, from being truly human, from being what they can and want to be. It is for this reason that so many of the blocks listed above are present in so many different organisations. So, blocking people from performing to their potential is not so much about bad management as about management itself. There is something amiss with our understanding of and application of the concept of management.

So now we have a real challenge and dilemma:

- We need people to perform well.

- People don't always do so.

- Part of the reason is that we, as managers, actually prevent them from doing so.

This means we have to take a look at why this may be so and, more importantly, what we can do about it. What can we do to improve our managers in their roles as managers? What can we do to improve 'managing' as such?

Chapter 13

COACH – The Key to Unlocking the Beauty and Potential in People

'Beauty is truth and truth beauty, that is all ye know
on earth and all ye need to know. Beauty has its
own authority.'

– John Keats

To deal with all of these blocks to creativity you might think that we have to look out for each one and work hard to not let it take effect. That we have to have a kind of checklist in front of us each day to make sure we are not blocking ourselves or others. This would be a very tiresome and, indeed, would form a negative agenda. Nor is it necessary.

We talked about our great power to transform people by how we are around them. In the case of my friend buying the car in the previous chapter, she handled one particular situation well by having a positive effect on the salesman. But what if we wanted to work like this all the time? What if we wanted to transform people all the time, especially those who work with and for us?

There *is* a way.

Can you recall a few moments or experiences in your life when you were engaged in something which was really memorable, satisfying and fulfilling? Some job or task or project – inside or outside of work – that went really well, that was very enjoyable? It may have been very successful too. It can be something that happened last week, last year or fifteen years ago.

Now, spend a little time thinking what was it about that event, job, project, experience that made it so special? Think of a few characteristics that marked it out in your memory as a good experience.

From asking people this question for more than twenty years in companies of all sizes in all parts of the world, I have narrowed the answers down into the simple mnemonic – COACH.

So what is COACH?

- **C** is for Commitment to clear, challenging, shared and exciting goals or vision.
- **O** is for Ownership of the task, job, assignment, project, etc.
- **A** is for Awareness of what is going on or what is needed, or acknowledgment of what has been achieved.
- **C** is for Confidence and trust – in yourself, in others or from others
- **H** is for Healthy relationships.

Take a minute to check which or how many of these elements played a big part in the satisfying or successful project I asked you to think about earlier.

You might take these for granted, but each of them has an invisible but enormous power contained in it.

Let's take a look.

C – Commitment to clear, challenging, shared and exciting goals or vision

Everyone agrees with the importance of clear goals and powerful visions but not all are really aware of the power they have or really trust them.

When you create a vision of what you want, you have actually already created something new. No, I hear you say, it is only an idea, an image, a picture in the head. It's not *something*. Yes, but that picture in the head did not exist before you created it and in that sense it *is* something, something new, something freshly created. And what good is that, you reply? A lot, I say and to prove it I dip into the world of sport because it is a world where the results of what we do and how we do it are immediately visible.

Have you ever seen a player taking a penalty shot at the goals in soccer or rugby, for example? They put the ball down, walk back their routine number of steps and get ready. They look at the ball, at the goalposts, at the ball and again at the goalposts and then at the ball again. They do this, not to check where the goalposts are, or to be sure that no one has moved them. They do it because they are visualising the ball sailing between the posts. And they do this because they know that being able to see it clearly in their heads will be half the battle of actually doing it in reality.

Conversely, you can almost predict some who are going to miss in penalty shoot-outs in soccer matches. They walk to the ball as if to the gallows, condemned, scared and terrified – of what? Of missing. And this is what they are seeing, themselves *missing*. And of course they do.

So our visions and goals have a huge effect on how we perform and behave. When we get people committed to clear, challenging goals and visions we give them enormous power. How we go about doing this is covered elsewhere. For now, let's be clear that challenge and commitment to an exciting goal or vision will provide the energy and power for people to realise new levels of performance and fulfilment. Doing this in a group and getting a group committed to a goal or vision of the future is enormously powerful and creates a new dynamic and power within that group.

O – Ownership of the task, job, assignment, project etc.

So often I hear from people that what made their achievement so memorable was that people really depended on them to succeed – 'It was up to me.' 'I was left on my own.' When people feel important, counted upon and fully responsible, they grow and achieve new levels of performance.

This is probably the most challenging issue to handle in the normal work organisation, where traditional lines of hierarchy and control very often dilute or destroy any sense of ownership. This happens for a variety of reasons, some good and some not so good. Often we are so concerned that things go well that we are too afraid to hand over full responsibility and ownership to our people. This very behaviour leads to a poorer performance from the person which in turn justifies our not having handed over ownership in the first place.

You can imagine the scene:

Middle Manager: Oh, by the way, that important meeting is taking place on Friday at last. Just thought I'd let you know.
Senior Manager: Oh really! Yes that *is* a big one. I see. I think I might go along to it and sit in. Is that OK with you?
Middle Manager: Sure, of course, no problem.

At the meeting the Middle Manager defers on a few occasions to the Senior Manager on questions that she believes the Senior

Manager would handle better. This becomes a pattern and the Senior Manager plays a more and more active part.

The Senior Manager thinks to himself: 'I am glad I decided to come to this meeting. A lot of questions would not have got answered had I not been here. I had better start coming to more of these.'

The theft of ownership can also happen by managers giving advice to their people on what to do or on how to handle a situation. In so doing they are unaware of the damage they have done to the sense of ownership and responsibility of the person involved and, of course, it becomes a self-fulfilling prophecy and a downward vicious spiral.

Watch how you can do this when giving someone a job to do – you can half give it and retain the ownership yourself.

The job of every manager, as we will see later, is to develop the KWA of their people – to ensure they Know what to do, Want to do it and are Able do it.

A – Awareness of what is going on or what is needed, or acknowledgment of what has been achieved

This is the most difficult to understand or appreciate of the five characteristics of great performance and transformation of people. And it is also the most magical.

It is based on a strong trust in the natural willingness and tendency of people to act in accordance with what they see and understand. So, if we are able to help people to see what is really going on, they will have a far better chance of behaving and performing well. Of course, there are no guarantees here but there is an enormous power in reality and truth and in the difficulty human beings have in not acting in accordance with what appears to them as reasonable and real.

The reason why this is so powerful and important is that most times we are not fully aware of what is going on around us and even to us. We get blocked by others, and we also block ourselves with our fears, prejudices, wishing and hoping, and by our denial of what is really happening. And because our awareness is partial, our response and behaviour is partial and poor. Once we become really aware, it is all easy.

Again, sport is a wonderful medium through which to demonstrate the power of awareness. When I coach people in sport, I base most of the improvement to be achieved on simply increasing the person's awareness of something – of what they want or what is going on in their own body, or what the problem is. For example, I remember coaching a girl in England some years ago who wanted to improve her backhand in tennis. I could see that she was trying to hit backhands from a very unbalanced stance. So, after finding out what she meant by improving her backhand and what she wanted to be able to do better, I got her to put her attention on something that was going on as she was hitting backhand shots. After a little while she reported to me that she was experiencing a tightness in her arm. Over a short period, I got her to focus more on this and to become more aware of it. In that short period she readjusted her stance to a much steadier one and began to hit firm and good backhands. Just the awareness on its own brought the cure. I often experimented in my own tennis game with putting my attention on *anything* while I was serving – the back of my knee, the hair on the back of my neck, whatever, and the serve would improve. It sounds crazy, but it works. Awareness is everything.

There are so many experiments and stories about how this applies to the work situation, but it really comes down to allowing unpolluted information to get to people and letting the rest happen. By unpolluted I mean information without any noise in the system which interferes with it. For example, we are not satisfied with letting people know that the market situation has become difficult and challenging for us, we have to add on a tag that begins 'We must…', and this distorts and destroys the pure awareness we were trying to create. Working in this way has to be tried to be believed. Awareness itself brings the cure, the improvement. If you don't believe me, try this:

Do some stretching exercise that you occasionally do or think you should do. Stretch as far as you can go without doing damage to yourself. Then stop. Now do it again but this time when you reach your limit, put all your attention on the point of pain. Don't try to make it easier or harder, just feel the pain and enter into it as much as possible, feeling it as fully as you can. Then notice how you can stretch much further.

We cannot spend enough time making people aware of what is happening in their environment at work without tagging on warnings or admonitions or plans for action. It will take practice to be good at this, to be able to simply let people get the relevant information and then let them respond to it. You will be surprised at the results.

C – Confidence and trust in yourself, in others or from others

This element is one that runs through all the other ones. It is one of the toughest because it is about what is the single most common problem in the world – fear.

While fear may seem like something that will require a long time to overcome, this is not so. You might think that you have to deal with the cause or source of the fear before you can be rid of it. This would be like thinking that to get rid of your fear of spiders, you will have to rid the world of spiders.

There is an easier and quicker route.

Ultimately the fear we experience is in *us* so it is there we have to deal with it – on the inside, not on the outside. It is our own images and words that we have to do something about rather than the poor harmless spiders. Doing this involves dealing with the voice in the head.

You know the voice in the head? That voice that starts up when you are in a tough or tense situation. Have you ever given a talk to a large and important bunch of people? And someone important looks decidedly bored or annoyed...and they get up and leave. You might think things like: 'He does not like it and I didn't explain that very well. I should have prepared it better. This is bound to come against me and everyone else has noticed it too and will be talking about it and about me. I hope the rest of it goes well but for God's sake sharpen up and get your points across better and more succinctly, if it is not too late already...'

There are two questions to ask about this particular incident, as an example:

1. What was really going on?

2. What was happening when you were doing all this worrying?

1. What was really going on?

Suppose, as may very well be the case, that the 'important person' was not at all bored but had remembered they had forgotten to make a very important telephone call (important people make very important telephone calls!). They waited for the right moment, when they felt that they had got the main points of your presentation, and decided to leave, while feeling bad about having to do that.

2. What was happening when you were doing all this worrying?

While you were doing all this fretting, you were not concentrating on your presentation and performance. And, because you were not doing that, you were not doing it very well...probably. Then, what happens is that your fear brings about the very reality you feared.

This is a serious problem that needs to be addressed because it will not be confined to this one event or even to such events in general. It will arise in all kinds of situations where you are not feeling confident or secure.

Author Timothy Gallwey, in his *Inner Game* books, calls this worrying voice in the head Self 1. He does so to point out that if there is a conversation going on, there have to be two people present. He first came across it when he was playing tennis because he realised he was not playing good tennis when Self 1 was very active with its advice, forebodings, criticisms and blaming. As a matter of fact, he became completely convinced that the more present Self 1 was the worse he played; the more Self 1 was absent, the better he played. He set out to come up with a way of dealing with Self 1 in tennis and in life.

But Gallwey discovered something else. He was coaching someone one day and after a while he left her to go and coach someone else. When he glanced over at his former pupil, he realised, to his dismay, that she was now playing far better tennis than she had been when he was alongside her, 'coaching' her. It was disappointing of course for him to realise how fruitless his efforts were, but all was not lost. Again he set out to find out why this was so and to do something about it. What he realised was that his pupil had her own Self 1 working away and now, lo and behold, she had another one – him. He as the external Self 1 was feeding and promoting her own internal Self 1 so that she had a double barrage of unhelpful interference with her tennis game.

Gallwey set out to establish a new and healthier relationship with his tennis pupils to deal with this negative effect, and we will come to this in the next section – healthy relationships.

With regard to dealing with our own Self 1, we have to simply go back to our previous letter 'A' for Awareness. It is as quick and as easy as that – become aware of Self 1 and it will disappear.

Let's go back to our scenario above, when you are giving the talk and the important person walks out, and apply our awareness:

1. Be aware that it is likely that Self 1 will arise in a stressful moment like this.

2. Be aware of it when it does arise and recognise it. Do not resist it or regret it or beat yourself up for this happening, as this is Self 1 at it again but now on a different topic.

3. Don't deny the feelings you have but simply recognise and acknowledge them.

4. Be aware of what you want to achieve with the talk and recall why it is important and valuable.

5. Focus on what you are covering in your presentation.

It is as simple as that.

It does require some courage and faith to do this, as it does not appear to make sense. But trust that awareness brings the cure. Nothing more is required. Follow these steps in every situation of nervousness or tension and they will work for you.

H – Healthy relationships

This is an enormous topic and, in a sense, is the subject of this whole book – managing and handling people. It is about understanding how the role of managing can be handled in a way that, far from damaging the previous four elements, actually supports and promotes them. It is about managing people in such a way that they are and feel treated as equals and adults. By equals I do not mean necessarily being on the same level or being equal in responsibility or decision-making obligations, but equal in the sense of not feeling inferior. While you might throw your eyes up in horror at reading this, either because you don't think it is possible to achieve that or because you would never treat people as inferior, believe me it does happen and happens very frequently. It is a very common experience for employees to feel inferior and so develop either a poor view of themselves, or resentment towards those who are treating them so.

The reason it is so common is that people identify their relationship with the manager with other relationships in life where a superior–inferior dynamic predominates. At work people often feel and behave like children and with some considerable justification for feeling and behaving like that.

The Transactional Analysis model says that we each have a parent, adult and child in us. In other words, we each have a parent, an adult and a child hiding inside us that affect how we behave in particular situations. Some situations evoke the child in us, causing us to feel hurt and annoyed, to sulk and so on. In some situations we behave as parents, telling people what to do, correcting, not trusting, interfering and so on. And, hopefully, a lot of the time we behave as adults – trusting, respecting and treating people as responsible adults. However, everyone else equally has a parent, adult and child in them so the relationship dynamic looks like this:

Me	The Other Person
Parent	Parent
Adult	Adult
Child	Child

In work situations, the Parent–Child is a very common relationship because of the position of authority of the manager or boss. Unfortunately, the Parent–Child relationship is a very comfortable relationship and both parties can enjoy it and want to continue it.

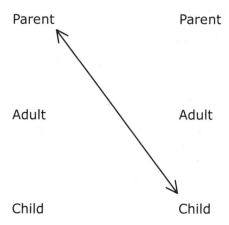

13.1. The common relationship.

So, what is wrong with it then, you might ask?

Well, adults should not be treated nor behave like children for their own sakes and for the sake of those around them. In mercenary terms, we are not going to get too much from them if they lack the responsibility, maturity, beliefs and attitudes of adults. In personal terms, it is bad for them too, irrespective of how comfortable they might feel within such a relationship.

When people on my coaching programmes doubt the validity of what I am saying about this, I do a little role play with one person from the group on some issue of performance or about their overall performance. Often this happens within the framework of a pretended performance review. What I do simply is to berate and abuse them about an aspect of their performance. What is amazing is that they accept it from me. Before the eyes of their colleagues I severely criticise them in the most disrespectful way and I normally bring it to a close with the words: 'Tell me. Is that the best you can do? I need to know.' Invariably they nod, acknowledge their failure and give assent to my effectively writing them off.

What is interesting about this is that, in twenty years of doing this, no one has ever challenged me back. No one has ever said: 'Come off it. Don't talk to me like that.' When I ask why, people always cite fear as the main reason. Of course, it is not a real situation and so in real life the person might behave and respond differently but, even with that, it should be relatively easy for them to get out of it or to take me on.

The other interesting thing about this is that when I ask the group why the person accepted such abusive treatment from an outsider, they answer: 'Because you were role playing.' And when I ask them: 'And what role was I playing?' They say: 'A manager'.

Aha! So now we have it. It is OK to be disrespectful, abusive and unfair if one is being or acting like a manager. The person in the role play does understand how to behave because they recognise from experience the behaviour I am exhibiting.

I would venture a guess that most manager–employee relationships are inherently unhealthy and considerably disrespectful, and abusive behaviour takes place unnoticed by either side.

What can we do to develop healthy relationships with our people as managers? One powerful way is through the principles of COACH – always.

Sometimes people can feel that this is a weak role for a manager to play but COACH-ing is, in fact, the most powerful and empowering way to engage with people in any situation in life and is the easiest way to ensure that you are developing a truly healthy relationship with your team.

When you behave and relate in a COACH-ing way, the relationship in terms of Parent, Adult and Child, that we looked at above, changes.

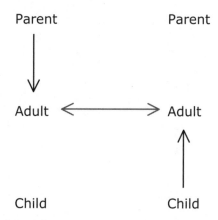

13.2. The COACH-ing relationship.

Both manager and 'employee' or team member move to behaving and feeling like Adults.

COACH

So these are the five principles around transforming people and bringing out the greatness and beauty in people. We know they work because they work when people use them with us. This does not mean that we have to go around checking ourselves against the COACH principles for everything we do but it does mean that these principles must underpin and guide all we do. Above all, COACH must inform and guide how we structure our organisations and work, and how we plan and allocate assignments. These five principles can act as a guide to us in all our work and in terms of the management style we adopt. If we are failing to operate in line with any one of these principles, our overall effort and work will suffer, our people will suffer and our organisations will suffer. On the other hand, if we operate in this way everyone will gain, but most of all we ourselves will benefit because we will find ourselves operating and behaving in a truly human way. I will be referring to and building on these five principles throughout the rest of this book.

The point of all of this is to make people more powerful, in other words, to give them more power so that they can be and do more than they are currently doing, for their own sake and for the sakes of the organisations to which they belong.

'Power' is often abused word so let's take a look at it because this book is really about increasing our power and that of those around us.

Chapter 14

Power – The Heart of the Matter

'We all have a moral responsibility, whether we
like it or not, but people in power – in the military,
in politics, in professions, whatever – have an
imperative to care, or at least to exhibit an officially
acceptable analogue of care: Duty.'

– Iain Banks

The different kinds of power

All managers need power. As managers we need to influence
people and when we influence another person we are using some
form of power. So power *is* important. The question is – what do
we mean by 'power' exactly? And what kind of power do we want
to use or is best to use?

The word 'power' often gets identified exclusively with physical
force or with some version of positional or hierarchical status.
In business situations it is this latter form of power that is most
used, often supported by some form of sanction, be it legitimate or
semi-legitimate. The fact that most ordinary day-to-day dealings
and transactions get carried out without recourse to these kinds
of power can be easily forgotten. Or it may be that getting normal
things done is not seen as having anything do with power. In fact,
these transactions take place through the use of *other* kinds of
power, equally legitimate, often more effective and certainly more
pleasant than coercive or hierarchical power, but which we don't
rate as power and we take for granted. Just reflect on the many
things that people around you do or that you ask people around
you to do or that you simply expect them to do everyday. Don't
skip over this. Take just five minutes and I bet you will come up
with a long list of things people do for you every day because of
the presence of this very different form of power. Even before I

finish my breakfast I can list ten examples of things that got done in my house without the use of any kind of physical, hierarchical or coercive power:

- I had clean towels that got washed for me at some stage without my asking for them.
- My wife enjoyed a warm shower because I paid an electricity bill (without any pressure).
- The fire got cleaned out by me without any orders from my wife.
- I had a fruit salad prepared for me and gave no orders for it to happen.
- I cooked porridge without the need for any direction to do so.
- A pot of tea got made without anyone being told to make it.

And so on ... (and I am only at breakfast).

These are all very minor and simple examples of one person doing something for another person that they might not feel like doing, but that they do because of the presence of a particular kind of power. That the person taking the action actually *wants* to do it does not mean that there is no power at work. In fact, as we will see, this is the most perfect form of power.

But this is an example of only *one* kind of power.

What kinds of power are there and which do you most often use and like to use?

Let us take a very simple example.

Some years ago, the English soccer team came to play Ireland in Landsdowne Road, the famous rugby ground, in a so-called friendly game. The game was ruined by violence off the field, mostly caused by English supporters, some of whom came with the clear purpose of causing trouble. Let's look at this hypothetically. There is a group of Irish supporters in the neigbouring section to the English troublemakers and these Irish supporters have had not only abuse hurled at them but also cans, bottles and a few stones. Some have been hit, some are afraid but a sizeable group have united and are out to settle matters themselves and get revenge. They are about to invade the English section. The superintendent in charge of the police (Gardai) who are on the scene is intent on stopping them. What power can he use to do this? Well, he has about ten different kinds of power he can use. Let's look at them:.

14.1. Kinds of power.

1. Physical power

This power uses might and physical force to get someone to obey or do something. It may involve the use of fear or threat and so could stop short of having to resort to physical force.

Usual forms of expression include: force, power, arms, threats, warnings, physical violence.

In terms of the example above, the police simply use physical force to prevent the Irish group from entering the English section, using batons, shields and their united strength.

We rarely have to use this kind of power in organisations unless we have to appeal to security to take someone off the premises or call in the police for some serious incident. But this form of power can lie behind the whole basis of our authority in some cases. If I give an order and it is not obeyed, I will use a discipline process. If this is not respected, I will appeal to a court, which may mean the person could be forcibly put in jail. While we don't think like this in the normal run of affairs, subconsciously that understanding is behind much of the power we use. And while people over whom we use that power of discipline might not think it all through to the point of going to jail, at some level they know they will lose out and so feel a real sense of powerlessness. This applies to most of the kinds of power we use as described below.

Of course it is necessary for law and order to have some kind of sanction as otherwise there could be chaos. However, if this is the only basis for our power then those who have this kind of power can do what they like and there doesn't have to be a rationale or justification for what they 'order'. This kind of power may work, but as we will see there is a big price to be paid for it.

2. Threatening power

This kind of power makes it very clear that it is in the best interests of the other person to agree in order to avoid unpleasant consequences. Whether directly or indirectly, this power points out the consequences of not cooperating and it backs the other person into a corner or attempts to do so. This form will often be supported by some kind of physical, political or hierarchical power.

Usual forms of expression include: Warnings, threats, advice, admonitions and ultimatums.

In the example above, the Police Superintendent makes it very clear to the Irish group that if they attempt to cross over into the English section of the stands they will be arrested.

In companies this power is often used in the typical disciplinary procedure which is very often based on threatening people. This power is underpinned by the physical power described above, which comes into play if the threats are not heeded.

3. Hierarchical power

This kind of power uses clout, rank or authority to get things done. It makes clear who is boss and that what is being said is an instruction to be followed and obeyed. The basis for the power is clear and confirmed or supported by stripes of some kind – symbols of office, titles and various forms of sanction.

Forms of expression include: Instructions, commands, orders, 'advice', 'requests' and rules.

The police uniform says and does a lot in our example. Prior to the arrival of the police there was probably a self-appointed leader in the Irish group. He felt he had full authority but this got superseded by the higher hierarchical power of the police This alone may do the trick in convincing the Irish group to stay put. They recognise that there is a higher power present.

As has been said, hierarchical power will use some form of the first two powers mentioned, however distant or removed they may seem to be. The organisational chart, whether visible or invisible to staff, plays a powerful part in establising hierarchical power in companies. Pecking orders become very clear and people pull rank.

4. Political power

This is the 'wheeler-dealer' kind of power. It points out that 'this can work both ways' and 'marks the other person's card'. The person wielding the power may have an influence over the other person's prospects when they need help or when they might lose out if favours are being granted. Promises are made that the person will not to be found wanting when that situation arises: 'If you scratch my back, I'll scratch yours, and if you don't, I'll scratch your eyes out.'

Usual forms of expression include: deals, bargains, offers, requests, explanations and warnings, indirect and hidden.

This is a bit difficult to spot in our example but the Police Superintendent could have done a deal with the leaders of the Irish group along the lines of getting their cooperation in return for the police arresting or beating the trouble makers.

This kind of power can happen most often between people at similar levels in organisations but can also be used with staff that work for you or with trade unions. It is a dangerous and risky game to play. I had a manager once who warned me about playing this game with our trade unions. He told me of the family who were visiting a wild-life park where there were notices not to stop or to approach the animals. This one family did stop and a bear approached the car. The child in the back seat wound down the window and proceeded to feed the bear jelly tots. All was well. Everyone was happy as long as the jelly tots lasted. But they didn't and when they ran out the bear reached into the car and plucked out the kid and headed off with it. The moral of the story, my boss told me, was that you can't blame the bear. He just didn't know when or where to stop. And so it is with favours. Make sure you have an endless supply of jelly tots. It's a dangerous game, but a very common one that we don't often even know we are playing.

5. Emotional power

This involves appealing to the sympathy of another person and referring to the difficulties you will experience if something does or doesn't happen.

Forms of expression used: Stories, body language, distress, sadness, tears, pleas, requests and complaints.

This may be a bit far-fetched, but the Police Superintendent in our example could have pleaded with the Irish group and explained the awful predicament he was in and how much trouble he would get into if a bigger row developed. Or, through pleading and adopting a soft approach, he might appeal to the good nature of the leaders in the Irish group.

This may work in a company or organisation on some occasions but it will not always work and it will not work in the same way consistently. People will get tired of or immune to our sad stories about potential job losses, closures, etc. and our appeals.

6. Rewarding power

This type of power has the resources and wherewithal to entice the person to do something for a benefit or reward. The protagonist may know what the other person needs or desires and how to satisfy this. He or she then makes it very attractive for the person to comply.

Usual forms of expression include: Promises, offers, enticements, financial rewards and manipulation.

The Police Superintendent in our example, not that he would, could have bribed the leaders of the Irish group to go away and have a hell of a night on the money in Paddy Cullen's pub.

This is a very common source of power that organisations use. More will need to be said about this later. For now let me say that rewards *underpin* and support effort but are not the most effective or all-embracive motivator. They are external to the work being done or the effort being made.

7. Personal power

This kind of power appeals to the relationship in question, the friendship, the good and bad times together. It deals in favours and good turns and expects to be able to cash in on previous good turns. If you want this power, you try to be warm and close to the other person.

Usual forms of expression include: Conversation, chat, friendliness, kindnesses, listening and explanations.

This is easy for the police who often use this kind of power, and unique charm, with people – 'Ah, come on lads. Cut it out...pleease!'

This is a very frequently used power in the workplace. It is also a very important one. It is probably true that nothing will get done well if relationships are negative. The opposite, unfortunately, is not true, namely that having a good relationship with a person will guarantee that they will behave in ways that we like. It is too weak a base on which to operate. This is one of the most commonly misunderstood dynamics in organisations and I will say more about it in Chapter 19.

8. Charismatic/inspirational power

This power sets an example and inspires people to do what they might not otherwise have done or wanted to do. It leads and influences. It gets people to identify with a higher cause and with him/herself as representing that cause or goal.

Usual forms of expression include: Example, speeches, visions and personal value statements.

An inspiring Superintendent might lecture the Irish group and tell them of the history of peace in Landsdowne Road and how they should not blemish the proud record of Irish supporters. He should tell them about how proud they should all feel at their ability to not respond to taunts from louts.

This can be very effective in terms of influencing people. How effective it is and how long-lasting it is will depend on the genuineness of the good or cause that the leader is expounding. As we know, charismatic leaders can also get people to do what they should not do. It can be seen as a personal quality that one either has or does not have, but this may not be so and we will re-visit this point in Chapter 18.

9. Rational power

This kind of power is based on clear arguments and reasoning, and discussions and debates with the other person. If a person want to use this power, he or she counters points put forward by the other person, and talks and explains a lot. He or she loves the cut-and-thrust of debate and believes in a rational solution to everything.

Usual forms of expression include: Arguments, debate, reasoning, explanations, point scoring and logic.

Again, in terms of our example, this is an easy one for the police – they can simply point out what will happen if the Irish fans cross the barriers and how silly and awful it will be.

This is naturally a very effective kind of power if we are able to show people that what we are putting forward or asking makes sense and is the right and logical thing to do. However, it can run the risk of endless debate and we may fail to be able to convince people of the strength of our arguments. It can smack of being too democratic. It can easily get mixed up or combined with other kinds of power like hierarchical power. Managers can give lots of reasons for things and consciously or subconsciously do so from their hierarchical position. I had a very strong experience of this once when I called a meeting of the entire workforce to address them on a serious industrial relations issue. Previously I had persuaded them in similar circumstances to listen to and act on reason – or at least on my version of it. However, this time when I went to the cafeteria to give my message, I found the shop stewards outside the door telling people not to attend. I was predictably very annoyed at my impotence to get my message across. Later, I summoned the chief shop steward to my office and demanded an explanation for his behaviour. He was very honest with me and said: 'We could not let you talk to them. We knew you would convince them again.' He was using his positional power to block my rational power!

10. Awareness power or the power of meaning

This power makes the other person aware of the facts and reality of the situation; it explains the need and importance of the issue and trusts the other person will respond. It respects the other person's ability to make up their own mind and leaves a lot up to them. And it believes the facts speak for themselves and has confidence in this.

Usual forms of expression include: Explanations, listening, questioning, clarifying, learning and descriptions.

The police may ask the leaders of the Irish group what they think will happen if they encroach on the English enclave.

This power is based on trust in the facts or reality of the situation and lays this out for people to see clearly, and invites or encourages them to respond accordingly.

Can you identify with or recognise most of the above forms of power?

Of course these are never absolutely discrete in their application in reality. Personal power will be present in most of the other forms, as will rational power. In various transactions there may also be movement from one kind of power to another. For example, a person may start off using reasonable (rational power) and if it is not working resort to hierarchical or political or some other form of power. But, notwithstanding this, there will be a predominance of one power at work in each situation. In fulfilling your role, you may generally have recourse to one kind of power or have it at work in the background behind the more obvious or visible form of power being used.

Let's put this outline to the test now to ensure it makes sense in your situation. To do so, I will ask you to carry out some exercises to ensure the efficacy of what is being said.

Exercise 1

Find examples for each of these kinds of power, either in your own or other's behaviour:

Kind of Power	Example
1. Physical	
2. Threatening	
3. Hierarchical	
4. Political	
5. Emotional	
6. Rewarding	
7. Personal	
8. Charismatic	
9. Rational	
10. Awareness	

Exercise 2

Which of these kinds of power do *you* use and in what situations:

Kind of Power	Situation
1. Physical	
2. Threatening	
3. Hierarchical	
4. Political	
5. Emotional	
6. Personal	
7. Rewarding	
8. Charismatic	
9. Rational	
10. Awareness	

Exercise 3

What effects do each of these kinds of power have on the other person? Find out by checking what effects they have on you!

Kind of Power	Effect
1. Physical	
2. Threatening	
3. Hierarchical	
4. Political	
5. Emotional	
6. Personal	
7. Rewarding	
8. Charismatic	
9. Rational	
10. Awareness	

Exercise 4

What are the upsides and downsides of each of these kinds of power?

Kind of Power	Upside	Downside
1. Physical		
2. Threatening		
3. Hierarchical		
4. Political		
5. Emotional		
6. Personal		
7. Rewarding		
8. Charismatic		
9. Rational		
10. Awareness		

Exercise 5

Which of these kinds of power do you prefer and which do you find easiest to use? Rate both of these from 1 to 10 in each case, where 10 is your most preferred or easiest option.

Kind of Power	Preference	Ease
1. Physical		
2. Threatening		
3. Hierarchical		
4. Political		
5. Emotional		
6. Personal		
7. Rewarding		
8. Charismatic		
9. Rational		
10. Awareness		

Which Power to Use

This is really up to you in each particular situation and there may be situations where you might use each type of power. But all ten are not equal in their effectiveness or in their effects. You will have noticed this in Exercise 3 above.

To clarify this, suppose for the moment that each of the types was equally effective in getting the job done, what then would the differences be between all ten and why would you prefer one over another?

We could use all kinds of criteria for evaluating and rating each of the ten, such as which is nicest, which is strongest, which is quickest, which is easiest, which is clearest, etc. Valuable as these and other criteria might be, they might not be critical or essential for performance, either by the individual or the organisation. Using vague criteria like these or deciding on this basis might not provide a sufficiently sharp tool to differentiate the ten options. So what would?

As already mentioned in Chapter 13 and other parts of this book, based on a considerable amount of experience, I have identified five elements that are present in all good performance, whatever meaning you like to give to 'good'. These are:

- Clear, challenging, shared and exciting goals or targets.

- Ownership and empowerment in regard to the task, job or activity.

- Awareness of what is involved, what is happening and acknowledgement of and recognition for achievements.

- Confidence – in oneself, in others, from others.
- Healthy relationships of trust, equality and maturity.

Underpinning all of these ingredients is the quality of freedom, as we saw when I talked of creativity earlier. Freedom is what gives people their power and fulfilment and, to the extent that it is absent, power and fulfilment will be missing or at least diminished.

So if we rate how well these five elements are respected or enhanced by the various powers we would get interesting results. Take a minute to enter your own ratings for each of the ten types of power. How well do they protect, respect and develop our five ingredients? You could use a 1 to 5 rating, where 5 corresponds very well to one of the five ingredients and 1 corresponds poorly.

Kind of Power	Clear & Shared Goals	Owner-ship	Awareness & Achievement	Confi-dence	Healthy Relation-ships
1. Physical					
2. Threatening					
3. Hierarchical					
4. Political					
5. Emotional					
6. Personal					
7. Rewarding					
8. Charismatic					
9. Rational					
10. Awareness					

I can't give you the 'right' answers.

But, back to our element of freedom, which underpins each of the five ingredients. I think we can evaluate each of the powers in terms of the fundamental criterion of freedom (see figure 14.2).

It is important to be clear about which kind of power you are using or are expected to use. If we use personal power when people expect bureaucratic or hierarchical power, this can be confusing to everyone concerned and may actually reduce or minimise the power we have and may need to deploy in the actual situation.

As you can see from figure 14.2, I believe that the last three types of power – charismatic, rational and awareness – truly respect the freedom of the individual, which is the most critical

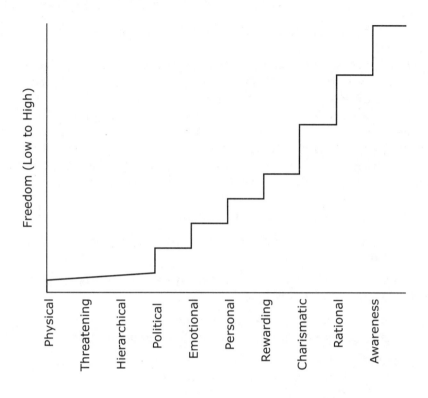

Kind of Power

14.2. What kind of power gives you the most freedom?

thing in every sense and for everyone's welfare, including that of the overall organisation. The challenge will be how to live this out and put it into practice in a business and organisational context. This is a core part of this book – to seek ways of influencing and getting things done through respecting the freedom of the individual. And it is not because this is best for the individual but because it is also best for the organisation. This sounds good, doesn't it?

The Power of MAGIC

The question remains, however – how can we manage and operate these three forms of power: Charismatic, rational and awareness?

These forms of power could be used to inspire (charismatic), convince (rational) or enable (awareness) people to behave in a particular way. We could put anything we like into these boxes of 'charismatic', 'rational' and 'awareness', as many charlatans, demagogues, fraudsters and preachers do. So is there anything new in this?

It is true that this model, like anything else, can be abused, as too can these three levers of power. And if they are abused they will actually lose their power. They will only be powerful in the long term if they are based on some sound principles.

This means that for us to be truly powerful in working and behaving in either of these three ways, we need to ensure they have truth and goodness behind them. By truth and goodness I mean five ingredients or qualities: MAGIC qualities!

1. **M**eaning – the need to be meaningful and to make sense.

2. **A**uthentic – the need to be genuine, true, real, sound and accurate.

3. **G**ood – the need to ensure that what we are after is good, good in itself, good for others and good for us.

4. **I**mportant – that what we are doing or what we want has significance, will make a difference and has consequences.

5. **C**orrect and **C**aring – that what we are about is the right thing to do, is a caring thing to do and is done with care.

So, what I am saying is that if we work to ensure that all, most or at least, some of these are present in all of our dealings then we will be able to present them in a charismatic, rational and awareness-creating way, and that this will give us enormous power.

This is what we are after – to be more powerful and impactful in all we do in every aspect of our lives, so that we are able to do and achieve more, and make things happen as managers and human beings.

When we work in this way we are increasing power, not just our own power but the power of the people we manage or lead.

What does all this mean in practice?

First of all, most managers will not perceive a need for any of this! They will feel perfectly powerful already in what they do. They decide and communicate their decisions or simply tell people what is to be done and people generally have no problem with that and get on with it.

This is true. But is that response from people the best one in every sense? Is it the best from the company's viewpoint in getting the most the person can give in terms of effort and quality of thought and intervention? And is it the best for the person in terms of their own welfare and happiness? We are repeatedly saying that welfare and happiness go hand-in-hand. If one suffers, the other suffers too.

We saw from the graphs above that the straightforward use of hierarchical power does not measure up well in terms of delivering on the principles of COACH. Nor does it do well in respecting and using the freedom of the other person.

In *The Future of Management*, Gary Hamel presents a scale that represents for him what most inspires people to work well:

- Passion: 35 per cent
- Creativity: 25 per cent
- Initiative: 20 per cent
- Intellect: 15 per cent
- Diligence: 5 per cent
- Obedience: 0 per cent

So, again, the knee-jerk reaction to fall back and rely on hierarchical or positional power scores badly here. On the other hand, the application of MAGIC, through being charismatic, reasonable and increasing awareness delivers on each one of these.

So how does one put these principles to use in the day-to-day? We simply trust the meaning, truth, goodness, importance and correctness of what we are doing and remind ourselves and people of it in everything we do.

Let's now take a look at the whole area of leadership as this will cover a lot of what I mean by using these kinds of power.

For now let me just say that we are looking at a form of power that is healthy and that fits with what it means to be human, while allowing us to use power in a good *and* more effective way.

Chapter 15

Manage in a Human Way – Just Lead

'The words leadership, vision and common purpose
have replaced the words control and authority
forever.'

– Charles Handy

We have looked at the various kinds of power and in particular
at three forms of power that will allow us to manage in a more
human and more effective way. I trust that by now it is clear that
by 'human' I am not referring to managing in a soft or so-called
nice way. I am talking about managing in a way that *invites and
challenges* people to be human and *makes it possible* or easier for
them to be so. In this way, they perform better for the good of the
organisation and for their own good, and are 'happier' or more
fulfilled as people.

Working with this kind of power affects how we manage and,
in fact, involves a substantial change from how we have traditionally managed. Much of our managing has not been done in
a way that enhances the humanity of the people managed. And
this for a very 'good' reason – that it is not seen as a key goal of
business organisations but as a secondary one to the goal of business success, most times seen as exclusively financial success.
As a result, a huge percentage of people at work are not being
challenged to develop as human beings. At best, people development is seen as a possible fall-out of how we manage and not
as a goal or criterion for how we manage. There is a perceived
dichotomy between what is good for the company or business
and what is good for people, as we will see later in Chapter 21
and elsewhere. Despite the nice rhetoric, work, and the people
who do it, are seen in many instances as a means to an end. The
oft-quoted TGIF ('Thank God it's Friday') is used to refer, not to a

189

welcome rest after an exhausting but exciting week's work, but to a sense of relief at the prospect of two pleasurable days away from the weekly slog before getting into another week on the treadmill. Real living happens at the weekend, or when on holidays or even with retirement. Of course, this is not universally true but there is some truth in the statement that for very many people work is not enjoyable or fulfilling. Work has been given a bad name and much of the cause of that is due to how people are managed.

To be clear, I am not talking here only of *bad* managing. I am questioning the whole approach to managing throughout this book. I am claiming that there is something quite fundamentally flawed in how we have learned to manage people and that there is a better way to be found and practised.

So, what is this better way?

Put very simply it is about basing how we manage and influence people on a different and better form of power. I now want to expand on what I have already covered in Chapter 14.

Using hierarchical or positional power

When we manage people in the sense of getting them to do things to further the interests of the business, we typically use a particular kind of power. It is because of the power we have that we can make things happen in the first place. Of course we use various kinds of power at different times but underpinning all of these is what I am calling hierarchical or positional power (see Chapter 14). What I mean by this is that we get legitimacy from telling people to do things. We take this so much for granted that we hardly notice it any more.

Let me try to make this a bit clearer. I have a neighbour. We are good friends. We meet at various times during the week when he is going to work or we are both outside doing some gardening or golf practice. We are of similar ages. He has been longer in the neighbourhood than I have and in that sense he is my 'senior'. He is a strong character and is involved in the local football club and other community activities. Sometimes I ask if he will attend a Residents' Association meeting but he rarely does. He declines the invitation or request. Now suppose I told you that last week I instructed my neighbour to get into his car and drive to Athlone – a two-hour drive – to attend a meeting and I told him what he had to do at that meeting. And he did it without complaint. Why would he have done it? Suppose I were to tell you that the reason is that he works with me in a company and I am his boss at work.

See how it all changes? It changes because I have a power at work that I don't have in my neighbourhood. This does not permit me to behave in the same way in my neighbourhood. So this makes it very easy for me to give him an instruction to spend six hours of his life in a certain way, going to a meeting. In the community where we live, I would not dare instruct him to go to the meeting as I don't have any hierarchical power over my neighbour in the community. I could use other types of power such as personal power where I ask him as a favour to attend the meeting as we saw in Chapter 14.

Ups and some downs of hierarchical power

So, hierarchical power is clear and effective – once we understand the rules and the pecking order, all works very smoothly. It is useful and, indeed, necessary in an organisation to give certain members of a group this legitimacy to organise and get other people to do certain things. It also has some downsides. One of the greatest weaknesses of this way of managing is that we could be getting people to do things that they may not think are right, good or the best and so they may not really want to do them. It can be worse than this in that we can get people to do what they believe or know to be wrong. We have numerous tragic examples from history where the most appalling things were done by people who were 'following orders'. While these may be regarded as extreme cases, the same principle applies irrespective of the seriousness of the instruction or situation when a person is doing something purely because someone else has told them to do it. In trivial matters such as 'close the door' or 'call me later' there is no issue at stake as the actions are neutral or free of any serious implications. The trouble is that we extend the same behaviour into more complex and important areas and issues, and give much more complex and problematic instructions with the same authority and simplicity as we do when we say: 'Close the door!'

If people accept it, and are perfectly willing to go along with it, then what is the problem?

In this book I talk about managing people in a human way. Telling other human beings to do something without any reference to what *they* think or to how *they* feel does not represent for me a good and acceptable way of handling people, even though it is common and absolutely acceptable as we have seen above. Notwithstanding this, it is inherently flawed. In a sense, it is violent as we are by our actions ignoring the views or wishes of the other person. Nor is it good for business.

If – as a neighbour – I ask my neighbour to come to a Residents' meeting and he has something on that he wants to do and regards as more important, he simply will not go. If – as his boss – I tell him to go to Athlone, even though he has something else that he wants to do and may regard as more important, he will go. Not because he thinks it is right or important but because I told him to go. What I would never get away with in 'normal' day-do-day life I can get away with at work because of the hierarchical relationship and the power that I have.

There are a few problems with this:

1. It is wrong, unfair and unjust to treat a human being in an inhuman or non-human way – wrong for them and wrong for us.

2. We will not get the same 'returns' from people in terms of quality work when we fail to treat them as human beings because to work well they need to feel and act as full human beings. (See Chapter 3)

But is there a better way?

So, what do we have to do and how do we have to manage in order to handle people in a human way? Is it possible? Is it desirable?

Throughout this book I am attempting to demonstrate that it is possible and that it is desirable. Let's focus here on the first question – what do we have to do to manage in a good and human way?

What is the right or appropriate power to use when managing people?

Meaningful power

As mentioned in Chapter 14, it is the power of MAGIC – meaning, authenticity, goodness, importance and correctness.

How is this arrived at? What would MAGIC mean in a company? In any organisation, to establish what all these things mean we need to spend some time in two areas.

1. First of all, working on what the company or organisation is about, what it is trying to do, its purpose. If we can do this and do it well then this will give meaning to everything that gets done in the company. It will provide a raison d'être for instructions, plans

and projects, as people will see how they fit with and contribute to the overall purpose of the organisation or company. In other words, what I do and am expected and asked to do will make sense to me as I see how it fits with what the overall purpose of the organisation is. It will have meaning and I will be able to do it because it is meaningful and makes sense, not because someone has told me to do it.

2. The second area where we need to spend time as managers in order to instil MAGIC into what we do and manage is the area of goals, wishes, objectives or vision. We are all familiar with this but we don't always practise it in the sense of establishing a vision and communicating it well and then living up to it. We take it for granted in that we set poor goals or token visions and also in that we don't spend enough time and effort communicating them to people and ensuring people understand them, buy into them and work to them.

I don't want to spend time on how to set goals and establish a vision here, as enough has been written on them already. All I want to mention is the importance of ensuring that the goals and vision are meaningful and not just token flowery words to hang on a wall.

The Goals Triangle

I believe mission and vision statements should not be framed and hung on walls if only because some parts of them, like goals, will need to be frequently revisited and revised. I say this because it cannot be that I am able to set something in stone or even in a frame and not need to adjust and change it with the changes that constantly surround and pound me. I see mission and vision as live and dynamic processes involving a tension between three elements:

• What is *needed*...out there'?

• What are we *able* to do?

• What do we *want* and *want* to do?

Graphically these look like figure 15.1. Because what is needed will in some senses remain the same and in some senses change, it draws or extends the triangle in one direction.

In turn, this puts pressure on the other two elements.

15.1. The Vision or Goal Triangle.

As *needs* change I will be required to be *able* to do more than I currently can.

New needs may also affect what I *want* and can attract and invite me to go after more or new things.

Any over-indulgence or exaggerated attention to any one angle or corner will distort the whole and damage the entity. Too many companies have floundered on the rocks of their pet products, services or plans as they were unable to let go of them even though they had become irrelevant and redundant. Others failed to take on the new skills and competencies needed to meet changing needs and to deliver what people actually want.

Equally, simply doing what we like doing and are good at without adverting to what is truly needed and of value, while pleasant and enjoyable, will be destructive in the long term.

Sticking with this dynamic process will ensure that what we are about in our companies will make sense to people, will appear as meaningful and good and of importance, and will thereby contribute to them feeling and being more human at work. The involvement of as many people as possible in the actual process of creating and operating the dynamic itself will greatly add to their sense of humanity. It is clear that it is not wise or even possible to do this on one's own.

Real visions

I am sure that you, like me, are tired hearing of visions and what they can do, because you realise they very often do not achieve all they are supposed to achieve. A lot of time is spent shaping and fashioning a vision statement. We hone it and tune it and round it and sharpen it until we are very pleased with what we have to share with the rest of our staff or workforce. Very often they are underwhelmed with our brilliant work. It can seem too neat, too slick or too rosy. Some of this may not be so much about the actual vision itself but because they know it will not really mean too much in how things are managed and done. They know that it will get framed, shown off, occasionally read by visitors in Reception and, apart from that, play no real part in the day-to-day reality. Often, too, they will see it as good and attractive but not too relevant or pertinent for them or their lives. This problem needs attention. It is too frequent an occurrence to ignore and the effects are too serious.

This calls for authenticity and courage – authenticity to believe that the vision is actually good and important for our people and courage to challenge them to go after it and make it a reality.

A balanced and rich life

15.2. The balanced life.

We have to believe that what is good for the company is also good for the various aspects of people's lives. Below are the eight ways in which the company has a very big impact on the lives of people:

1. How the company is will affect and contribute to people's *careers and their career progression.* A strong and successful company will offer more opportunities to people for promotion and progression. A caring company that values its people will seek to develop and promote its own people and look for opportunities for them.

2. How the company is will contribute to their *personal and professional development.* As the company develops it will need new skills and competences as it faces new challenges. A company can never stand still; it needs to change and develop and in so doing can bring its people with it. A well managed company that cares for its people will want to reward the loyalty of its staff by giving its people opportunities to grow and develop.

3. People are proud of where they work and what they do at work. What one does and where one does it contributes to the sense of identity and pride a person feels and so the welfare of the company does and will impinge on one's *social status* and how one feels within the *social community* and the family. If you are in any doubt about this, talk to someone who lost their job and what it did to their relationships and to their own confidence and sense of well-being.

4. Apart from providing resources to create the wherewithal for people's *hobbies and interests*, the demands of work act as a necessary foil for other interests, be they sport, arts, physical activities, DIY, etc. The balance is everything and the company can act as the centrepiece around which various interests rotate and play their part in the whole. Playing golf is great but not if you have nothing else to do.

5. It is not difficult to see how the welfare of the organisation will positively affect *one's family.* It can, of course, have a negative effect too if it robs the person of family time. But a well-managed and successful company will enable its employees to provide for their families as well as giving them the opportunity to fulfil their familial roles.

6. Naturally one's *financial welfare* and all that brings with it will depend to a great extent on the company's financial welfare. Wise company management will be creative in making these links strong and visible.

7. By *personal development* I mean a lot of things and among these are values, the spiritual, life skills and character. Spending on average eight hours every day in an environment necessarily affects how a

person is. There are many challenges of a personal and relational nature that a person has to deal with. There are also many calls to be made that affect values, ethics and what is good and right. Work will present challenges of a spiritual nature too, in terms of the meaning of the work, and its effect on the community and the world. How the company is and how it handles these topics will affect the person and the person's development.

8. The opportunity exists for the company to help people derive personal and professional *satisfaction from their work*. This is a huge responsibility on a company and on management. People entrust themselves and their lives to us for eight hours every day over two hundred and forty days of the year – by far the greater percentage of their lives. As managers we have a real responsibility to ensure that this enormous part of people's lives is meaningful and satisfying.

How the company performs, then, how successful it is, but also how well it manages its people has huge repercussions for people's lives. For that reason the vision is not just something that belongs to management or shareholders. It has great implications for every aspect of the lives of those who work within it.

Because of all this we must make sure that in handling the communication of the vision we really believe this. We have to make the links for ourselves and we have to be happy that the vision we are sharing does have the capacity to play a positive part in enriching people's lives.

We also, as I have said, have to be courageous. We have to be able and willing to look people in the eye and invite or challenge them to go along with the vision as something that is important in every sense and not just in a commercial one.

This is not to imply that one should prepare a vision based on one's own in marvellous isolation from the rest of the organisation. The views, feelings and input of others will greatly enrich and help to build a truly powerful picture of what is best for the company or organisation and will win all minds and hearts over to make it a reality.

Managing to and living the vision

Once the vision is set it becomes the source of meaning and direction. If it is well prepared and well communicated, it will become the centre of all managing thereafter.

What do I mean by this?

I am back to power! The power that we will use, once we have a vision that is rich and meaningful for the business and for people, will be the power of meaning – a power that functions on the basis of what is good for everyone. Once we have got this by doing good work on the vision, ensuring that it is meaningful for everyone, we are gifted with enormous power. This power is the whole power of MAGIC – what is meaningful, makes sense, is authentic and attractive, is good, is important and is correct or right. With this we have infinite power in all we do.

How does this work?

It works by identifying the MAGIC or meaning in everything we do, every instruction we give or request we make. In this way we are asking people to do things, not because we have asked for them but because they are what is right and best, etc. Apart from being absolutely respectful of the other person, it also helps the other person to understand and see the sense in what is being asked and so gives them the power, the sense and the will to carry it through. This is enormously empowering and helpful. It allows us to make every thing we do and ask for meaningful and enjoyable for our people. We are bringing sense and fulfilment into their lives and giving them the wherewithal to do it or get it done. As the conductor and writer Ben Zander says: 'We can awaken people to all of life, full, passionate, total life.'

What if they do not see the meaning in it or agree with it?

The onus is on you as a manager to work hard to make sense out of whatever is being communicated. Equally, you have to be open to the possibility that you may not be right or that a more sensible or meaningful option exists. This calls for greatness. While it might appear that it is a reduction or diminishment of your power to hear and take on board ideas or suggestions that you had not thought of, in fact it will increase your real power. On top of that, if you are open to learning and to what makes most sense, you will end up doing the right and best thing. Even better than what you had intended. In other words, the decision or direction that will be taken will be a better one. Is this not huge? It's elephantine – as we saw in Chapter 5.

I was running a leadership programme for managers in RTÉ, the national television station in Ireland, some years ago. I was making this same kind of point when one of the managers who also happened to be a representative of the Managers Staff Association said to me, 'You know, Brian, a manager does not have the right to make decisions. A manager only has the right to make *good* decisions.' What he was saying, in effect, was what I am saying here – that our authority comes not from our position or from our 'stripes' but from our wisdom. We have the right to ask people to do certain things because they are the right and best things to do and they make sense.

You may feel as you read this that to follow this would mean some kind of climb down on your part, a loss of status, a loss of influence, but the opposite is in fact the case. By appealing to what people know to be meaningful and right, you will grow in influence and status. People do see through us when they go along with our decisions and these decisions don't make sense to them. If we are always open to what does make sense, what is right and best, then they will respect us much more. Then, when some decision of ours runs counter to what they think or want, they will be much more willing to go along with it, as is mentioned in Chapter 24.

For example, I could tell a member of my team – like my neighbour – to go from Dublin to Athlone, 100 km away, and he would go.

Well, suppose instead of just *telling* him to go to Athlone, I were to explain to him that:

- As he knows, we have a goal to grow our wonderful business and get more clients interested in and benefiting from our services.

- There is a meeting in Athlone of an association of buyers who want to explain what it is they will be looking for from suppliers in the coming year and what business they hope to do in the coming year.

- We need to have someone good there to hear what they have to say and to represent the company and I would really like him to go.

Now, gifted with this information and aware of the need, he will go to Athlone as he would have done if I had instructed him to do so, but in a very different frame of mind, indeed, as a very different person. He will go because he wants to and because it makes sense to him. He will go as an empowered person. He will go as a free person doing what he believes is best. He will go with a clear purpose and goals that he understands and shares and wants.

He will go taking ownership for the outcomes of the meeting. He will go fully aware of what is involved and what is required. He will go feeling that I have confidence in him to act as our trusted representative. He will go feeling good about himself and about the relationship he has with me.

You may recognise in this the COACH principles we discussed in Chapter 13: Clear and shared goals, ownership, awareness, confidence and a healthy relationship.

Only ask and do what is good for people

I was running an influencing skills programme in Spain some time back and I made the statement that we should never ask people to do something that is not good for them. Or, put more positively, we should only take decisions that are good for people. You can imagine the reaction I got. All kinds of examples and instances were put forward where this could not apply – redundancies, no pay increase, failure to be promoted, disciplinary situations and so on. Of course there is an element of bad news in all of these cases and in many other similar situations. However, if in each of these situations the decision being taken is the right and best one, then it has also to be the right and best one *for the individual involved*. This is tough to take on board.

Let us take an example to try to make sense of it. Suppose we are a theatrical musical group. We put on musicals. It is what we do. We all gain from the success of our musicals in every way, financial and otherwise (see the discussion on the balanced life earlier in this chapter). We have a new musical that we are putting on, and you, as the manager or leader, have to decide how many you need to take part and also who will play the lead parts. This is going to spell bad news for some people – those who will not be chosen to take part and those who will not be selected for the principal parts. This could be seen as a situation where your decisions are simply bad for them. But is that really so? If we all agree that it is the success of the musical that will ultimately benefit us all, then people can be brought, albeit reluctantly, to accept that this is the right and best decision overall, and so the best and right decision for *them* also. Or, suppose one of the musicians is not performing well, should we not confront that situation even if that may involve some 'bad news' for the musician in question? If this is the good and right thing to do, then it is good for everyone including the person negatively affected. Ideally they themselves should reach that tough decision themselves – that they are damaging the overall cause and so should do something about it even if that something means leaving the group. Because people don't always know that they are not contributing to the overall welfare, and therefore their own welfare, or are not prepared to take the necessary steps that are required for the welfare of everyone, the manager often has to do this. The fact that it is the manager who is making the right decision does not mean that it ceases to be right and good for the person affected. This negative perception arises and gets taken for granted for two reasons:

1. Managers do not always make sufficient effort to ensure their decisions are the right and best ones.

2. Managers do not always make sufficient effort to communicate their decisions as being the right and best ones and so often feel guilty about them and handle them badly.

This happens because of the mistaken concept we have as managers of the power we believe we have and can use which, again, is hierarchical or positional power. We need to make sure that our decisions are based on criteria other than that *we* want it done. This is challenging and we need to constantly remind ourselves of the need to only take good decisions, to only give good instructions. How do we do this?

Don't forget the MAGIC at your disposal

We will be able to ensure our decisions in any business situation are good once the decision is put through the MAGIC test. And every decision should go through this process to ensure it is a good decision. Without any exaggeration, this means that we can manage every situation in a human way for the betterment of everyone – the business, the people and ourselves as decision makers and managers.

So in fact I could get my neighbour to go to Athlone even if he did not work for me. I could tell him of a funeral that I think he should attend, or a wonderful concert that he would really love, or a very exciting talk that I think he should not miss, or a symposium on local communities that would be of great interest to us all and that I cannot attend. If these are valid reasons, he would *have* to go. But not because I told him to. In this way I am actually helping him to see what might be the right and best thing to do – for him too. This is a shift in management style from telling and instructing to educating and explaining. It is called leadership. The best way to manage in a human way is to lead. It is easy. It is also very important. We will now look at how managing in the usual or traditional way can be damaging to people and to performance.

Chapter 16

Healthy Management

'To do what is commanded, *because* it is commanded, even if this is by God, is always wrong.'

– St Thomas Aquinas

'Profit is like health. You need it but it is not what you live for.'

– St Luke's (advertising company)

As part of our search to find out how we can manage to be human, we have stumbled into a problem and a challenge. In this regard, I am saying a few things:

- Being human is about doing justice to ourselves as human beings and performing – in the broad sense of the word – in line with that.
- Many of us fail to perform in line with our real potential as human beings.
- Some of this is down to the fact that we get blocked from performing in line with our true potential.
- One of the ways we get blocked is that our management blocks us.
- Managers block us, not always because they are bad managers, but just because they are *managers*, because there is something flawed with the notion of managing as we traditionally understand and apply it.

Managing can do serious damage to health

This would suggest that I am saying there is something unhealthy about management. That is exactly what I *am* saying. In fact most of what we refer to as management is unhealthy and damaging. It is unhealthy for the managers themselves but even more unhealthy and damaging for those managed.

Let's go back a step to what we normally understand by managing people. The reason we have managers and supervisors to manage people is that we believe that, without them, people would not work on their own, or work as well on their own. We believe they need managers and need to be managed. This is in fact true but not for the reasons we normally believe.

The three reasons why we believe people need managing is that we believe that without a manager they will:

- Not *know* what to do.

- Not *want* to do it.

- Not be *able* to do it.

As I mentioned earlier, I was in a large restaurant in the Plaza Oriente in Madrid, Spain some time ago and as I ate and drank I watched the waiters at work and also watched their restaurant manager. The restaurant manager, in his role as manager of the waiters, was probably operating out of one or all of these assumptions (most managers do). He believed he was needed because without him, his waiters would not *know* what to do or would come across situations which they would not know how to handle – customers with strange requests, customers not attended to, customers not seated where they wanted to be. Or he believed he was needed because without his presence they would not do what they should or as well as they should because they didn't *want* to. Without him they would not do what they ought to do because they didn't want to make the effort, or didn't care enough, to ensure customers' needs were met, to take away plates when people were finished eating, to check if customers were happy with their meal or needed more wine. Or, he believed he was needed because they lacked the skills and *ability* to wait properly and so needed him, the expert, to guide and help them to do it, to do it well or to do it better – to know how to handle special requests, to deal with problems that arose, to deal with a shortage of tables. Dealing with these three needs, then, became the key role and function of our restaurant manager, as they are of every manager. But it is *how* managers deal with these three possibilities or realities that matters.

Let's look at them.

Knowing

The assumption is that people do not or will not know what to do. They may not know all that is happening or what is required. They may not have the big picture and so need to be told what is needed – 'Tidy off those tables and then get the plates ready for the evening meal'; 'Get those tables moved over there and the layout ready for breakfast.' They may not know all that their job entails or involves. In the case of the waiters, they may not know of a special event that is coming up or of a change to some aspect of the restaurant or the menu. The manager will point out to waiters, then, what to do. He will answer questions they have. He will direct them to certain tasks. He will correct them and point out things they need to do or do differently. This is quite a big and busy job for a manager.

Wanting

The assumption here is that people will not work or work as well as they could and should unless they are managed and supervised. The waiters may take too many breaks, wandering into the Plaza to have a smoke or to observe the tourists. They may work too slowly. They may not give the clientele, including myself, the attention and service we need. The manager is necessary, then, to encourage them, motivate them and maybe admonish them if that is called for so that they give good service. Without him, the service might be awful. He is critical.

Ability

The assumption here is that people will not be able to do their job without help. They will not have the skill, ability, confidence, organisation or experience to do the job. In the case of my Spanish waiters, this would mean they are not skilled enough in taking orders, in treating customers well, in understanding the menus or the wines. The manager may be very experienced and have been very good at waiting, and so may be able to do things and handle things better than his team of waiters. The waiters may simply not be able to do the job as well as the manager and so need managing.

So, there we have it – a very clear role for the manager to play. And without a manager it is obvious how much could go wrong.

Self-justifying management

But suppose, just suppose for a minute that the waiters worked hard to make sure that they *did* know all that was involved in the job and what was required. And suppose they were a very motivated and mature bunch and so wanted to do a good job for the restaurant and themselves. And suppose they became very skilled and capable and were well able to do the job perfectly. What then happens to the manager? Is the manager then no longer needed? Or are we saying that this is impossible and can never happen? Surely not!

But it is here where managing can and does go horribly wrong. If the role of manager is confined to 'managing' and propping up or supporting, then it means that these three needs have to continue to exist so that the manager has a meaningful role and a raison d'être. See the dangerous dynamic? The role of manager is dependent on people not knowing what to do or not wanting to do it or not being able to do it. This might seem a pernicious thing to say but I believe it is the reality more often than not. A very dangerous vicious circle develops whereby managers need people to not know, not want to perform or not be able to perform in order to justify their existence and role. And they create that very situation and often do it well and with great disguise.

You might say that this is ridiculous, that no one would think or behave like that. However, it does not happen at a conscious level. A whole subconscious dynamic develops. Managers actually expect people to not know, not want and not be able and this creates the reality of people not knowing, not wanting and not being able. A stable relationship exists where all are happy and reconciled but which is quite unhealthy and negative. It is a bit like what happens between parents and children where parents expect children to do wrong things and children duly comply to fit with this expectation.

A new approach to management

There is a better way. It lies in a completely different understanding of what managing is about. Of course, there is a need to manage people in situations where some do not know what is required, where some don't want to do what is required, and where others are not able and need help to do what is required. But managing cannot be built *only* on these situations, for all the reasons mentioned above.

This is where it gets exciting.

Let's go back to the Plaza Oriente and to our waiters. Let's suppose they are a smart bunch – they know the job, and have found out how many are expected for dinner and what the chef has planned and prepared. Suppose that, apart from being smart, they are a responsible and motivated bunch and so are really keen to do a good job and give the customers good service. And, on top of all that, suppose that they are an experienced crew and need little or no guidance or help in getting the job done and giving customers a top class eating experience and service.

Our manager or head waiter is hanging around but he is not twiddling his thumbs. He is busy too, not watching the waiters or making work for himself, but looking at what could be done better and what new things could be done to take the restaurant on to a new plane and make it even better. He is doing this because it is what he wants to do and likes doing, but he is also doing it because he knows what his managers want, what they need and what their goals and wishes are for the restaurant. He has some idea of the resources that are available for this and knows that he can make proposals or requests for additional resources if they are needed and make sense. Of course he will also spot things the waiters can do better and will share these with them either there and then or later.

Now he would be a very foolish head waiter or manager if he tried to do all of this on his own. He has the heads of eight waiters available to him to contribute ideas and suggestions to improving the restaurant. The waiters' input will be uniquely valuable as they are in daily contact with the customers. They will spot lots of ways to improve things.

But they will only do this if they are:

1. On the look-out for things

2. Requested and encouraged to put forward their ideas and given the opportunity to actually submit their ideas

3. Confident that something will be done about them when they do put their suggestions forward

Putting these three things in place is the responsibility of the head waiter:

1. He will need to let the waiters know the desire on the part of managers or owners to improve things, the need to do so and the benefits from doing so for the restaurant and for them.

2. He will need to make it easy for them to contribute their ideas by establishing some formal mechanism for doing so and handling that mechanism well and in an open-minded way.

3. He will also need to take the ideas put forward seriously and act on them and, where he doesn't or can't, come back to the waiters to let them know what happened and why.

In this sense the manager (head waiter) acts as a link between the waiters and the restaurant managers or owners. More than a link, he is a conduit or whirlwind, bringing information, challenges, visions, goals and needs to the waiters, and ideas and suggestions to management. In this way everyone in the restaurant is connected and linked. There are no ceilings, glass or otherwise, only a dynamic interchange and exchange that informs and enriches everyone's function and enriches the whole. In this model there is one goal to which everyone subscribes and contributes, be that through actual work or ideas. Change, improvement, betterment, progress and growth become the order of the day, and the goal and focus of everyone. Everyone wants to do better, to be better. Successes are shared and celebrated. Every job is infused with the meaning of the whole. All share in the success and in the problems. There is no hierarchy but a differentiation of responsibilities, which of course will be rewarded differently.

All of this creates more meaning for everyone in the restaurant. Everyone's job is seen in the overall context and so they understand the importance or relevance of what they are doing. The only enemy is the competition; everyone within the restaurant or company is seen as an ally or a friend. Everyone's role is understood by everyone else and is recognised and appreciated. The person responsible for safety is seen as a great help and not a nuisance. The quality person's role is seen as a critical contribution and safeguard and not as a brake on getting people served. The owners and senior management identify with the frontline waiters and want to understand how they feel and what they think as well as sharing some ideas with them.

Meetings take place with people from all different levels to look at problems and opportunities. New ideas and projects are always worked on with multiple levels of people present so they can be tested on a cross section of people as early as possible. Every manager at every level is focused on improvement and betterment.

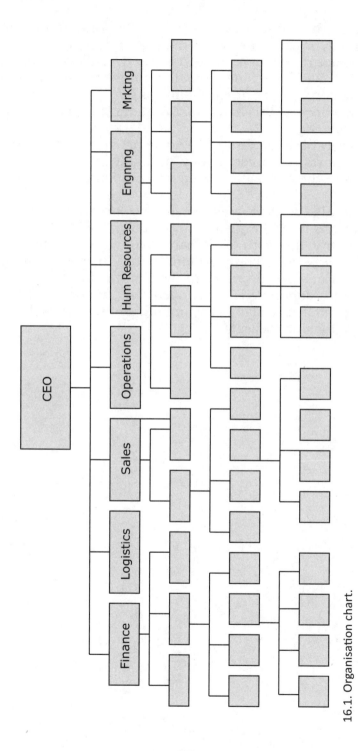

16.1. Organisation chart.

Of course the day-to-day routine has to continue too but this occupies only a portion of what managers do. Their main aim is to put in place a system and mechanism that allows people get on with the job. With everyone's goal to improve things, there is little need for supervision or much monitoring.

So, where does all this leave us? What am I suggesting or recommending you do?

Well, several things. First, add some art and life to your organisational charts. At present they probably look a bit static. No movement in them. No life. See figure 16.1 for an example of such a chart.

There is also a clear message in the format that the people higher up are over the people lower down. 'Well they are,' you might say, but the word 'over' can have many negative associations, like 'superior', 'better', 'dominating', 'in control of' and 'in charge of'. Each of these affects people, making them feel 'inferior', 'worse', 'dominated', 'controlled' and 'instructed'. So, even from the geometric design of the organisation chart we have given people a damaging message.

16.2. Pecking order.

But what can we do? Let's draw the organisational chart more like it is, with life and movement in it. How about a whirlwind model, or a cyclone, vortex or spiral model into which the organisation chart roles are inserted? Now we have movement – up

16.3. Dynamic organisations.

and down and around. Everyone works in all directions, up and down. There are levels of responsibility, action and relationships. But levels are crossed as everyone is connected to everyone else. What matters is the movement, the dynamism, and this is all about change, energy, improvement, progress and growth. This is the life of the organisation – constant improvement, searching, adapting and changing. Management is all about change and improvement. It is ironic that 'change' is such a problematic issue for so many organisations when it is the most fundamental thing in the universe. Many of these problems come from the concept we have of organisations and of management, based on ideas of control, the top-down flow of information and decision making, superior–inferior relationships, and a perceived need to manage and maintain status quo. We need to seriously question and fundamentally review each of these concepts. A first step might consist of drawing or capturing the organisation chart in a more dynamic and live way. I put this forward as an easier and probably more effective option than re-designing the organisation.
What does this mean in practice, apart from improving our drawing skills?

It means many things.

1. It means that there will be no ceilings between different levels. Regular meetings of two and three layers of people from these levels will take place and this system will operate right throughout the organisation.

2. It means that all managers will be more like leaders and change agents than supervisors and overseers. Their aim will be to make their teams and departments as autonomous and independent as early and as much as possible. This may never actually be fully achieved but the goal and the focus will be based on achieving it.

3. It means that team working and collaboration are not just luxuries but the lifeblood of the organisation. Team working will operate across levels and between different levels. This is critical for the achievement of maximum autonomy and minimum organising and controlling.

4. It means that the organisation is listening – to what is happening, to what people are saying. It invites the views of everyone in the organisation to help ensure wise directions and good decisions are taken at every level by everyone.

5. It means that change is initiated and promoted from every level in the organisation in the drive to respond to developments and to constantly improve.

6. It means that everyone is aware of the goals of the organisation in carrying out their function, works towards their achievement and shares in the successful realisation of them.

7. It means that learning and expertise development are sought after and are given enormous attention in order to create maximum autonomy, independence and performance.

8. It means that people want and seek feedback in order to improve their contribution and their performance.

9. It means that managers take risks in trusting people to do their jobs and this trust enables and empowers people to do so.

10. It means that no one loses sight of the world outside because everyone sees their job in that context and is aware of customers, markets and suppliers through the one-piece organisational structure.

This healthy form of managing is about achievement, making things happen and bringing about a new state of things. At its core is a desire for betterment, for improvement of the existing, as covered in the section and chapters on creativity. This it seeks to bring about through helping people to understand their roles and equipping them to fulfil them as responsibly and autonomously as possible. It is not about managing people but about exposing people to the challenge to make things better, inviting them to take part in successfully facing that challenge and equipping them to be able to do so. It believes that the challenge itself will drive performance if people are allowed to see it for themselves rather than being pushed by a manager to do a job.

It is healthy because it is good for everyone and is based on a belief in the goodness and potential of people. It is healthy because it is outward looking. It is healthy because it is built on common and shared goals pursued by all in a spirit of team working and unity.

Look at what this does to the 'blocks to creativity' already covered in Chapter 12:

How We Block Ourselves	How We Block Others or How Others Block Us
1. Fear of making mistakes, of getting it wrong, of not making it.	1. Goals and objectives not clear enough.
2. Fear of getting outside our comfort zones.	2. Not enough attention and listening.
3. Our lack of self-belief and confidence in ourselves.	3. Poor management style.
4. Our inadequate skills level and knowledge.	4. Lack of trust.
5. Lack of clarity and focus on what we really want; poor goals.	5. Lack of recognition.
6. Blaming others, the organisation, our manager, life.	6. Insufficient information and involvement.
7. Not spotting or taking opportunities around us.	7. Management over-control.
8. Poor relationships and turf wars that distract us and waste energy.	8. Too many rules.
9. Failure to take responsibility for things.	9. Too much criticism.
10. Lack of persistence; giving up or settling for.	10. Lack of support and tools.
	11. Lack of respect.
	12. Lack of trust in people.

All of these blocks are dealt with under this form of management. They should all disappear. There is no room or place for them in this new way of working. There is no need to avoid them or to work hard to stop doing them. We just need to take on a new way of seeing 'managing' and the rest happens. The new way is to see our role as KWA managers (helping people to Know, to Want and to be Able) and as being about making everything better, every day. This is perfectly in line with our vocation as human beings, with what makes us most human. Once we do it, we will manage to be human.

While this may be an attractive way to manage, it may seem to lack realism. It may present an image of managers without teeth, without real power. It might seem that it would work in some ideal kinds of situations but not in normal situations, in real life. Let's look into this a bit more in Chapter 17.

Chapter 17

Organic and Live Organisations

'It is better to have lived one day as a tiger than to
live all your life as a lamb.'

– Anon

When I talked about a different form of organisation chart in
Chapter 16, I was attempting to capture on paper something that
is actually live. This is not an easy task. I was and am doing this
because organisations are alive; they are live entities even though
we often see and manage them as if they are inert, lifeless things.
For this reason, I want to take a look at the difference between
organic or live organisations and traditional organisations.

The traditional organisation

The traditional organisation is seen and treated as something that
has to be managed and controlled in the sense that, if one did
not do all of that managing and controlling, nothing much would
happen or be carried out in a right or good way. In this way,
the people who do the work know what to do and do it because
managers *tell* them to. The level of detail in this 'telling' can vary.

To use the example of the restaurant in Plaza Oriente in Madrid,
which we described in Chapter 16, the manager or head waiter
can simply get his people, the waiters, to look after and serve the
customers that arrive. Alternatively, he can:

- Issue them with their instructions for the day based on what *he*
  knows is coming up.

- Assign responsibilities to each of the waiters for the day.

- Tell them what they need to know for that day.

- Intervene when things go wrong or when he sees them going wrong,

- Correct waiters for doing things in a wrong way and discipline them if that is needed.

- Be available to address problems and answer questions that arise.

- Step in and help out occasionally when he sees the need.

- Inform the waiters of what is coming up next, for example, a group or party coming in for dinner.

- Move waiters around in the restaurant as he sees the need.

- Liaise with the kitchen and other people in the hotel or restaurant around needs.

The problem with the traditional organisation

In the traditional organisation, the manager (like our head waiter) believes he has to be there. If he were to get sick, he would immediately get someone to replace him. Otherwise, who would look after all of these things? It would be chaos.

Yes, it would be chaos because people have been trained and developed in attitudes and a culture of ignorance, irresponsibility, lack of ownership, ineptitude, incompetence and inferiority, etc. for years. In a phrase, none of the COACH principles are in place:

C. Clear, challenging, shared and exciting goals

The waiters are not clear about the overall goals or where *their* goals might fit in with these. As a result of this, the waiters will form and follow their own separate and individual goals. These may be things like:

- Getting the work done more easily.

- Getting time for their breaks (and the more of these and the longer they are the better).

- Getting the easiest and avoiding the toughest jobs.

- Outside-of-work interests.

- Maximising earnings through tips or overtime which can come from things going wrong or slowly.

- Doing as little as possible which may mean not wanting to hear customers' complaints or about their needs and ignoring other waiters' customers.

- Turning a blind eye to other problems that have arisen or are looming.

Of course they want to get the job done and keep the boss, the head waiter, happy and off their backs, but this has to fit in with their own goals and a daily game takes place between these two sets of goals.

O. Ownership of the job – the tasks and responsibilities

Ownership is reduced and kept to the narrowest of responsibilities or duties. The overall ownership of the task in hand, of the main purpose or goal, is not felt or taken on board. Once each waiter does his or her bit, that is all that matters, and how well or poorly it all goes is not their problem. Anything arising or occurring outside their narrow area of focus is not their concern. Individual tasks are seen as such and not seen as part of a larger and more meaningful purpose. The overall welfare, success or failure of the restaurant is remote from them, not up to them and, indeed, may run counter to their own interests and goals, as was referred to above. Looking after customers is a kind of side-show to their real lives and interests. If there isn't a table for a party of six that has arrived it is someone else's job to sort it out or it is just too bad. A costly 'wrong' or misunderstood order is just too bad. A group of older people who want to linger over their meal are a nuisance and disruptive of the schedule.

A. Awareness of what is needed, happening and planned

The waiters are aware of all of what is planned and happening, but indirectly through their manager, the head waiter. As a result, there is no real awareness of the reality of what is going on but all gets channelled as instructions, requirements, orders and requests. How staff are made aware of things and from whom has major effects on the quality and nature of their awareness. For example: 'A large party will be arriving for lunch' gets distorted from a given reality to an 'order', if they hear it from their manager as 'I have a large party arriving for lunch.' Reality has been fundamentally changed by how it got channelled or communicated. All developments for this event – the party arriving for lunch – will be expected to also come through the manager and, if they don't, they are simply not seen or understood. The world is reduced to what is described and outlined by their manager.

Nor is there awareness of many other things at a higher level, such as the contribution this party might make to results, to the image of the restaurant, to the overall goals of the restaurant and so to the welfare of everyone, the waiters included.

In other words, let the dog see the rabbit!

17.1. Dog & rabbit.

We can remove the power of a real and felt challenge by getting in its way through indirect explanations of what the goal is. We explain what it means instead of letting people see, hear and feel it for themselves. The difference, while it might appear slight, is actually enormous.

C. Confidence – in oneself, in others and from others

The waiters lack confidence in themselves in terms of their work duties. They have learned that they are not capable of taking big decisions or making calls. While they all take far bigger and more serious decisions every day in their homes, families and the social groups they belong to, they are very clear that they cannot and should not do so in the restaurant. They get confirmed in this belief by the fact that the head waiter appears to want them to go to him with questions and that he treats even the simplest of questions with great seriousness and gravity. Once or twice some people took initiatives but these were not well received. The fact that they are never left on their own is further confirmation that they are not expected to be able to decide things and make moves on their own. They have become quite comfortable with this arrangement and don't feel like taking risks or responsibility. As a result, virtually every issue and problem is brought to the head waiter for a decision.

H. Healthy relationships, adult to adult

The hierarchical model reigns and each person knows his or her station. The head waiter has a lot of power over the waiters and they see and recognise this. Whatever he says goes. Sometimes, while they can see that it does not make sense, they know that one does not question one's superior. How each waiter is evaluated is based on the opinion of the boss or head waiter. For that reason it is important to please and satisfy the head waiter as it is he who decides bonuses and the distribution of the tips, which is based on merit. While they generally get on well unless something goes wrong, the waiters defer to their manager on virtually everything.

While this may appear a bit extreme in parts, the general principle behind the above way of managing is sound and is at the root of all traditional management practices. Nor is it believed that there is any real alternative to this system. Many pretend to operate in a different way but the same old belief system will be always at work deep down. The dividing line between what is called the mechanistic, traditional approach and what is called the organic, quantum approach is subtle but absolutely decisive. One, the mechanistic, is driven and controlled by a manager or nothing happens. The other, the live, autonomous and dynamic organisation, has a life of its own and only needs 'feeding' and some 'looking after'.

The organic organisation

As I wrote and thought about this, I looked out my window and in my neighbour's garden I saw he had wooden garden furniture in front of his Leylandii trees. I pondered the difference between the two – the furniture and the trees. I asked myself: What makes the trees different? I came up with twelve differences:

The Tree	Furniture
1. The tree moves (has an inner life and develops on its own.	The furniture has no inner development; it is dead.
2. Grows continuously.	No growth, apart from what gets added on from the outside.
3. Changes and has an inner knowledge or wisdom to change and adjust to light, water and wind.	Is changed. No internal knowledge or wisdom to adjust. Gets blown over in the wind.
4. Trusts in itself and has confidence that it will cope with most things. A broken branch will either get repaired or replaced.	No trust in itself – passive and a victim. A broken piece of furniture will remain broken unless fixed by someone.
5. Relaxed and quietly relentless in its growth and renewal.	Listless and waiting; slowly decaying.
6. Appears dead but a life is there that never dies.	Lifeless.
7. Innovative – grows in different ways and gets around problems of obstacles to the light, etc.	No innovation. Will always remain the same.
8. In touch and in harmony with its environment; shares with, adjusts for and cooperates with birds, soil and air.	A foreigner or stranger to the environment with no interaction or relationship. Gets rotted by moisture from the earth.
9. Complex in how it works, operates and lives.	Simple, inoperative and inactive.
10. Each tree is unique. No two trees are identical.	Standard and can be replicated over and over.
11. Thinks of the future and of continuing life.	No future, only this.
12. Part of something greater, a whole, a greater purpose.	Isolated, cut off, on its own, for itself.

While both of these two 'personalities' are the same size and have some things in common, there is a fundamental difference between them as captured in the above twelve points. The tree is alive, intelligent and responsive. The furniture is dead, stupid and passive.

It is obvious that it is preferable to work with an organisation model based on the tree rather than the furniture. Apart from being preferable, it is also more accurate as organisations and people are vibrant and alive. Yet, we treat organisations, people and teams of people more like the garden furniture than like the intelligent, flexible and autonomous tree. What is at stake with most organisations is not so much whether they are alive or not but where their life comes from and how they channel their life. There is life at work in any group of people. The unfortunate thing is that life may be channelled in different directions from the goal the organisation is pursuing.

Two agendas

To get back to the Plaza Oriente – the group of waiters may be full of life. They may have great sport and fun among themselves, have nicknames for managers and for the head waiter, play little games among themselves about who does what in the restaurant, scheme around getting overtime, share tricks to get away with doing things in easier or deviant ways, enjoy a whole alternative value system and culture among themselves, plan and live through outside-work experiences, invent ways of dealing with or avoiding awkward or demanding customers, and have cliques and sub-groups that control what really gets done and bring deviants who want to do more back into line. So there is no shortage of life but it is created around the wrong things.

In parallel with all of this, or even against it, will be all of the management actions that are designed and intended to get the waiters to do what is required. The two may coincide at times but the management action will run counter to the real 'life' and energy going on in the group of waiters. Every initiative of management – the formal agenda – will be measured against the other agenda, the informal or 'real' agenda, and accepted, resisted or tolerated depending on how well it measures up to this agenda. This never gets articulated and the waiters will play the game of going along with the management messages, but it will be at best lip service as most of these are seen as manipulative ploys to curtail the energy in the group and to control them and keep them in line. Indeed, the fun and enjoyment being had from fighting with management may be so strong that *this* becomes the main driver for people – the battle with management. Ironically, going against management decisions and initiatives can be the principal source of energy for the workers. While ordinary and minor decisions may be accepted, big decisions, changes and fresh initiatives become great sources of identity, energy and excitement for the workforce but for the wrong reasons – as a cause to be opposed and resisted. For example, some trade unions would get their raison d'être from working with employees to resist the imposition of changes on them. Many of us get our identity from what we hate. For workers, management can give them their identity as workers. This is less so than in the past but is still true. Rarely can this resistence be articulated but that does not mean it is not at work, opposing and resisting management decisions, much to the bafflement of managers.

When there is some problem and something goes wrong because of some behaviour of the waiters, a new rule or procedure is introduced to deal with it. For example, 'In future, all waiters have to work until closing time and shall change into their own clothes on their own time and not on company time.' Another loophole closed! And on it goes: Deviant waiters and managers plugging holes to put a stop to the deviation.

When 'management' come up with a better way of serving customers through a more sophisticated system, the waiters see that this will mean a change in their work practices and so they raise it as a negotiating issue if they belong to a trade union. Management are astounded that something so obviously beneficial could be resisted and challenged, and so the industrial relations game or circus begins. The main issue is that there are two agendas at work and in conflict – that of the restaurant or company one and that of the waiters or workers.

When the eventual agreement is reached – if it is – then management will police the new agreement and a new game commences with two opposing agendas and energies again at work – to implement the agreement or to get around it. Rules and a mechanistic approach to everything are used in order to get people, staff or workers, to behave in a particular way, to fulfil their duties. Behaviour is being sought and pursued through a mechanistic, rules-driven and external process, imposed and demanded from the outside. The agreement gets pushed to the limit, topics that were not anticipated or adequately covered get raised and new discussions and debates develop. All of this takes time and energy and, all the time, life in the persons of the waiters finds new ways to express itself and have its fun.

The breakdown

But, one day, there is an electrical power-cut. All systems collapse and gas cookers and ovens have to be commissioned and got working again. It is chaotic in the kitchen. In the restaurant mayhem also reigns. The usual systems are not working and the head waiter is caught up trying to manage orders and revise menus. The waiters are equally thrown into chaos and end up doing all kinds of things to get people attended to and served. Everyone does everything that is needed. They organise themselves, order each other around, liaise with the kitchen, find out what bookings have been made and arrange how to handle them. They deal with problems and complaints and control the whole environment. Any customer needing attention gets it immediately, from whichever waiter happens to be near. Messages, requests and orders all get communicated between the waiters and the kitchen. Normal break times are changed and some are not taken at all. None of the waiters has ever worked harder. At the end of the day everyone is tired but a great feeling of satisfaction and achievement is felt by everyone.

The following day, the electric power is back again and all is back to normal. The waiters are back to their old routines. They wait for directions from the head waiter, go to him with problems, handle their own tables, take extended breaks, carry on conversations about everything except work, apart from, that is, how awful their managers are.

What has happened? What has changed people so radically in such a short space of time?

People want to live

People want to live just like our tree does. They want life. They want excitement, challenge and enjoyment. They do not normally expect to get it at work and work is designed to *remove challenges*, uncertainty and risk. So, when people at work see that their work is not going to be filled with meaning, challenge and excitement, they go in search of fun, challenge and excitement in other places – like our waiters who find it in breaks, working as little as possible, engineering overtime, outwitting management, etc. All great fun. The only problem is that this life is contrary to the direction and energy the restaurant wants. Management, faced with this, resort, as has already been said, to more controls to cut off avenues of escape from the responsibilities of work.

Creating the live organisation

So, how can this be avoided? Is it possible to manage in such a way that there is only one energy at work – the good of the overall organisation?

Yes, it is possible, but it calls for a fairly radical shift in how things get handled and how managers see and handle their roles.

To find out how to bring this about all we need to do is to refer back to our COACH model. In other words, we are going to manage only in line with COACH principles:

- **C** is for Commitment to clear, challenging, shared and exciting goals or vision.

- **O** is for Ownership of the task, job, assignment, project, etc.

- **A** is for Awareness of what is going on or what is needed, or acknowledgment of what has been achieved.

- **C** is for Confidence and trust – in yourself, in others or from others

- **H** is for Healthy relationships.

Rather than getting into the theory of this and how it might work, let's go back to the Plaza Oriente and have a look at what is happening in the restaurant. A major change has taken place and the restaurant is being run along COACH lines.

Everything looks the same on the surface as it was on our first visit but under the surface it is quite different.

The waiters have met and planned their day. They did so based on the list of bookings that have been made, some of them directly to the restaurant which they themselves have taken and some which one of the waiters gets every day from the restaurant reception area. They have also checked what day it is and if there is any reason – special occasion, weather, day of the week, past experience – which might lead to numbers being up or down.

At their meeting they have also:

- Reviewed the previous day's work and results in the context of how it ultimately affects the welfare of the restaurant and so their own welfare.

- Reviewed some problems that arose the previous day and have fixed them or put in place improvements to deal with them.

- Allocated responsibilities for the day based on workloads, development and learning needs, and special circumstances.

- Agreed to try out some improvements that have been raised at the weekly meeting and discussed with the head waiter.

- Looked at some possible scenarios that might arise during the day so that everyone is prepared.

While they each have their key responsibilities, they overlap where that is needed and the focus and effort is on getting the job done. Of course, things go wrong, problems arise, surprises happen but they solve the problems themselves and, where necessary, make notes of points that they will need to bring up at their morning meeting and at their monthly meeting because they will require longer discussion and some problem solving. Because the numbers are especially large that evening, they decide to open up another room which is an extension of the restaurant, and this they decide and organise themselves. Some of the more experienced waiters accompany and support and guide two new recruits and will review with them what they have learned and the problems they encountered at the end of the day. One waiter needs to leave early and they accommodate this among themselves and some stay back to make up for his absence.

Because it is a very busy day, some know they will not be able to take their full break but this does not matter; the day is going well. Regular customers are recognised and given that special treatment and new customers are given enough attention so they return. All know that the better the day is the better it will be for them too. They are looking forward to the end of the month to see the results.

The leader of the group has been involved all day in the restaurant but was also involved in liaising with the hotel management and attended a management meeting in the afternoon to discuss some new plans for the restaurant. He presented the results of a meeting the waiters had the previous week to put forward some suggestions. There are some things they want to change that they believe will improve the service and make the restaurant more efficient and receptive.

Characteristics of the organic intelligent organisation

The restaurant is now an organic organisation, which means:

1. It is a vibrant, live, dynamic restaurant run by the waiters who are passionately interested in doing a good job.

2. It is driven by a shared goal that all understand and have bought into.

3. It is a flexible entity that adjusts and responds to circumstances and needs as required.

4. The staff are constantly trying to improve and grow and be better.

5. It is a united entity with each person supporting and working for the other.

6. The staff get their information directly from the customers and from what is happening.

7. The staff need no direction or to be told what to do.

8. It is an exciting and fun place to work.

9. The staff control themselves by their desire to do a good job and provide a quality and efficient service.

10. The staff are forever inventing and searching for new and better ways to do things.

Just like the tree, the group of staff is alive and responsive to its situation. Like the tree, it is intelligent with a clear goal and the ability to create ways to accomplish and achieve that goal.

The role of the manager in the organic organisation

But, if the waiters behave like this, what is the role of the head waiter – their manager? Is he redundant? No longer needed?

Not at all. The head waiter or manager has responsibilities under three main headings:

1. Working to ensure that his waiters *know, want* and are *able* to provide the level and quality or service required and desired (see Chapter 16). This will, of course, vary from person to person and new people will need more assistance than the more experienced ones. But his focus must be on this – not on getting the job done well every day but on ensuring that his people know what has to be done, want to do it, do it well and are able to do it. This has to be the focus always – enabling and empowering people to be as autonomous as possible in their areas so they can take maximum responsibility for their work.

2. Working on improving the overall operation in his areas of responsibility so that it is constantly made more effective and efficient.

   This improvement work will have three main sources:

   i. Problems, issues and failures from 'below' – i.e. from the operation itself. In the case of our restaurant, it may mean noting that there are space issues on the restaurant floor or that the flow of customers needs looking at or that there has been a drop off in customers at lunch times at weekends.

ii. Ideas, needs or new requirements from 'above', i.e. senior management or the board or owners. They may want some improvements or changes to the positioning of the restaurant because of a need for better returns, or because of some new direction being followed.

iii. Changes, needs and opportunities from the outside, i.e. customers, markets and competition. There may be a need to get the restaurant to a new level of service quality in order to get an added advantage over some new or existing competitor.

3. The third area of responsibility is to provide a link and flow of information between senior management and the staff so that relevant information flows both ways and the whole operation is one seamless unit working to shared goals and a clearly understood reality.

The intelligent organisation

Do you think this is far-fetched? It is not at all. It is how people really want to be and really are. And it is how most managers are and want to be as well – consumed by what they do and achieving their goals. Why not get everyone equally consumed? It is easy. We just have to stop managing or managing as we have been traditionally doing and begin to manage in an organic way, a human way. In this chapter I have used the example of the tree as representing life in an organisation. Imagine how powerful it will be to develop and trust this life at the human level, with its richer forms of intelligence. And imagine life operating at group level, with the combined intelligence of a group of people. The wonderful opportunity that is available to us if we can learn to manage and lead in this way is to create a truly intelligent organisation.

Creating such an organisation is the responsibility and privilege of managers performing as real leaders, and it needs to come from and be led by the top of the organisation. If it does not operate at this level it is likely that different agendas and in-built conflict will again predominate and block good will and real intelligence.

Chapter 18

The Facilitating Leader

'Don't be an Idiot.'

(The word 'idiot' comes from 'idios', meaning 'own' and 'private'. Therefore an idiot is someone who is unable to learn from others.)

The term 'facilitating leader' sounds like a bit of an oxymoron! Or is the word 'facilitating' used to soften or sweeten the role or title of leader? Is it just plain impossible to link these two words without each damaging the other? 'Facilitating' weakens 'leader' while 'leader' despoils 'facilitating'?

What if I were to say that a facilitating leader is a more powerful leader?

More powerful? Do you not mean more accepted, more involving, nicer?

No. I mean more *powerful*, in fact. And, yes, as a result of reading this chapter, you will probably be more accepted, more involving and even 'nicer' than you already are. But, most importantly, you will be more powerful.

Ah, now I get it. By facilitating my team or group, I will get more commitment from them by making them feel more involved, respected, important, included and so on?

Yes. That is true and is an important outcome. People will feel all those things you mention and that is a very good reason for leading in a facilitating way.

But if doing all these nice things does get your people more on board and feeling important and included but, at the same time, slows down your work and decision making, or makes you appear weak and uncertain, then it is a big price to pay.

That is the main problem managers often have when they involve, consult or facilitate staff. It seems to weaken them as managers, making them less decisive and authoritative, and leading to slow, compromised and often poor decisions. Yes, if this is so, it is definitely far too big a price to pay.

For this reason, many managers do not see it as essential to facilitate their meetings and their people. It can be sometimes nice to do so on certain relatively unimportant issues, but not on the day-to-day or really serious and important ones.

Thought as much! See?

But what if the main reason for facilitating as a leader is *not* to win people's commitment or buy-in or good will? What if the main reason is to get their ideas, contribution and input? What if we believed that doing so actually leads to our making better decisions? If this were so then facilitating and involving people would seem a good idea and might even be a necessary one. In which case, facilitating and involving people should be 'mandatory' or compulsory practice and a pre-requisite skill for every manager.

Let me repeat once more the wisdom of the manager in RTÉ (see Chapter 15): 'A manager does not have the right to make decisions. A manager only has the right to make *good* decisions.'

This means quite simply that we have our jobs as managers because we are deemed sufficiently wise and experienced to make good calls and good decisions. It is our wisdom and ability to make good decisions that give us our authority not our rank or 'stripes'.

So, for this reason, we would be very foolish and, indeed, irresponsible if we did not listen to the ideas of our people so that we take really good decisions. For this we need to facilitate them, to get them thinking and giving their ideas.

But people expect us to make decisions, to be decisive, to give the lead

They do and even more than that they expect us to make *good* decisions. They will respect us more and will support our decisions more when they see that they are good ones. Of course, feeling they have been asked and involved will also help them support the decision, but that is an added benefit.

But this is like some kind of democracy? Surely that is not appropriate for most businesses?

Yes, it is not appropriate. But this is not democracy, at least in any traditional sense. When facilitating one's team or group, the aim, of course, is to get as much consensus as possible. If this happens, great – and it often will. But it will not always happen. Often it will not be possible to get full agreement on issues and when this happens the manager or leader decides. In fact, the manager or leader will always decide with varying degrees of agreement or consensus with the group.

But is it not a sign of weakness for managers to frequently ask their people for their ideas? It is a good thing to do in certain workshops and participatory forums but not in the normal running of a business

No. In fact, as mentioned, it makes managers more powerful! The better the decisions managers make the more powerful and effective they will be as managers. They will have more options, more confidence, feel more support and enjoy more respect.

So should we hold meetings as often as we can, if this is a better way to manage and lead?

It depends on the complexity of the issue or the size of the problem or opportunity. Managers need to know when they need to use the resources of their team or others and this will depend on the nature of the situation. This is generally not a difficult call to make. It will rest on how difficult or intractable a problem is, how big the opportunity is or how multi-faceted or complex the issue is.

Is there not a danger of creating potential division between people because people are bound to differ, and the more often they are exposed to issues the more divided they may become?

This is a risk but it is not a reason for avoiding getting people together. And differences can be minimised. More importantly, working in this team-like way will actually improve relationships. A group will not become a team simply by being thrown together. This needs to be worked on. Every issue that is worked on must be clearly linked to the overall goal or vision and people need to be reminded of this. Everything has to be worked on within the mission or purpose or goal of the company, department or section.

Making this clear at the outset of any meeting will ensure that everyone is aware of how important the issue is and how it fits in and contributes to the welfare of the company or area (department, function). This becomes the criterion that will be used in terms of making decisions on particular issues.

Does this not go against the grain of what we have learned about managing?

Playing a facilitating role does go against the grain of much of what we have learned about managing with its emphasis on individual accountability, decisive decision making, making calls, the buck stopping with us and so on. This shows itself in two understandable reactions:

1. We feel some fear and nervousness in engaging with groups of people or with our team as it can diminish our image or sense of power.

2. It can be difficult to lead and facilitate groups.

With regard to the first point, I hope I have already adequately dealt with it in terms of showing that we end up being more powerful by facilitating.

In regard to point 2, yes, it can be difficult to play this role and to get the balance right. By 'balance' I mean finding the right place between chairing the meeting in a tight, controlling way, and facilitating it in an open way. It is for that reason that I am using the words 'facilitative leadership' or the 'facilitative leader'. This is attempting to get across that I will move between two poles:

- That of ultimate decision maker in the meeting, with whom the buck does stop.

- That of the facilitator, guiding the thinking of my people or the group.

While these two poles might appear to be 'either/or', in fact, as I have pointed out, the two are complementary and help each other. The more I facilitate, the better my decision making will be. The clearer I am with my team or group about my role, the easier it will be for them to individually and freely give their opinions, knowing that there is someone who will work to combine all the different views into a consolidated viewpoint and possible way forward.

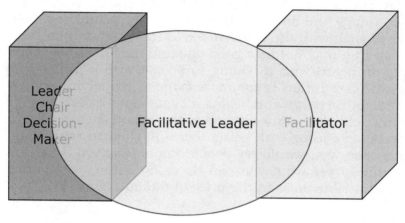

Leader
Chair
Decision-
Maker

Facilitative Leader

Facilitator

18.1. Facilitative leadership.

This role calls for some unique skills which are difficult by virtue of being simple!

What are these core facilitating skills?

There are approximately ten basic skills and processes that the facilitative leader will require to get maximum contribution from people in order to resolve big problems and get exciting breakthroughs:

1. Presenting a problem or issue in all its complexity, mystery and difficulty without coming up with a thought-out answer or solution

As managers, we need to be clear and decisive and we feel we need to be so all the time. Not knowing what to do, uncertainty, being lost or stuck, being unsure are not states that sit easily with us. We like to get to some definite position or state of certainty. This runs the risk of premature closure of the discussion without adequate investigation of an issue or situation. To get the contribution of our group or team we need to stay open and present problems, challenges and opportunities from a position of uncertainty, not knowing and being a bit lost or stuck. This may sound strange but life is full of problems that don't have any easy or quick solution. It is going after a solution to these kinds of problems that will give the greatest gains. A huge gain is made just by deciding to go after a difficult problem or issue.

Let us take a topical issue. Your company is facing huge challenges from the recession and cannot continue to operate at current cost levels. The temptation is to come up with a solution and so you go and find one. But it is OK not to find one...yet. It is better to stick with the problem for a while rather than rush to a decision that may not be a good one and may fail to bring critical people on board with it. Going to people with a problem rather than with a solution is far more honest, respectful and engaging. It creates energy and begins a challenging puzzle that people welcome and that can only end with its satisfactory resolution. And you will end up with better ideas on what to actually do! So, in this case, you would let people know that you want to have a meeting to see what you can do or do better to maintain the health of the business in the present difficult climate.

2. Objective and purpose

People come to meetings with all kinds of notions and agendas in their heads. Some come to be with other people, some come to fight with other people, some come to complain and some come to defend themselves. The fact of the matter is, a meeting means different things to different people. For that reason we need to make clear to everyone what the real purpose of the meeting is and what the objectives for it are. This means that at least all are in the same room for the same reason and so there will be a better chance of making progress and of the meeting being a success. Without this, it is quite possible that there will be very different thoughts going on in people's heads. We need to create an agreed purpose.

In our example this will mean clearly stating or writing up that the purpose of the meeting is to come up with better ways of managing costs so that the company remains viable and is more successful. And you will make sure that all are clear about that purpose and in agreement with it by explaining or eliciting the reasons why doing this is so important to the company and for them.

3. Climate and environment

People can also come to meetings in very different moods or an overall mood or atmosphere can enter the room without anyone knowing. This will have a big effect on the performance of the individuals and the group. The facilitating leader can affect this atmosphere by the tone they set, by how they kick the meeting off and by how they keep the meeting focused and positive.

Setting the right tone seems so obvious but it so rarely happens. We need to get everyone into the room, really into it and not with their minds and hearts still outside clinging to some 'more important' or more relevant topic. For this to happen we will need to convince people of the importance and value of the meeting and not proceed until all have taken this on board. We will achieve this by explaining why the meeting is important in itself and why it is important for them. This needs to be done well.

In our example this is easily achieved. In an objective way you can give people clear facts about the actual situation, point out possible outcomes if it is not addressed and check with them that they understand this and why it is important for each one of them too.

4. Guidelines and ground rules

As in any situation, people may have different views on what is appropriate or not on in terms of behaviour and process at a meeting. Some basic ground rules are important and these will vary from company to company and from situation to situation. Respect for ideas and for people, accepting and recognising differences, the importance of contributing and not dominating are some of the basic ground rules that will normally come into play and help the effectiveness of the meeting.

In the case we are looking at, you may need to stress the importance of differences and of the need for everyone to be open to any approach or idea. For this to happen, people will have to respect all ideas and refrain from knocking the ideas of others.

5. Involving everybody in the search for a good solution

This is not difficult but does need attention, discipline and some care. We can find it difficult to do because, as I have said above, we can operate from a basis that we are supposed to know and to have the answers. It calls for humility and honesty to ask people for their ideas. We fear that we may not like what they say and so want to steer things and people in particular directions. We can also get lost in the topic and get enthused by certain lines of thought and so tend towards the viewpoint of one and neglect those of others. Some people need to be invited and encouraged to contribute for a variety of reasons. If we fail to do this we run the risk of losing some of the rich differences of viewpoint that will make a contribution to the overall performance of the group and to the quality of the eventual decision.

If you apply this approach to your costs problem above, you will be surprised at what you get. The challenge in doing this is that you fear, again, that people may come up with suggestions and approaches that you will not welcome. But if you search for ideas throughout the area or organisation, you will have an enormous brain at work on the issue that will come up with suggestions that neither you nor your own team could ever have thought of. While it is you who make the decision, you do so gifted with the wisdom of your people.

6. Encouraging and welcoming differences

This can be the most challenging and the most rewarding aspect of facilitating. It is challenging as it can be difficult to hear different opinions to our own. We are back to the elephant model once again and no apologies for repeating this basic truth and principle.

18.2. Elephantine working.

The story, once more, is based on the old myth of the Blind Men of Hindustan who come across an elephant.

They each have a different opinion of what it is they have stumbled upon. But this is more than an opinion – they are all *sure*, they are all *certain* that they are right. And they know the others are wrong. They are all certain because their view is based on their experience and so they are 'obliged' to believe this thing is what they feel and think it to be. They are limited and, indeed, confined to their particular experience. So what can they do? They can stay where they are, happy and convinced about their particular version. Or they can make an effort to advance, to learn more, to see what more there might be. What does this involve?

A lot! It involves sharing their different experiences and views. And sharing involves two things – talking and listening. By far the more difficult of these two is listening. It is not easy to listen to 'nonsense' or people being 'wrong'. In fact, nearly always, people who are 'wrong' in your opinion are people who have a different perspective from yours because they have had a different experience from you.

This is what you need to do when you facilitate – encourage people to share the different perspectives and get people listening to them. Often the truth will fall out of this exercise. Sometimes you will have to put that truth together from combining and mixing and matching the different viewpoints. When you do this you get something far greater than any one truth or viewpoint; you get something huge – an elephant! The insights that emerge from the coalescence of different opinions are enormous. On top of that you build a stronger and more respectful team.

Applied to the example we have chosen, you may, at some stage, find yourself facing enormous differences of opinion and with strong emotions behind them in your quest to cut company costs. This is great! Some will want to cut salaries and others to cut staff. Some will suggest dropping some products or services, others will want to drop expensive suppliers. There will be no one correct answer but you can synthesise the various proposals and come up with something that is far greater than any one of the individual points of view. To do this it is important to stick with the differences. Like every idea, they will all be wrong in some respect but they will all be right in some other respect. Find the common threads and knit them together into a powerful rope that will resist all challenge. And don't forget that you too may be certain you are right. But being certain and being right have little in common so you would be an 'idiot' not to check out your opinion by listening to other people's.

7. Note taking, recording and summarising

This seems a petty role but it is an important one. We all like to be heard and very often we keep talking until people have agreed with us because that is the only way we will feel heard. Just try this with someone when they are talking to you. Look at them but don't acknowledge what they are saying with words, nods of the head or anything. Watch how disturbing this is for people and how they will keep on talking until they get some acknowledgement of having been heard.

Of course, when we talk so much we stir up the opposite reaction in the people listening to us to the one we intend because we can give the impression we are ramming our idea down their throats. We then get conflict and disagreements and all because someone wanted to have their idea heard and themselves validated. The way out is so simple – find a public way of recording the main points being made. In this way people can actually see what they said recorded and they will feel heard. It does not mean that it is a great idea or that we are actually going to implement it but at least it has been noted and heard. This can be done in several ways, like using a flipchart or typing them up on a screen using a projector. This simply means that you are running the meeting in public.

In the example we have chosen, it may not be easy for people to say some things because they may be very contentious and run the risk of being criticised. Some may fear that if they mention cutting salaries that others will jump on them and a big discussion will ensue. Writing ideas up means that they have been heard and will be considered. Nothing needs to happen yet about them and so there is no need to get into a big and contentious discussion at this point about how a particular idea might work or if it is a good or mad idea. This makes it easy for everyone to voice their ideas without fear of rejection or any pressure that it has to be implemented. It also allows you the space to go over the various points, merge some, select others or simply take them away to look at in order to form a comprehensive plan around making the company more competitive and sustainable.

8. Time management

Groups can be irresponsible and one area where this can happen is that of management of time. Normally everyone leaves it to everyone else. Each person thinks that they are only taking up a little part of the meeting and so is not the problem. But all this time spent on individuals adds up. For this reason, good time management is critical. The overall time for the meeting should be agreed and set and then monitored and controlled throughout, so the objectives are met within the agreed timescale.

In our example you can agree how much time will be spent on the meeting up front; you can map out the various stages of the meeting and then let people know how the meeting is progressing. This will free people up to be really at the meeting and, at the same time, keep people aware of the need for energy and efficient working.

If you see that the meeting is going to run over you make people aware of this or re-schedule the meeting to continue at another time. This may appear restrictive but it can be very educational in terms of helping people to appreciate time and to make the best use of it. Otherwise a lot of time and energy may be lost.

9. Decision making

Some decisions will be easy and some will be difficult. Who will take the decision and how needs to be managed. If there is one problem owner or 'client' for the topic then it is that person who will be handed the right and the responsibility to decide as they are the ones who will have to implement the decision. Often there is no one problem or issue owner and it is you as manager or leader who will have to make the call. This needs to be made clear to the group so they do not feel defrauded from having made their contribution and seeing someone else decide. This needs to be handled clearly and firmly, making clear:

i.   That this is how it will be done.

ii. What the decision is.

iii. What the reasons for going this route are.

iv. That the alternative views are also valuable.

v.   That all are being asked to get behind the decision, whether it accords with their own view or not.

This will be important in the case of reducing costs. People may have strong preferences for particular routes and strong dislikes for others. While the session will have been participative and could give the impression that it will be a democratic or consensus-based meeting, it is important that people understand that some one person or group will take the decision because they have the ultimate responsibility. They will need to be helped to understand that this does not mean that their input has not been considered or that it was not important.

10. Care: Care for people. Care for ideas

Finally, throughout the meeting the facilitating leader needs to be aware that everyone in the room is a sensitive human being with their insecurities, vanities, needs and passions, and all of these have to be cared for. We *are* our ideas so when our ideas get criticised, we can feel criticised. This is not to say that one has to be too gentle with people but criticism can be done in a good and healthy way. Often humour is a powerful tool to use to help people deal with moments of difficulty.

In our meeting on costs, it will be your job as facilitator to ensure all ideas are respected and that the people giving them are too. This will create a positive and strong dynamic that will allow and encourage everyone to contribute and to take risks in putting forward new and exciting ideas to improve the management of costs in the company.

The X Meeting – the basis for it all

Being able to play this role of facilitating leader is one of the most powerful skills a manager can have for all the reasons mentioned above. It empowers the people in the group and also will empower you as manager or leader.

Being clear about what facilitating means is important for all meetings that a manager will lead but most of all it is important for what I call the 'X Meeting'. The X Meeting is the meeting where the leader sets out his or her stall. By this I mean that at the beginning of the year or on some key date, such as the beginning of a new project, they meet with their team and go through with them:

- What their purpose is as a team (mission).
- What they want to achieve (goal or vision).
- What they need to do to get there (strategy or plan).

Now I know this sounds pretty ordinary but that it is done and how it is done will make all the difference to everything that follows and is implemented in the company, the area, the department, the team, and so on.

Later, in Chapter 21, I will deal with what I call the Two Pillars. I have already dealt with what I call the Two Pillars of Dichotomy in organisations where a false dichotomy gets created between the welfare of the company or organisation and the welfare of the people, the staff or employees who work in and for it. The X Meeting banishes this dichotomy for good. This is brought about by working with the group to invite them to share in the achievement of a really worthwhile goal. The goal or vision is initially created by the leader or manager and will be one that will meet the needs of all the key stakeholders – customers, owners or shareholders, employees, the community and suppliers. One way I have used to visually depict this is to put the company vision or goal in the centre and then describe what will be happening in the case of all five stakeholders when the vision is realised

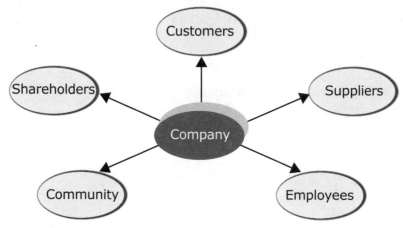

18.3. Balanced scorecard.

Suppose we were talking about an hotel. The vision might be:

'To make all our visitors feel at home in an environment of luxury, comfort and attention.'

We would know this was realised if:

- **Customers** are actively seeking information on the hotel for return visits for themselves and are making excited recommendation to their friends.
- **Employees** look forward to each day as an opportunity to give new people a quality hotel experience.
- **Owners** are seeing results beyond their expectations and using much of these for the development of the hotel and new hotels.

- The **community** is delighted to have the hotel in its neighbour-hood and sees it as a most valued citizen.

- **Suppliers** are forever seeking new ways to better serve the hotel out of a desire to promote the welfare of the hotel and their own.

This has to be well done. There are so many visions hanging on walls full of nice words and empty of any passion. Your vision has to be you, to represent you and your values. If not, people will sense or smell it from you. It has to be something that you would do a lot to achieve, that touches your deepest desires and that is in line with your dreams, old and new. It should score well on all of the three points of the Goals Triangle, as applying to the company or your part in it:

- What is it that is really *needed*?
- What do you really *like and want*?
- What are your *capabilities* or *competencies*?

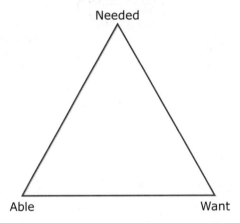

18.4. Goal and Vision Triangle.

If any one of these is missing or is very weak, this will distort and weaken the vision or goal.

When you do this well, it will also touch the hearts and deep aspirations of your people and you should design and share it in such a way that it does.

Sharing it is important and this too has to be done really well. I often give the example of a theatre owner or director sharing their vision for their theatre with their actors. It would be something like:

'I want us to be the best theatre in this city.'

What do I mean by that?

- 'I mean that we want to put together performances that have the theatre full every night... Not full of dead people, but excited, thrilled, engaged people.
- I want a buzz at the interval, and at the end with people discussing and sharing their experiences in a delighted way as they leave and make their way home.
- I want us to put on plays that are different, that mark us out from the rest, that challenge us.
- I want these plays to show up the talent in this room, in this theatre.
- I want us to do well financially; I want you all to do well financially.
- I want us to be recognised by the critics and also by the award givers in X and Y and Z.
- I want every actor and every person in the theatre to be excited and proud to belong to our theatre.'

The same kind of message could be given to a football team, a band, a team of architects or to any group of managers or employees like your own.

This is what the X Meeting does and that is why it is so important.

We can be truly passionate about this message because we believe it is good for every aspect of the lives of those listening to us and working in the company. I say this because of what I call The Balanced Life, which we looked at in Chapter 15.

What I mean by this is that we balance a lot of things in our life and this balance is important. Our company, where we work and the entity to which we commit so much of our time, effort and resources, plays an important part in our life and, indeed, affects every aspect of our life. I am not saying that it is or should be the centre of our lives but it is central. Because of this, the welfare of our company will affect every aspect of our lives and can help provide a good balance between all the various aspects.

18.5. The Balanced Life.

And the lines are double-headed arrows – they go in both directions. So, the company can play an important part in ensuring that people get satisfaction from their work in the interests of the company and of the person. The company, because it plays such a large part in who people are and what they do, will affect people's social relationships, how they view their role and perhaps their sense of identity. But management in companies need to be aware of the life that people have outside work and to respect this and respect them as people in this sense.

In terms of the other areas of life – family, professional development, career, personal development, hobbies and interests and, of course, financial – the welfare of the company will affect the welfare of each of these and in turn people's welfare in these areas will benefit the company and its welfare.

The leader believes this, upholds it at all times and steadfastly refuses to let anyone else hold or operate to any alternative view. In other words, the leader works out of a mindset that what is good for the business is good for people and vice versa. This is obvious. By insisting on high performance from you, for example, as a leader, I am actually doing you a service. How? Well in the first place, your welfare is closely linked to the welfare of the organisation and, second, to make demands on you and to expect you to do better is also good for you in terms of your own personal and professional development.

There should be no excuses tolerated for failing to do everything in our power to make this happen. This message has to be delivered with real, genuine conviction. The trick to convince people that you care is to *really* care! Nothing else will work.

Before the X Meeting ends, there is one more task that has to be done. The leader should ask each member of the team, there and then, to give some thought to the role that they each need to play to achieve the goal or vision. The manager or leader asks the individuals to make a note of what is the unique contribution they need to make to help everyone to get there. Nothing more is done about this at this point, but the manager reminds people that he or she will be meeting with each individual as part of the Performance Development System (Performance Review) to go over these points. For now, while it is fresh, it is good to give this some thought.

Realising the goal or vision

With this done, it is time to begin to plan how to make the vision a reality, to make it happen. This can and should be done with the group or team, getting their input and ideas on what you need to do. This calls for the manager playing the role of facilitator and leader. The skills of facilitating have been covered above and here, again, they need to be coupled with those of leading. This involves several activities:

- The manager will facilitate the group so that there is a rich contribution of ideas from everyone on what is needed to make the vision a reality.

- The manager will also contribute ideas so that their contribution is not lost.

- The manager will challenge ideas in a healthy way to ensure that good thinking is being done.

- Finally, the manager will summarise or shape the strategy, either there and then or later when there has been time to assimilate it.

This strategy, when finalised, will become the plan of action for the year and will dictate all that gets done by the team. But it is never really finalised! It will be changed, added to and enriched in the light of what actually happens. It will not be a plan that the team will stick to, irrespective of what happens. This calls

245

for a healthy balance between the plan or strategy on the one hand, and reality or what happens on the other. This is always a challenge: Are we flexible, open-minded and responsive to what is happening and are we courageous enough in sticking to our plans and not losing our nerve? This is a call that has to be made. Again, it is a question of being faithful to two poles or pillars at the same time: The pole of the strategy or plan and the pole of reality or what is actually happening.

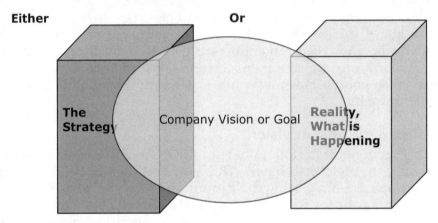

18.6. Managing the Two Pillars.

This impossible challenge is made possible by being faithful to the vision or goal and using it as the ultimate yardstick or arbiter of what to do.

It is very easy to get caught up in holding on to one pole and ignoring the other. If this happens, returning to the goal or vision will allow you to work between the two.

And, the two poles actually help each other. The pole of the strategy or plan will serve as a very useful tool with which to test and find out about reality and what is going on, and the pole of reality will test, refine, enrich and develop the strategy or plan. This creates a powerful and healthy dynamic once one has the courage to be faithful to both poles or pillars.

Regular or monthly meetings

While this dynamic of strategy and reality will get handled essentially at the monthly or regular review meetings, it will be happening with each development on each passing day. But a formal check-in and review of how the strategy is working and what is going on in the wider world in general will be a core activity at the monthly team-review meetings. These meetings also need to be handled well. At a monthly team-review meeting, the vision or goal has to be formally brought to the table again, to remind everyone what the whole thing is about, what 'we' are about and how the meeting is intended to help us to get there. Then the meeting considers and works on the various topics that get put forward and does so in a creative way, as described earlier in Section II of this book.

Chapter 19

Performance Reviews, Appraisals and the Performance Development System (PDS)

'Good timber does not grow with ease; the stronger
the wind, the stronger the trees.'

– J. Willard Marriott

To paraphrase Charles Dickens in the opening to *A Tale of Two Cities*, performance reviews and appraisals are the best of things and the worst of things. They can do a lot of good if designed and handled well and they can do enormous harm if designed and handled poorly. Often they are 'just OK'.

I say this for a variety of reasons. In my considerable experience I have found the following. Check if you recognise your experience or situation here.

1. Appraisals rarely, if ever, get done on time.

2. Managers find it hard to give criticism and feedback and find it even harder to take it if it comes their way.

3. Some managers find it too easy to be critical and lose their people or their minds and hearts in the process.

4. People feel judged, watched, rated, measured by superiors and resent and mistrust this deep down.

5. You frequently end up with both sides feeling uncomfortable and resentful.

6. Appraisals sometimes do more harm than good by taking personal accountability for the work away from people and replacing it with the goal of satisfying one's manager or management.

For greater ease of communication, I am going to deal with this in a dialogue format. I hope the questions I pose here are ones that are on your mind too.

So what is wrong? Why don't appraisals work?

1. They are based on a flawed philosophy of communication.

    This is along the lines of: 'I tell you something and you absorb it, understand it and follow it.' Life doesn't work like that! Information is not a thing you hand over like a pen or an apple. Communication is about uniting two minds, not handing over pieces of information from one person to another.

2. They are based on a superior–inferior relationship which in itself inhibits and blocks improvement.

    It is never nice to feel or be made to feel inferior. The conversation – or so-called conversation – is taking place between two people in very different positions of hierarchy and power.

3. They are judgmental and nobody likes being judged.

    The word itself – 'appraisal' – is 'loaded' in that it implies that one person is doing something to another, i.e. passing judgment.

4. They try to do too many things at the same time, many of which are in conflict.
    For example, they try to:

    - Identify areas for improved performance.

    - Identify training or development needs.

    - Provide information for promotions or succession planning.

    - Decide levels of pay increases or bonuses.

    - Address problem areas, either in terms of performance or behaviour.

    It won't be easy to get people to recognise that their performance needs improving if doing so means they won't get a bonus or promotion.

5. They are too sporadic and infrequent.

    They should happen once a year, at least, but often don't for different reasons. So much gets lost between one meeting and the next.

6. They frequently block and hinder normal, day-to-day communication about performance.

Managers can postpone or hold off on necessary conversations with some people until the performance review or appraisal, and they note and store points for discussion at that point.

7. They have a negative bias and negative expectations.

   Often they operate on the basis of finding out and identifying what is *not* being handled well enough and focusing on these as a way to get improvement.

8. They frequently categorise and rate people and often do so very crudely.

   Sometimes rating systems 1 to 5 or A to E are used, and are used badly and unfairly. It is a crude way to categorise a whole array of behaviours as part of performance.

So, why would we need appraisals or performance reviews at all? Haven't we done very well without them?

Yes, but you might have done better if you had them. And you will do better if you have them now.

This is because the performance of your company, like that of any organisation, is linked fundamentally to the performance of the people in the organisation. But helping people to perform better will involve answering some fundamental needs that all people have.

What kinds of needs?

1. People need *recognition.* We all want our efforts and good work recognised.

2. People need *attention.* We all need to feel we are important and matter.

3. People need *feedback* or *endorsement.* We all need help from the 'outside'. We don't see or know all the effects we are having on others.

4. People need *opportunities to just talk.* We all want to be listened to and heard.

5. People need mechanisms to express *views, needs* and *complaints* without having to ask for the opportunity to do so. We don't like to have to always raise issues and ask for a forum to do so.

6. People need to be *stretched, challenged* and *motivated* and have *high expectations.* We all have more in us than we often believe.

7. People need and should have *an input* into how they are seen. Otherwise we feel we are being judged behind our backs.

Managers also have needs:

1. Managers need to understand *what is happening* with their people and in their areas or responsibility. We can easily lose touch.

2. Managers need to understand *their people.* We can jump to conclusions and operate snap-shot management.

3. Managers need to understand how <u>they</u> *are performing* and in what areas they need to change and be more helpful. We need feedback too and to be aware of how we are affecting others.

4. Managers need feedback on the *system, structures* and *operation* in the company. We need to continuously question these to ensure they are helping.

5. Managers need an opportunity to *express their views, ideas, expectations, requirements, disappointments*, etc. and to be able to do so in a normal, easy way. We don't like to have to summon people to special meetings to address issues.

6. Managers need the discipline and opportunity *to listen*, show they *care* and *are interested*. This does not always come naturally to us.

So, how much improvement might we get from appraisals or performance reviews?

If you only got 10 per cent improvement in staff performance you can work out what that would mean in terms of costs, quality, new ideas, results and efficiency. It could be like having ten extra people in a workforce of a hundred!

You will get a lot more than 10 per cent improvement, however. In some cases you might even get 100 per cent improvement.

But some companies have a performance appraisal system and they are not over the moon about it. I am not sure performance appraisals work or make a great difference.

You are right. They don't. For all the reasons I mentioned at the outset.

So what is the alternative? What system would not succumb to these pitfalls?

I believe the system I use with companies – the Performance Development System (PDS) – is the best alternative.

What is this?

It is a system whereby a manager acts as a coach to members of their staff to help them become clear about their roles, their goals and their objectives; to help them also to be fully aware of how they are performing in pursuing those objectives – where they are doing well, where they need or want to improve, where they need help, and how and where they want to develop both themselves and their careers.

But is it as simple as that, i.e. acting as a coach?

Yes, it is as simple as that and it is in the simplicity that the difficulty arises.

Managers need to be trained to handle the role of coach, a role that does not come easily to everyone.

Is there a system or format to follow?

Yes, a very simple one. It operates in two stages and at two levels:

1. The level of the area, function, department or group.
2. The level of the individual.

Why would we have a departmental or team review if we are only talking about a PDS? Does it not apply to the individual?

This two-level approach described above is important as no one operates or can operate in complete independence from others – hence the need to look at the team or group role and objectives, as well as the individual ones. From this, the individual can better identify their own unique role and objectives.

So it would be nonsense to think you could look at someone or their performance in isolation without having reference to:

- The group they belong to.
- The people on whom they depend and with whom they work.
- The goal or purpose of the endeavour they are involved in.

So how exactly does the PDS work?

1. First, let's look at the area, function or departmental review.

    This consists of the area, functional, departmental or team manager holding a meeting with the staff in his or her area to get them thinking and sharing how they see the role of their department, setting objectives for the area and planning how they are going to achieve those objectives. The manager summarises what he or she has heard, enthuses about it, shares their own vision and goals, fills in any gaps that might exist, and builds an exciting picture for what the area is going after. This is similar to and may coincide with the X Meeting described in Chapter 18.

    Once this has been done, the group can subsequently, during the course of the year, meet to evaluate and review how they have done against their objectives and what areas need more attention. (This is described in more detail in Chapter 18.)

    This might seem strange in a performance review or development system but it works very well, because in working in this way people are identifying with the overall goals of the area or department and so understand their own role better as well as that of the other people in the group. In reviewing the performance of the total group, people will advertently or inadvertently be looking at themselves and how they are doing, and what they need to do in order to be able to perform better and to develop as people and employees. So there is a lot of reviewing of performance going on. And it gives the *managers* a chance to get across some powerful leadership messages and understand a bit more about how their people operate and think, so giving them better leadership and support. On top of that it is a great help towards building teamwork and co-operation among individuals in an area.

    This will set things up for the individual meetings.

2. The individual meeting: Half the battle is done with the group review but the time spent with the individual is critical also. It is very important to ensure that this is not just an appraisal in another guise. At this meeting the *individuals assess themselves* against their role, responsibilities, objectives and aspirations.

What? Assess themselves? Surely it is the role of the manager to tell the individuals how they are doing?

Well, no. We are drifting back to the old appraisal system again. People assess themselves and this works far better than traditional appraisal because:

1. People will normally be far harder on themselves than a manager would ever be.

2. People know more about how they are performing than a manager does as they are with themselves all day, every day. And by virtue of the fact that it is they who are doing the talking, we can be assured they understand what is being said and what are being identified as problems.

But what if they get it all wrong? What if they miss big things or hide things?

They don't! There may be occasions when individuals do this but we can treat these in a special way and not build a system based on the few who play games knowingly or unknowingly.

Graphically it looks like this:

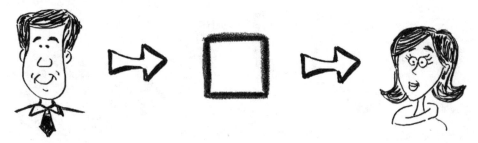

19.1. Traditional performance appraisals.

Typically, when you 'appraise' someone, you prepare the proposal beforehand, filling in all the blanks, especially under the heading 'Areas for Improvement', maybe having it checked and signed off by your own boss. If there is a rating system, this also needs to be agreed with your boss. After all, you can't have too many '2' ratings ('Exceeds expectations for the Job').

Then all that is left is to 'do' the person's appraisal or 'give them' their appraisal. In more familiar and colloquial language, this is described simply as: 'Telling people how they are doing or getting on.' Like in the image above, then, we tell them how they are doing, we appraise them and they appear to accept that. We don't really know how much they understand or how much they really accept. And very often we don't want to hear objections and they often know better than to object. It would only lead to a conflict and it is not hard to know who will come out on top. So, in our picture, the manager gives the appraisal as it was prepared and so nothing that happens or gets said at the meeting has any bearing on the ultimate outcome of the meeting. We go into the meeting with one thing, a viewpoint, and we come out with exactly the same thing. Irrespective of whether what is said is good or bad, that very behaviour is fundamentally disrespectful to the other person and demeaning of him or her.

As mentioned above, when you allow people to assess themselves, most of the time they don't leave anything out. And in fact you will get a lot more from people when you handle things in this way rather than in the old traditional way.

How can you get more?
It looks like this:

19.2. Self-assessment.

In other words, you will get to hear from the person most of what you had intended saying and a lot more.

Why a lot more? Should it not be the same?
As mentioned, you will get a lot more from the person because they know a lot more! They know themselves better and are with themselves all day. You are only going on glimpses of them, which has not prevented you from forming your own opinion on how they are doing. And, of course, it is far better because what they say is theirs, i.e. they have ownership of it. For example, 'need to do better' is far more effective with an 'I' in front of it than with a 'You'. 'I need to do better in how I manage people' is very different from: 'You need to do better in how you manage people.' Just one little pronoun makes all the difference.

Does it always work as well as that? Surely there are times when the person reviewing themselves does not share or say everything for lots of reasons?

Yes, you are right. There will be times, especially in the early days of switching to this better approach, when people, out of fear, nervousness or suspicion, don't share everything.

19.3. Value of self-assessment and person talking.

But even if the session looks more like figure 19.3, you are still better off. Even if things are being left out, you can be sure that effective communication is occurring. You know there is communication going on because it is the person reviewing themselves who is talking, not you. And this makes all the difference. We know the person understands or agrees with the need to up their game because they say it themselves.

But what about the things that have been left out? Do they need to be brought up by the manager?

Not necessarily. You might not want to bring them up because they are not really all that important. Or maybe they are not really that important *now*, in the context of all the other things that have been said. Perhaps they have ceased to be important in the light of all that you have heard and learned.

Even if they are still important, you might make the decision not to raise them then, at that particular time, because they could eclipse or undo all the other valuable insights that you and the other person have gained. However, you might decide that it is important to raise them, that you have a responsibility to the company, to the project or team, to yourself and to the person to bring up and discuss some topic around the person's performance or behaviour.

But would bringing up the negative things not ruin everything and even de-motivate the person for the future?

You will always have these moments when you have to bring up an issue of performance or behaviour that in your view is unsatisfactory. As a result you can feel that you are not being the good and nice manager that you normally are. It is easy to see this situation as being potentially damaging to your relationship with the member of staff, that person's morale, etc. But it need not be so at all if you are clear that you are doing the right thing by everybody.

However, there will be times when it is critical to bring up important items that have not been raised for whatever reason. Once again, these may be because the person:

- Does not know about them.

- Knows about them but for some reason doesn't want to do anything differently.

- Knows and wants to do something different but is not able to or can't.

This brings us to a kind of Johari Window:

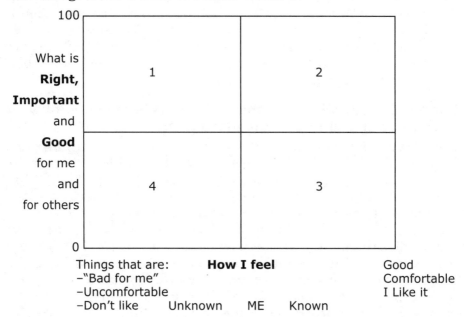

19.4. Decisions for life.

So, Box 4 contains things that are not important and I don't know about them or I don't like them or like doing them. *No big deal.*

Box 3 contains things that are equally unimportant but I am aware of them and I like them or enjoy doing them. *Fine.*

Box 2 is great – it contains things that are important and I also like them or enjoy doing them. *Well done.*

Then Box 1, which is the really important one, contains things that are important but which I don't know about or don't like doing.

It is because of Box 1 that we need to occasionally bring up things that have not been raised by the other person. They are simply too important to ignore or pass off. We have to address them.

And we do so along the lines covered in Chapter 23:

- Use subjective language.
- Talk of your responsibilities to the person, to others and to the organisation.
- Use the Two Pillars philosophy.
- Focus on the future and what you want in the future, rather than arguing about the past. (See Chapter 21.)

So, getting back to the PDS, if the person is doing all the talking and reviewing, what does the manager do?

The manager listens and learns, coaches and prompts, teases out and explores, recognises and commends, and challenges at times, i.e. challenges the person to go after greater things. And sometimes there will be need for some feedback and this gets given in a respectful and adult way, as described above. And there will always be a need to understand how the employee is in general and to find out how the manager may be failing to help them to perform as they would like to or is blocking them in some way.

This seems very simple to do – is it?

It is simple and it is in the simplicity that the difficulty lies, as we said earlier. This looks a passive role for a manager but it is really the most powerful way a manager can be present to an employee. To play the role, managers have to understand and re-learn some of the principles of interacting with others and of communicating and, for this reason, a grounding in coaching always goes along with the introduction of the PDS.

So why does the PDS work when appraisals fail so miserably?

The PDS works for very good reasons:

1. It is based on a relationship of equals and respect.
2. It is based on a sound philosophy of communication.
3. It is geared towards identifying strengths and successes and building on these.
4. It is characterised by listening, empathy and interest.
5. It is free from threat, fear and possible recrimination.
6. It has a single focus – to bring out the best in the other person and improve their performance, and to develop them as professionals and as people in their own interests and in the interests of the organisation they work for.

How would I go about setting a PDS up if I wanted to go ahead with it?

There are six steps to getting the system up and running and working well.

1. Acquaint people with the dynamics of performance reviews and performance appraisals so that they understand the difference between the various approaches and why appraisals have not worked. With this put to one side, it will be possible for people to understand the PDS.
2. Educate everyone about the system and how it works and the very clear difference there is between the PDS and an appraisal system.
3. Give managers a grounding in the principles, philosophy and skills of coaching.
4. Train managers in the approach, the system and some of the skills required, and familiarise all staff with the overall approach.
5. Introduce the system and support managers in the early days so that they get it right and don't slip into old appraising ways and approaches.
6. Run brief familiarisation sessions with staff so they understand the purpose of the system and the approach being followed so they understand and trust it.

And what if we already have a system in place? Should we throw it all out and start afresh?

I understand why it may be impossible and unnecessary to dump a total system. But I would want to make some changes to it and I would want to let people know about the richness of an alternative way of handling your current system. This is eminently achievable.

First, it would be very important to get people to an understanding of all of the points already covered in this chapter around the issues with appraisals handled in the traditional way, the need for the group review and planning meetings. Of course it would also be necessary to give people a sound understanding of the coaching philosophy and approach. With this and an explanation of how to handle the meetings in a new way, you would have a revitalised review system that really works!

Why is it called a Performance Development System?

It could just as easily be called a Personal Development System or a Professional Development System. Some organisations prefer to call it Personal Development System because they want to emphasise the importance of people development, which will, of course, ultimately determine the performance of the organisation. They do this because they feel and fear that there can often be too great an emphasis on performance in isolation from the development of people. If this becomes too strong, if there is a total focus on performance then the greatest asset of the company, its people, is being neglected and, in the long run, the company will suffer. It is great to want to build a bridge but even more important to know how to build bridges – hence the focus on developing people, and on the assets of know-how, knowledge and expertise. And, of course, as we have seen, to do this we have to also focus on performance as the main driver of improvement and development. But if you think in a truly Two-Pillar way, there won't be any issue or dichotomy anyway.

How do I know the PDS will really make a difference to how people perform? Will it really work? Will people actually achieve that 5, 10, 15 per cent improvement you talk about?

There are five sound reasons why the PDS will achieve what it sets out to achieve what I am promising it will achieve.

There are great G-A-I-N-S that people will get from the PDS because all of the following get clarified, identified and highlighted:

- **G**oals and expectations are clarified, reviewed and shared.
- **A**ttention and interest are aroused.
- **I**nformation and inputs are given and feedback is given and received.
- **N**eeds – organisational and managerial needs are identified.
- **S**upport is given to remove blocks.

G

People will improve because they are being invited, encouraged and challenged to set high goals and expectations for themselves.

One of the reasons why people do not realise their true potential and perform really well is that their expectations for themselves are too low, for a variety of reasons. The PDS gets people upping their expectations in terms of their goals, what they believe they can achieve and what they want to achieve. People are encouraged to set higher standards for themselves and to expect more from themselves. This is bound to make a difference in most cases.

A

We all need attention. It is the most basic human need and it does not disappear when we become workers or professionals.

The PDS ensures people get attention and feel attended to, looked after, that someone has an interest in them, that they are noticed and that they matter. This makes a huge difference at the critical subconscious and emotional level in people. Get this right and you are already half-way to a big improvement in how people feel and how, as a result, they perform.

I

People will improve because they learn and they get feedback on how they are currently doing.

We all need feedback. We are not aware of many things about ourselves and so need to see, hear and understand how others see us.

As managers, we also need information and feedback about ourselves and about the organisation, and we need to provide the facility for our people to give that input.

Much of the feedback comes from the people themselves, but in time they will welcome feedback from you as their manager and from others. It is hard to believe that this will not make a big difference.

N

People will improve their performance if they understand what their organisation needs from them.

People in organisations do not operate in a vacuum; they are part of a larger whole and need to understand the needs of that greater whole and how they fit into it and what is required from them. Feeling part of a team, of a larger group, or something greater than just 'my own little world' is tremendously enlightening and inspiring. It can bring out the very best in people and get them out of themselves.

And, in all of this, you, as the manager and person responsible for many others as well as for the organisation, will also have needs that should be known and shared.

S

Finally, people need support.

People will feel blocked in various ways and we need to find out what may be blocking them. It may be due to something about us as their managers, about the organisation or about the individuals themselves. Uncovering these blocks and removing them will make a huge difference to how people perform, do you not think? Imagine if someone helped you in this way!

Yes, that makes sense, but I wonder if it is really worth all the trouble? Apart from the individuals themselves, will it make a difference to the overall organisation, to the company?

Well, if it doesn't then it is not worth it. But of course it will make a difference. If we get the groups and individuals all developing as people and upping their performance substantially, it is bound to make a difference.

Even apart from that, it will make a difference at a more macro level. The PDS will have effects on the organisation at a strategic and structural level.

How?

The various meetings, both group and individual, will have serious impacts on the strategy and thinking in the organisation because people are formally being invited and asked to contribute their opinions. Likewise it will affect how the company is structured and organised as this too will come up in discussions on what is helping, or on what is blocking performance. Finally it will affect the culture of the organisation and will, by default, create an open, participative, challenging and exciting culture.

The learnings that are picked up from operating the system can be used to review how the organisation is being managed and directed. It is hard to get it wrong if the input of so many people is really listened to and considered.

Well, you seem very excited by it. Are you not being a little bit naïve and maybe expecting too much?

I am excited about it because I see the enormous potential it has to do so many things in an organisation in one fell swoop.

- It will dramatically improve the performance of many individuals and of the whole organisation.

- It will increase the level of satisfaction people have about their jobs and themselves.

- It is a powerful tool for bringing about change as it makes people more aware of the need for change and encourages them to look for ways to change themselves.

- It has an effect on co-operation and teamwork as it gets areas and functions communicating honestly about how well they are working together and supporting each other.

- It improves relationships by providing an effective way of dealing with the dissatisfaction we often have with people's performance and the disappointment we often feel with people around us.

- It increases the understanding of key people of what is happening in the organisation and so enables them to make more meaningful interventions and provide better leadership.

- And it is a truly human way to handle what could otherwise be an awkward, parent–child-type event. We can manage to be human in how we handle it, with all the results and outcomes mentioned above.

Yes, I am excited...very. And I don't think it is one bit naïve or over the top. Sorry!

And if the PDS doesn't work for some individuals and they still continue to perform unsatisfactorily...well, let's look at that next.

Section IV – When it Is Not So Easy to Behave in a Human Way

Chapter 20

Not Another Meeting? How to Make Our Meetings Really Worthwhile

'It is only through relationships that we exist in the universe.'

– Paulo Coelho

We have been looking at how it is possible to handle all kinds of situations in work in a good and human way and, as a result, in a more effective way. In this section I want to look at six common situations where we can find it difficult to respond and behave in a good way:

1. Some problems with meetings.

2. Dealing with unsatisfactory performance.

3. 'Managing up' or managing our bosses.

4. Managing ourselves and our own power.

5. Decision-making styles and approaches.

6. Dealing with 'difficult' people or personalities.

Meetings in General

Most people in most organisations spend a large percentage of their time at meetings. How large? In some cases it is definitely no less than 50 per cent, if all kinds of meetings are taken into account. How about you? Do a very quick assessment.

Even if the time you spend in meetings is less than half that, say around 20 per cent, that is still a lot of time – one whole day of the week, over two months of every year, one whole year out of a five-year stint with an organisation and, if you stay twenty years in the organisation, four of them you will spend at meetings!

- Is it enjoyable time? Most would say no.
- Is it time well spent? Is it productive? Again, most would say no.
- Is it important time? Most say definitely yes. What do you say?

So, if all of this is partially valid – and every piece of informal research we have done would back it up – then we have the serious dilemma facing us that:

> *Something that we regard as very important and that takes up a huge percentage of our working lives is frequently not enjoyable and often quite unproductive.*

If none of this is ringing bells with you at all then stop reading here and flick on to the next topic.

If it is making some sense, perhaps you might like to take the following little survey or self-diagnosis. Forgive the negative tone being used in this exercise. It is not intended to be either manipulative or provocative. It is only because, if you are still reading this, it means in effect that you agree there is an issue here. And, as it is a diagnosis we are after, we are looking at what might be wrong and so this exercise does tend towards the 'what's wrong' or negative pole.

The scoring will be very simple:

- Five points apply if the statement is true or nearly always true of your organisation or situation.
- Three points apply if it is true in part or is sometimes true.
- Zero points apply if it is not applicable at all to your situation.

Most meetings frequently suffer from some of the following. How about yours?

1. They rarely finish on time.
2. Items discussed are often given time out of proportion to their real importance.

3. Some items get squeezed in at the end of the meeting when people have either left the meeting or have lost energy. Some of these often require more attention and time than what they end up getting.

4. The agenda is established based on the previous meeting or 'what we always cover', or it is set by the manager or a senior person. Very often it does not cover the really important issues that need to be addressed.

5. Very often there is no real, clear and agreed objective for the meeting. There is an agenda but no real or meaningful objectives.

6. All items get treated in the same way with the same process, even though they require very different handling depending on the kind of topic in question.

7. Some topics don't get raised to avoid offending someone else or possible trouble for oneself, and so the meetings are harmless and ineffective.

8. There is often collusion on not raising thorny issues. Those who break rank on this 'get punished' subtly and informally and brought back into line.

9. Some people get involved in long discussions while others 'spectate'. These discussions often end in some form of conflict or don't end at all.

10. Frequently political game-playing, rather than the serious topics up for discussion, is where the real action and fun is, though nobody would ever admit to this.

11. People are afraid to raise their own issues out of a fear of being drowned in advice and help they cannot refuse and did not ask for. Others keep their head down to avoid getting extra work to do.

12. The chairperson is torn between controlling and involving, between listening and deciding, between democracy and autocracy – and so everyone else gets confused as a result.

13. The only roles at the meeting are those of the manager or 'chair' and 'the rest', unless a secretary is asked to take the minutes.

14. Many meetings drag on, sap energy, and divide and destroy team working rather than encouraging and promoting it.

15. Frequently the real meeting takes place beforehand or more often afterwards!

16. Decision making is difficult due to tension between a group decision and a decision imposed by the manager or chairperson.

17. Often people believe the major decisions have all been taken prior to the meeting and that all discussion is fictitious and so they just go through the motions.

18. Frequently the decisions that are taken never see the light of day in terms of any action apart from featuring in minutes that become the sole outcome of the meeting.

19. Meetings are not really seen as very important except for sharing information, and most believe it would not matter too much if they did not take place at all.

20. Some people get out of them as much as they can.

If you have got high scores, for example anything over 50, then I think you would agree it would be worthwhile doing some work on this topic.

And if you haven't, it might still be worth your while to read on in order to find out aspects of how you currently handle meetings that could be improved, with great results and benefits for you and others.

Reasons Not to Call Meetings

You might feel meetings are boring and talking or reading about them is even more boring. So you may feel little interest in continuing with this section. Some of that is down to the actual word itself – 'meetings'. This is a generic word to describe a whole series of events or things that we lump together. You probably have some image in your head now of some typical group that you often spend time with around a table. And yes, these are 'meetings'. But meetings are a lot more than this.

If, for now, we exclude meetings with one other person and leave that for a separate discussion, then 'meetings' are those moments or events when you are working with, engaging with, talking to or in discussion with a group of other people. I am purposely taking a broad interpretation initially in order to make some very general but important points about how we handle these situations. I am doing this in the context of this book because I am searching for practical and valid ways of handling management situations in a truly human way.

Would we be better off without meetings at all? Well, here are five reasons not to call or hold meetings, to hold as few as possible or to avoid them as much as possible.

1. Meetings often lead to conflict between people and can actually damage relationships. So isn't it better to avoid this risk completely in order to be on good terms with people?

2. You can end up forced to go a route you don't want to go and feel your hands are tied, or your lovely plans get thwarted or blocked. Freedom and autonomy are precious and should not be thrown away lightly. Is it not better to hold on to your own responsibility for things and do your own thing rather than throwing it open to everybody?

3. Meetings can confuse. Often the person who calls the meeting has their mind already made up about the outcome and, if they haven't, they shouldn't call a meeting in the first place. Why not be clear and keep things simple and let the boss or the most senior person decide?

4. Very often the effort to reach consensus involves some kind of compromise on everyone's part. Meetings work on the basis of the lowest common denominator and rarely are they innovative or creative. Surely it is better do your own thinking and so be more creative and open-minded?

5. Sometimes you can find yourself up against stronger or more powerful people who can pressurise you or even bully you, and you can lose your power and control. Is it not better to avoid such situations and avoid the meetings that cause them?

Let's take a closer look at these reasons, understandable as they might appear. In each case I want to attempt to turn it around by overcoming the valid concern and turning it into a means of making your meetings really rich places to be and truly worthwhile.

1. Meetings often lead to conflict between people

Conflict can arise at meetings because of a tension between looking after the relationship with people and going after a good outcome.

In most meetings and gatherings of people two things will be going on at the same time:

i.   The group and the individuals in it will normally want to remain on good terms with each other and with other members. We have a natural desire to be on friendly terms with people, be liked by them and enjoy pleasant relations with them. On top of that we often believe that, if we do not have good relations with people, we will not get a good result.

ii. The second thing going on will be a need to decide on a particular strategic issue or direction, resolve a problem, take a good decision on something, get a good outcome and so on. That is why the group has come together or the meeting has been called. It was not called for the first item above, namely to have good relationships and be friends with your colleagues. The meeting is about some need to change.

These two elements can often seem to be in opposition. Frequently one gets sacrificed for the other. Because we don't want to upset people, step on toes, make enemies, etc., we avoid facing up to issues that might upset people. We go easy on certain problems and even avoid mentioning them.

Let's take a simple example:

It is a routine Senior Management meeting, or it will be as long as certain hot issues don't raise their heads. Things are OK in the company in general, but orders are showing a consistent downward trend. Of course, there are general market conditions that are contributing to this trend. There are some good new players in the market and some of your products are not as exciting and sellable as when they first came on the market. The Production Manager believes that other things are true as well, such as the Sales Division personnel not being as sharp, hard-working and innovative as they could and should be.

The Production Manager also knows that Production people have a part in all this as there have been problems with delays to some orders and some recalls of faulty products. These have been taken on board and remedial action is being taken, but the pain of the failures still stings.

For this reason the Production Manager is reluctant to raise the issue of the performance of the Sales Division. Not only will it lead

*to a turf war of serious proportions but it will also recall the prob-
lems Production caused and this will be put back on the table as
one of the real factors in the downturn of the business.*

*Nor does the Production Manager feel that the CEO will welcome
the sales issue being raised as it will create huge conflict in the
meeting and afterwards, and it will be up to the CEO to try to calm
the warring parties.*

*As the meeting is about to start, the Sales Manager asks the
Production Manager how his/her son is doing after a recent viral
illness he has been suffering from and does so in a warm, caring
and genuinely friendly way. They then chat on about the economy
in general and other issues on which both fully agree. The meeting
begins.*

The dilemma the Production Manager faces is whether to raise
an issue that he or she genuinely feels is important and needs
attention but that they know will raise all kinds of other issues
and lead to serious differences and conflict.

Without saying what the beleaguered Production Manager
ought to do, let's take a look at some principles that are at work
behind this particular story.

There is an assumption here which says that challenging people
and being honest and frank around important topics runs a serious risk of damaging relationships. Put like that, the assumption
is a sound one. The mistake arises in the conclusions one draws
from such an assumption, such as: 'One should not be honest as
it will damage relationships.' Because challenging or being honest
runs a risk does not mean that it should not be done or that it will
always go wrong and cause trouble.

But the assumption becomes so general and fuzzy in our heads
that we slip into commonly accepted behaviours of being nice and
friendly and not doing anything that would damage relationships.
This becomes the norm and culture, and it creates a downward
spiral which makes it ever less possible to raise problems and be
honest about important issues. Graphically it looks like figure
20.1 on the next page.

So, we believe that the greater the risks we take in being honest
with people and raising issues, the less healthy our relationships
will be. For this reason, we sacrifice naming what really matters
to avoid offending or annoying someone else in the group on the
basis that we will make more progress on things if we are in good
relationships. Which is, of course, valid.

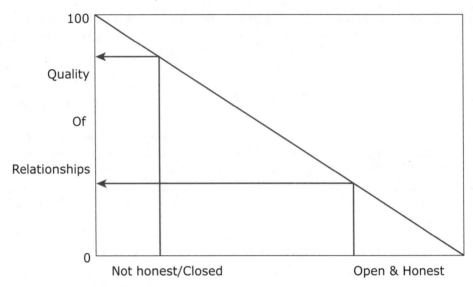

20.1. Relationships and honesty.

What is not valid is the assumption that to do this we have to be careful about being honest in the topics we raise and what we talk about. In fact, the opposite is the case!

Is it not true for you that in your best personal relationships you are able to be more honest with the other person than in your poorer relationships? Is it not actually a criterion of what you regard as a good relationship that you are able to be open, frank and honest?

In reality, we have to correct our previous graph. It should really look like figure 20.2 on the following page.

The more honest and open and frank we are, the better our relationships will be. Now this has to be handled with care. What we have to do is to move along the horizontal line and work at being ever more honest, all the time watching the vertical line of the relationship. We go as far over the horizontal line as we deem the relationship will allow. But, what happens is that, because we are caring about other people, they understand us and tolerate us when we are frank with them because they know and feel that we care for them too. Like all good things in life, there is a fine balance to be achieved between these two and managing this inbuilt tension is the key to creating a good and healthy relationship. The temptation is to give up on either frankness or the relationship rather than resolutely remaining faithful to both, always at the

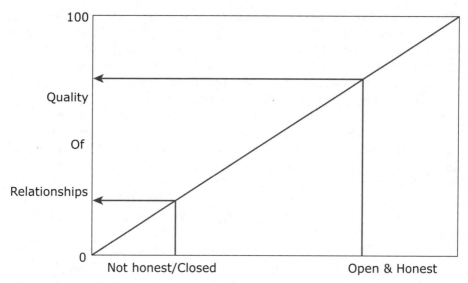

20.2. Relationships and honesty – the truth.

same time. This calls for good, courageous and human performance and there is no substitute for this and, equally, there is no
end to the benefits that come from such an effort. And the more
serious and important the topic is on the horizontal line, and the
more convinced we are of this, the greater ability and ease we
will have in airing it while maintaining a good relationship on the
vertical axis. In other words, the more convinced we are about the
value of something, the better our relationships with people will
be. If we work from this philosophy we will get the best of both
worlds, all the time.

If we return to our earlier example, this is the challenge facing
our Production Manager. I am saying that he has to take the risk
of raising the issue the company faces about its sales efforts. He
will do this in full awareness of the potential damage to the relationship with the Sales Division. And he does it with respect and
care for the people in Sales. If this is done well, not only will the
business gain from having a major issue tabled, but the actual
relationships between all the members of the Senior Team will be
strengthened. This approach has to prevail at every meeting and
it is up to the managers and leaders in the organisation to push
this awareness and encourage this behaviour. Part of this will
involve spotting any examples of attacks which have a political
motivation and, equally, to watch for revenge cycles that might

occur as a result of people taking risks in being open and honest. This, too, is a narrow path to follow but equally one that will bring untold benefits to both the performance and well-being of the organisation and to the relationships between the key people.

Far from seeing this issue as a reason to not call or to avoid meetings, I would propose that it is the very reason why meetings should be called and attended. I say this because it is in meetings that weaknesses, problems, issues, areas for improvement and opportunities will be best identified. Without them, there is a real danger of things being swept under carpets or not spotted at all. Meetings provide the opportunity to get several sets of eyes, ears, hearts and minds awake and in touch with reality in order to make the very most of that reality. No one individual, no matter how clever, will do this. It is impossible – 'None of us is as clever as all of us.' Meetings can offer or can be the most sensitive diagnostic tool with which to look at the health of the organisation. They can be the microscope looking for details in the present that need to be improved. They can be the telescope looking far into the future. They can be the well of energy and life in a company.

And, yes, they are challenging in terms of putting relationships to the test. But if these relationships are seen and handled as outlined above, where people trust each other and have a respect for each other and for what they are striving to achieve, then this courageous activity is what will bind them as a group and deepen their relationships and unity as a team. The pursuit of an over-riding or underpinning goal enables people to take risks with each other and to grow as individuals, and as social groups. The temptation to avoid this effort will always exist and this temptation needs to be dealt with. People, supported by each other, need to resist it and to take risks in the interests of growth – growth for the business and growth for people.

Why would you not get people together in order to achieve what all want? How could you miss such a meeting?

2. You can end up at or after a meeting forced to go a route you don't want to go and feel your hands tied

The perceived challenge to or loss of one's autonomy or freedom is a reason why some managers are reluctant to call or attend meetings.

When I was visiting the home of a friend of mine in South America some years ago, I noticed the strange behaviour of her hens. While there was lots of nice green grass and weeds nearby, the hens continued to pick in the same area which was becoming more and more barren. When I asked my friend why they didn't move into the more fertile area just a few metres away, she pointed out to me that each hen was tied by one leg to another hen.

'So...?' I asked.

Meetings can be like hens tied together.
Hens or people feel they can't move without the
other and so end up going nowhere at all.

20.3. How we hold each other back.

'Well,' she told me, 'when they go to move they each feel a tug on their leg and they each think they are tied to something so they don't go very far.'

So each hen was, in effect, holding the other hen back.

We can feel like this at meetings. We can feel held back by someone else and their expectations of us, and they can feel the same about us.

It is very common and indeed natural to feel that, by sharing an issue with a team or group of people, one will be forced to take into account the views and wishes as well as the biases of others. We can feel that we won't get our own way, that we have to compromise, and that we will lose our freedom to do what we want and believe to be the right and best thing to do. For this reason, people can avoid calling meetings or going to meetings where their preferred viewpoint on some issue might be challenged and resisted and changed completely. It is better to take a decision oneself rather than have all kinds of people snipe at what one sees as the only or best way.

The alternative is to go to the meeting but make sure that you have lobbied as many people as possible beforehand so that there is enough support for your way forward. Alliances can be formed and deals agreed around a table without anyone noticing it or at least being able to name it. In this way, one can generally get away with doing one's own thing without too much interference or dilution.

So, for all these reasons, meetings and one's own autonomy and freedom seem to be in direct opposition. But this is an illusion.

We hold on to this illusion because we believe that freedom means doing what *I* feel like doing, what *I* want to do. But, as we saw in Chapter 5, this is a very inadequate definition of freedom. Drug addicts are doing what they feel like doing and want to do, yet they are anything but free. So 'doing what we want' does not fill the bill in terms of describing what real freedom is. Sticking with the drug addict for the moment, being free for him or her cannot mean doing what they want in the sense of what they feel like doing, but being able to do what is best for them and for others. So being free means being able and wanting to do *what is best* for oneself and others.

Applying the same criteria to managing, we can quickly see that working in groups of people, while it may mean that one does not do what one wants or feels like doing, it will help managers do what is best for them and for others around them. In other words, it may help them to have more freedom in the correct sense of that word – able and wanting to do what is best. So it is not true that involving people in a meeting will reduce your freedom. It will increase it. (For now I am ignoring the situations where decisions are taken on the basis of a vote which I will cover later in Chapter 22 on decision making.)

This is not just a nice theory. You must have found yourself in this position very often. You feel clear about some course of action you want to take and are attached to it and you don't want anything to interfere with it or to change your plans. The last thing you want is for your nice plans to be challenged or changed and so you don't want to expose them to the critical eyes of others. And yet you have a sneaking feeling that others have different views on what you should do. But you don't want to entertain these, you don't want to be blocked on the path you are so keen to go down.

This is a moment of truth and some of the most fatal decisions in history got taken in exactly this way – leaders not wanting to expose their plans to others in case their plans got changed or thwarted. In essence, what is going on is that we prefer to go our way than go the right or best way.

If we go back to our earlier example and get inside the head of the Sales Manager at the Senior Management meeting. Let's say she has been having a hard time of it and things have not been going great. But now she has a plan to reorganise the Sales Department and move to a structure based on the main regions. She knows that anything she raises at the meeting will be questioned because of the difficult period Sales has been going through, and so she decides not to share the plan with her colleagues out of a fear that her plans may be challenged and even changed. Even though there are major flaws in her plan, some of which she is vaguely aware of, she plunges ahead.

On an issue of this seriousness it would make sense for her to check the plan out with her colleagues. Even if she was on exactly the right track, the confirmation and support of her colleagues for her plan would add to her own confidence and ability to implement and make her plans work. By involving others in her thinking, she would increase the chances of doing what is right and best for her and others. She would increase or improve her freedom.

I have said many times elsewhere in this book that our duty as managers is not to take decisions but to take *good* decisions. Meetings offer us an unequalled opportunity to ensure that our decisions are good ones by exposing them to the thinking of the people in our teams or organisations. It would seem stupid, even irresponsible, not to expose our thinking to a larger group. We owe it to others and to ourselves to question and deepen our thinking and decision making in this way. What a resource to have at our disposal!

3. Meetings can confuse. Often the person who calls the meeting has their mind made up already

Letting the boss decide is a good thing to do once the self-same boss decides well and takes a good decision. And, yes, sometimes the senior person who calls the meeting does have their mind made up and this can avoid confusion and reduce complexity.

It can also reduce the quality of thinking and so reduce the chance of a good decision being taken.

How can this be so?

It's like this. Usually at a meeting there will be a person who leads the meeting – we normally refer to this person as the chairman or the chairperson. This is usually the person who called the meeting and who has the issue or topic that needs to be addressed. Or it can be the senior person, the manager. Now I want to take a look at this role of the leader or chairperson in a meeting.

The chair or leader of a meeting has two critical tasks:

i. They are responsible for the topic – the subject matter of the meeting which we can refer to as the content.

ii. They will also be responsible for how the meeting gets handled – when it starts and finishes, and who speaks and for how long – ensuring it stays on track, etc. This refers to the process of the meeting.

So the chairperson has the task of managing both the process and the content. This can be a difficult task as either one can suffer, especially the process. Because of this, it is important that every manager and everyone who has to lead or chair a meeting are skilled in facilitation. (The key responsibilities of the facilitator are covered in Chapter 18.)

This is important because, unless the chair or leader is skilled in facilitating and aware of its importance, they will end up with their own ideas only, because they will only have focused on the content or subject matter. And, because they have a strong vested interest in the subject matter, ideas that don't fit with theirs or that don't seem to make such sense will be thrown aside. Other participants in the meeting will soon learn what the chair or leader is looking for and will only put forward ideas that they believe are likely to be accepted. Later on, they will go further and not even *think* of ideas that they believe might not be acceptable to the chair or leader. Nobody will realise this and the chairperson will feel very pleased that they have done a good job, especially since they like all the ideas they have heard – essentially their own, or in line with their own. The participants will all feel OK too, especially those who most coincided with the chair or manager. Some won't. Some will feel disgruntled and, for some unknown reason, bothered and unhappy.

But, quite apart from how people feel, the end result will be a relatively poor one as few if any really new ideas will have made it to the light of day.

If the chairperson or leader understands facilitation and the value of it, then they will be able to elicit many more ideas from the participants through inviting them to be involved and hearing and noting what they say. In this way, the chairperson, if also the manager, will have a richer array of ideas from which to choose and, in this way, will be better equipped to take better decisions. They will have more ideas and richer thinking from which to choose.

But this will not happen unless the manager who is leading the meeting is truly aware of what is involved in facilitating and is able to marry this role with the more regular role of chairing and focusing on the content.

A manager who knows how to lead a meeting in a facilitative way can avoid possible confusion at meetings, but, more than that, they can get enormous support and contributions to help them with their own thinking, planning and decision making. They get the best of all worlds – a great contribution of ideas from their people *and* without losing the right or responsibility to take the final decision. (For more details on this see Chapter 18.) By running a meeting in a facilitating way, you are getting in touch with an enormous resource of expertise, experience and thinking that is available to you, your department and your company. If all meetings are run in a well-facilitated way they will be truly places where surprises abound and things happen. Yes, there will be people who will want things all wrapped up before the meeting because they lack the courage to trust the wisdom and goodness of the group, but it is this that leads to much of the game playing that goes on at meetings and makes them places to be avoided. But this need not be so if good leadership and facilitation are understood and practised in the context of meetings. Ultimately the boss will decide, but it will be a better decision and one that enjoys the support of everyone.

4. Very often the effort to reach a consensus involves some kind of compromise on everyone's part

This, too, is a valid concern with meetings. Mediocre thinking and decision making will lead to mediocre organisations. And this can happen if the basis for reaching decisions is too often to compromise.

But it need not be so. In Chapter 8, we looked at ideas and how we can evaluate and select ideas on two bases:

- How valuable they are.
- How feasible they are.

We plotted these on a matrix as follows:

Idea Selection

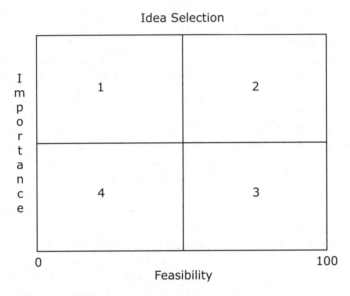

20.4. Idea selection value and feasibility.

The importance of this model is that it allows us to move from the bottom half of the matrix – safe and very doable ideas that won't change or improve too much – to the top half – powerful ideas that will make a real difference if we can make them happen. There is a real danger in going for ideas in Box 3. These ideas, while useful, will not take us far forward in our companies, nor will they be good or strong enough to deal with big problems. Understanding this model and applying it consistently will create a new atmosphere of open-mindedness and creative thinking.

The second notion we looked at in Chapter 8 in respect of good and bad ideas will also help. We said that there are no good or bad ideas but only ideas with some good in them and some bad in them. Remember the model or figure?

Let's take the clear space in the figure as the good in the idea then all ideas look a bit like this – lots of value and some bits that are not good or don't make sense or won't work. So, when we hear an idea, which side do you think we tend to focus on

IDEA

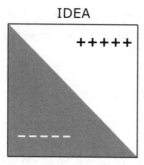

20.5. No good or bad ideas.

or go after? Yes, the shady or 'bad' bit. And we do this for good reasons, especially if we are managers or people with responsibility, because seeing what is wrong is our job. So, we have to watch for this tendency when we are looking for and hearing ideas. Our real challenge is to preserve the good and deal with or get over the bad.

This is important for meetings. If we don't operate in this way we will throw out a lot of ideas with lots of good in them because there is some bad there too. And there is no need. We can keep them all, look at them, combine them and find ways to remove the parts we don't like or that we think will not work.

Take a stupid example of a 'stupid' idea – 'open the window and throw this book out'. On the surface, this is not a great idea and is certainly not a great one for *me*. But let's look at the positives in it or find positive applications of the idea. Let's aim for ten, for a start!

i. Take a break from reading this.

ii. Open your mind to all kinds of ideas in this book and elsewhere and let them in.

iii. Spread or throw around some of the ideas and wisdom in this book.

iv. Distance yourself from some of the messages and points in the book.

v. Get some distance from this topic so you understand it better.

vi. Rely more on yourself and your own inner wisdom than on outside sources like books.

vii. Get rid of old ideas and prejudices and out-of-date thinking.

viii. Make an effort to learn and develop and take on new things.

ix. See how far you can extend and stretch yourself and continue to aim for more.

x. Relax and trust more and cease to worry about knowledge, or yourself or anything.

This is not to say that we should waste time exploring and searching for the value in every zany idea that comes up. What I am saying is that we need to become good at spotting the value in ideas and being open to look at ideas that at first do not appear doable or practical. With this understanding, there is no need for and no danger of meetings coming up with mediocre, compromise-based ideas; quite the opposite – meetings will be the place where you will find more creative ideas than anywhere else because of the wealth of different people and viewpoints present and because you can do elephantine thinking. Creating this atmosphere in the meeting is the function of the leader or facilitator/leader. Creating this atmosphere in the organisation is the job of the leader and everyone. This book is aimed at helping you to do that and do it well.

5. Sometimes you can find yourself up against stronger or more powerful people who can pressurise you or even bully you, and you can lose your power and control

This, too, is a valid concern. One of the difficulties for anyone who has a problem in their area of responsibility is that it can be hard to ask for help from the group or team. If you do, you can feel criticised and in trouble. In addition, people will, more or less, tell you what to do or what you should have done. For that reason, when you have a problem or if things are not going so well, the last thing you as a manager want to do is to share it with a group of managers or with your colleagues. You can feel and fear that your control over what gets done will get wrestled away from you by strong people who will pressurise you into going a way that you may not want to go. Or a group may gang up on you and put pressure on you to go a particular route that you do not want to go.

I came across this many years ago when I was working in a division of a large building materials company in Ireland. The Managing Director asked me to have a word with the Operations Director who, he said, never shared his problems with his other fellow directors. When I approached the Operations Director about why he didn't include his colleagues in his problems, he asked me why would he. He explained that it was a most complex chemical manufacturing process that used temperatures of 2300°C and so was quite dangerous. I said to him that it would help his colleagues to feel included if they were allowed to hear his issues and give ideas. He said he had no problem with this, except that, in the past, they only accepted that he had really listened to their ideas if he implemented them and put them into practice.

And, he said, 'I can't do that. Many of them are just not doable. And the others don't have the responsibility that I have. I have to wonder every night what is going on and hope that the process is working and, above all, that people will work safely. Success is worth nothing if one person gets killed. So, I can't tell them what is happening because they will want to give ideas and advice, and I can't listen to their advice because they will only accept that I have really listened if I put it into practice.'

See what is going on? The answer to this issue is *clientship*. Clientship refers to the person who has the responsibility for and ownership of a problem. This gets respected by others who can offer ideas and suggestions, while always recognising that the ultimate decision belongs to the client. This means that a person can share what they like with a group, knowing that the group will, at the end of the day, accept that the client is the person responsible and so has the right to decide what is best for their area, within reason of course. But most people are reasonable, especially if they feel respected and not cornered. So this means that anyone who has an issue can raise it in the group, get lots of ideas for it and do all this without feeling dumped on and also end up still being the person responsible for the particular issue or area. Sometimes, too, a person goes in talking about 'my' problem and leaves talking about 'our' problem. The notion of client avoids ownership getting diluted or lost which happens when a problem changes from being 'my' problem to being 'our' problem.

So now we have a system that gets the best of both worlds – the client gets lots of help, support and ideas, and the client retains the ownership and accountability. And so there need be no fear of losing control or ownership of your areas of responsibility. Quite the opposite! By sharing your issues and challenges with a group of people without any fear of being bullied or coerced, you will have even more control over all your areas of responsibility.

Summary

Meetings and social gatherings are where we are most ourselves, are most human and are most powerful. Yes, there are challenges but these are human challenges and each one is an invitation to be stronger and better as people and as managers. In turn, we can help others be stronger, better and more human in the process. I hope this chapter has shown how we can handle meetings in a good way that deals with some of the normal human frailties we have and unleashes the wonderful power we have for making great things happen together.

Chapter 21

Dealing with Unsatisfactory Performance or Behaviour

> 'It's a funny thing about life; if you refuse to accept anything but the best, you very often get it.'
>
> – Somerset Maugham

If there is one thing certain it is that you are going to come across situations where you are dissatisfied with the performance or behaviour of some of your people. Agreed? For whatever reason – so-called human nature, working conditions, the inadequate capitalist or economic system, you name it – you will come across such situations and people.

And even if they are unavoidable we often try to avoid them. We do so because we don't feel comfortable dealing with them or confident that we will handle them well. Often, attempts to address poor performance end in conflict and so there is a temptation to ignore them or tolerate them. After all, we believe the instances of poor performance or behaviour are relatively few, so why not live with them?

The performance of people in an organisation can look like figure 21.1.

So we have the vast majority of people who, while undoubtedly they could do better, are performing satisfactorily. Then we will always have the outstanding ones, who will be in a minority but are a joy to work with. And then we have the other minority, the ones with whose performance we are unhappy. Let's say, for argument's sake, these split into:

- 85 per cent good, steady performers,
- 10 per cent in the outstanding elite, and
- 5 per cent in the unsatisfactory category.

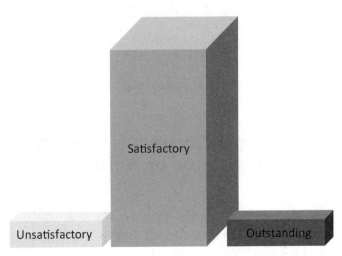

21.1. Performance patterns.

It is easy to keep going with a toss of the head and a dismissal of the 5 per cent as not being worth the trouble...and trouble they can be!

However, if we do this, things do not remain the same. After a while we end up with a picture like this:

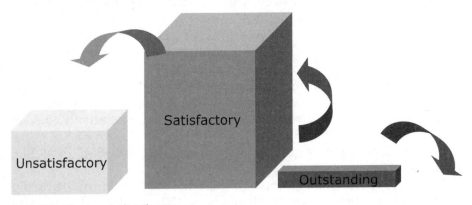

21.1.2. Performance distribution.

This happens because some of those in the middle (the 85 per cent) question why they should keep doing their best while others get away with doing little and nothing happens apart from the fact they keep getting paid. So they lose a bit of heart and consciously or unconsciously slip into poorer and poorer performance. Those in the outstanding category lose heart in an organisation that accepts such low standards and they drop their standards, or just leave. So there is a big price to be paid for not dealing with the apparently insignificant 5 per cent. Apart from all that, it is just not right to ignore problems like these.

There is also another price. When we don't deal with such people early enough it can take an inordinate amount of time to deal with them later on when we have to. We can often regret having let things go unattended for so long and not having put in the one little stitch that would have saved so many others and so much time.

Of course, it is not as neat and water-tight as it looks in my histogram model. There will be considerable overlap and some movement between the various categories so that there will be many more than 5 per cent that we need to manage. This is the biggest danger of all – that there will be a gradual erosion of stand-ards and performance, a slippage away from high performance and a leakage of real talent and potential.

It is not easy to deal with these situations or to confront someone whose performance is slipping. It is uncomfortable and possibly contentious. It can mean the end of what was or seemed to have been a nice, friendly relationship. Even though we are managers, we can feel challenged, criticised, blamed and abused for confront-ing people. We can get emotional, angry, upset, hurt and frustrated when we do so. We can get our way or not get our way. For these and other reasons we often want to avoid these situations. We turn a blind eye to them. We justify or explain away what is going on. We rationalise the situation – anything to avoid facing up to the awkwardness of dealing with the person or the situation.

So, serious and important as it is to address situations like these, the effort or pain involved in doing so prevents us from doing what we should do.

But this need not be the case at all. There is no reason why addressing these situations should cause us so much trouble or angst. Believe me!

Let us take a fairly common type of case. Suppose your situa-tion is a bit like this one:

You have a person working for you who has been in their position for quite some time and has generally done OK in what was asked of them.
However, their performance is no longer good enough.

*Some of this is due to the fact that standards have risen and there is need for everyone to up their game. Some of it, however, is about the person him/herself. While they **do** all that is asked of them, that is **all** they do and they don't seem to be interested in doing any more, in taking on any more or in putting their shoulder to the wheel.*

They are not in tune with others in the department who are eager to do whatever is required of them. You have made many efforts to involve the person and to get more commitment from them but they have not responded and now it is time to do something about it and talk to the person.

Others see this going on and some have mentioned the person to you as a bad example for others and the kind of person we don't want to have and can't afford to have any more. It is just not good enough.

So this is far from being an extreme situation. It is not dire. But it is not good enough. Let's say that, on top of that, your own manager is understandably putting some pressure on you to deal with the situation. So are others.

So what do you do? How do you handle it? You might feel it is a very straightforward case; you just point out to the person what is going on and what you and the organisation need. Just tell them and get on with it. End of story.

Or, you might be more subtle and ask them how they think they are doing and so elicit from them recognition that they could be doing a lot more and need to do a lot more than they are currently doing.

So, what's the problem? Well, part of the problem is that the person involved may have a very different view of things. Put yourself in *their* shoes:

I have been in my present job for quite some time now and I know it very well. I could do it with my eyes closed and I am very confident about what I do. I really believe this is a good contribution to the company and I deserve every penny I get paid. Yes there are some whiz-kids around who are more ambitious and very keen to take on more but I am not interested in going into the fast lane.

The company has got a lot out of me and now I am just going to do a good, sound job. On many occasions, hints were dropped and I felt I was being nudged or manipulated into taking on more but I resisted these efforts. I am not that interested in getting on and moving up the ladder and, even if I were, I would probably get overlooked as has already happened on a few occasions. While work is important, it is not everything and I am doing my bit. And that should be quite good enough for any company or manager.

So now we have two very different but understandable views of the same situation.

And this is even more complex if the two people involved have a personal relationship. Now the risk arises that the manger will understand the person and accept their point of view. They may do this because they don't want to lose a friend or the relationship, or because they believe that, ultimately, they will get more from the person if they have a good relationship with them. However, they will win little commendation from their own management for this stance, and will probably be regarded as a weak manager.

Faced with this possibility and wanting to avoid being seen in a bad light, the manager may take a different stance and enforce their view of the world and the situation on the other person and take no excuses, not wanting to hear any stories or explanations. Apart from very probably losing the relationship through this approach, they may also lose their reputation as a good and fair manager and the good will of others around.

While this might be deemed an unusual situation, with a lot of ambiguity around the person's performance, this is in fact always the case. Rarely, if ever, will two views of any situation coincide exactly. The chances of this happening when the complexities of work and performance are involved, along with all the other complexities of relationships, power and divergent interests, are slim.

For these reasons we often handle such situations poorly or we avoid handling them at all. We resort to some arbitration or legal board for resolution.

So let's go with the case described above and use it to find a way forward. You will be able to apply the learnings to your own situation(s).

There are at least three different approaches we could use.

Approach 1 – Coach

The approach we mentioned in Chapter 13, about going in and coaching the person on how they believe they are doing is a good one and a great start. This will give us vital information about how the other person views the situation and so will allow us to connect to that and match our viewpoint to theirs. The hope is that, with gentle coaxing and skilful coaching, they will arrive at a realisation that their performance is in fact not good enough. It's great if this happens and if it does then we are home and dry, while preserving the good relationship we had with the other person. However, if the person fails or refuses to acknowledge how things are, then we are faced with another problem. Sometimes all the best coaching in the world fails to get the person to realise or accept that their performance is unsatisfactory.

Approach 2 – Learn and find out

We could take an even more gentle and respectful approach and simply use the meeting to find out how the person is thinking and how they see things and why. Then, gifted with this information, we can subsequently plan what to do about it. So, we are not seeking a change of behaviour or an open confession but just an increased awareness for ourselves of what is going on with the other person. Armed with this, we can decide later what to do about the situation. This might mean having another meeting with the person to look for greater mutual understanding.

Approach 3 – Tell

A third approach is to do what we also mentioned earlier – simply tell the person what we see going on and challenge them with the unacceptability of their current level of performance. We let them know that their performance is not good enough and give them the evidence we have for this.

So it bears repeating that these are three valid ways of addressing the situation, going from very mild to strong:

1. Coach the person to an awareness that their performance is not good enough.

2. Go into the meeting to find out what is going on in the person's world.

3. Tell the person that their performance is not good enough and why this is so.

Think a little before you act

But, when we go to deal with an issue like this, sometimes we go too far too quickly. We presume too much. Suppose the case is a bit different from the one we just looked at. Suppose the issue is with the leader of a team where, while the results and performance are fine, there are other problems. There have been numerous complaints that some people in the team have been badly treated, disrespected, shouted at and made to feel inferior. You are sufficiently satisfied that your team leader is mistreating some of her team members. You decide to deal with it and to talk to her. What would you do? How would you handle it? Take a second to think of this before reading on.

One obvious way – and you may have come up with a far better one – is to let the person know that this kind of behaviour is not acceptable. You could say that, while you are pleased with the overall performance and results of her team, you are not happy about how she is treating some of her team members. You let her know what you understand or know to be happening and you make it clear that this way of handling people is not acceptable, and so on. Then hopefully you will get a commitment that she will mend her ways and handle people with respect in the future.

This is a very short-cut version and, yes, I am sure you see better and more complete ways of dealing with your team leader. I only want to make a point about what the kind of influence needs to be, which in this case is the influence of awareness as we discussed in Chapter 13. In this case it is simply that you, as her manager, are asking her to behave differently and you expect her to change as a result. This is fine and may indeed work.

But let's back up a little. Remember what we said earlier: Every person who has a problem will fall into one of three categories:

1. They *don't know* they have a problem.

2. They do know but *don't want* to do anything about it.

3. They know there is a problem, want to do something about it but *can't or are not able*.

The first thing we have to do before addressing the issue with the team leader is to find out to which category she belongs.

Is it that she is not aware of how she is behaving or is it that she thinks that it is normal and OK? This is quite probable and is very frequently the case. Or is it that she does know but enjoys throwing her weight around and likes her image as the dominating leader of the team who can put people in their place and get excellent results from doing so. Or, finally, it may be that she has bad habits or has a short fuse, or is impatient and intolerant and gets stressed under pressure.

Having decided to which category she belongs we can address the issue in a more accurate and helpful way.

If it is Category 1 and she does not know, then we can find ways to let her know what she is doing, the effect she is having on people and, if necessary, why this is not acceptable.

If it is Category 2 and she does not want to change, we will have to help her find some good reasons for changing. If painting the picture of the bad effects she is having on her team members and other such promptings isn't working, we might have to let her know that, frankly, her behaviour is not acceptable to us and then proceed to get her to commit to working and behaving in a more acceptable way.

Finally, if she simply can't or is not able to do something about the problem (Category 3), then we have to help her. This could take various forms such as advising her, supporting her, getting her mentoring or counselling, finding her a different job, or reducing or adjusting her present one.

The point is that it is not wise to decide on a particular approach until we know to what category a person belongs.

What makes this more important is that it is not always obvious to which category a person may belong. Why is this so? Because people in Category 2 (don't want to change) will often pretend they are in Category 1 (don't know or are not aware of the need to change)! This is a good first line of defence for people, and, unless you are persistent with them, it may actually work. So we cannot take it at face value when a person protests their innocence or ignorance about their performance or behaviour. While not directly challenging their innocence or ignorance, we should move on quickly to what they plan to do about the issue now that they do know about it.

Even more complicated is Category 3. People in Category 3 (can't or are not able to change) will often claim to be in Category 2 (don't want to change). They do this because some people do not like admitting they are not able or are not up to the job. They would prefer to pretend they are not interested. Many years ago I had a Production Control Supervisor whose job it was to ship parts to Opel in Germany and Vauxhall in the UK. Our part, the wiring system, was a critical component and, in fact, the first component into the car shell. A shortage of our component could quickly stop the plant and a stoppage of just one hour could amount to a cost of $1m. When things were tight and we were struggling to meet deadlines, I had regular meetings with the Production Control Supervisor. First thing in the morning he was summoned to my office and had to tell me, the Managing Director, what he had shipped the night before and what he planned to ship during the day. He was back in after lunch to give me more information and assurances. Of course, I was showing a lack of confidence in him with some justification. But, in addition, I was treating him as belonging to Category 2, not wanting to do anything about the problem, and pressurising him to perform. In fact he belonged more to Category 3 (can't or are not able). He needed help, not more pressure. If I had given the situation and him more time and thought, I would have come to understand that he was outside his competence level and so avoided a lot of time wasting and frustration for both of us.

Sometimes managers feel that they are doing their job if they criticise a poor performer or tell them that they are not performing well and demand that they perform better. We can behave a bit like our friend here – judging, criticising, being disappointed but not helping, not giving him the ladder.

21.2.. Manager's role to HELP.

Sometimes managers do not realise that their job is also to help. People in Category 3 need help and it is important to spot that and provide whatever help they need.

So, before taking any action in terms of dealing with either unacceptable performance, as in our first example, or unacceptable behaviour, as in the second, we need to find out to which category the person belongs as this will help to make our intervention more focused and effective.

To check that this is making sense to you in your situation, please take a few minutes to identify people you know who fall into each of the three categories. These people can be inside or outside of work.

- Namely someone who has a problem but *is not aware* of it.
- Someone who has a problem, is aware of it, but *does not want* for some reason to do anything about it.
- And, finally, someone who knows they have a problem and would like to resolve it, but *are not able to*.

Doing this will enable us to deal with them in a more human and so in a more effective way.

Move from looking at the past to looking to the future

The thing is that, even with all of this, there is no guarantee that the person, the alleged unsatisfactory performer, will realise or accept that they have not been performing well or even satisfactorily. This can happen for a lot of reasons – different standards, low self-awareness and downright fear or defensiveness. People do not like being accused in the wrong and sometimes we don't like being accused in the right. Have you ever made a mistake when driving and have someone get irate with you and blow their horn? It's bad enough having made a mistake but to have someone notice it and berate you for it makes it doubly painful and annoying. This also applies to poor performance. The challenge can double our defensiveness and denial.

So, even after having used these three approaches we may not yet succeed in getting the person to accept that their performance in the past has not been good enough. Nor do we have to! It is not the *past* we are concerned about but the future – future behaviour and performance. It is fine to use evidence from the past to persuade the person that there is a need to improve, but it is not the only way. We can skip the arguments about the past and go straight into the future. This is simple and it is magic. In the case of the underperforming employee that we have been looking at, it goes something like this:

Manager: It seems we are not in agreement about how you have been performing. I believe it has not been good enough and I have given you reasons for that belief and you disagree. Ok?
Employee: Yes. I disagree completely with you about how my performance has been in the past while. Completely.
Manager: That's a pity but let's move on. If we were sitting down for a chat in, say, six months' time, can we agree now how you will be performing then so that there will be no disagreement between us at that point? In other words, how will you be performing in six months time so that we are both in full agreement that your performance is quite satisfactory and, indeed, more than that?

So then we hear these from the employee. We get them describing what really satisfactory or good performance would mean in their case. We might have to help them by reminding them again about what it is we are trying to achieve in our areas of work or in the company so that they can fill in what their particular contribution to it needs to be. Or we might need to add in one or two things that they have missed and insist on these. Then we can summarise what the person has said, play it back to them and agree it.

The key is to focus on the future rather than on the past.

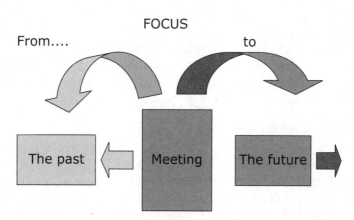

21.3. Move from focus on past to focus on future.

1. We are avoiding an impossible tangle over the past and the difficult struggle to agree what actually happened in the past. Even
non-stop cameras on the employee 24/7 would not resolve this.

2. We are getting the employee to create an image of how their
performance will be in the future.

3. In doing this they are actually committing to tackling it and
making it happen. It is they who are saying it, not us.

4. We are preserving a healthy and respectful relationship in a
spirit of win-win.

This approach, of focusing on the future rather than the past, will
work especially well in the many cases where there is potential
ambiguity or no way of measuring. For example, in the case of our
team leader above, if she challenges your view that she is treating
her people in an aggressive way, you can avoid trying to prove or
convince her that she *has been doing it* and move to the future.

> Manager: Look Anne, we are disagreeing fairly strongly about
> how you treat your people. I believe that you are aggressive
> with them and you deny this. How would we handle this in the
> future so that we are never in this kind of disagreement? If we
> met again in two months what would be happening that would
> tell us that you are handling your people really well and not
> being overly aggressive with them? How would we know?

She then begins to list a few clear indicators and you can add in
a few of your own and 'hey presto' we have a list of key behaviour
areas for her and a commitment from her that she is going to
meet them. You could top it by saying: 'You know I am really
looking forward to meeting with you on 24 May to hear how you
are getting on and to see that all these things are happening.'
And, again, you have got the commitment without damaging the
relationship at all.

The job or the relationship?

This latter point is important. It keeps coming up. We mentioned
it at the outset as part of our reluctance to engage in challenging
poor performance or poor performers. Let's look at it now in more
detail. We have talked about this in Chapter 18 but it is important to re-visit it here.

What happens is that we dichotomise. We dichotomise two things: The task, job or company on the one hand and the person, individual and relationship on the other.

We feel that these two are often opposed to each other, that if we emphasise one, then we risk damaging the other. So, if we drive the company's goals and needs very hard, we will risk ignoring and damaging the relationship with the other person. Or we believe that we need to look after the relationship with the person or with people in order to get them to perform well. After all, people who are not happy or don't feel cared for will not perform well, and will not be loyal, dedicated and committed.

We often hear people use this language – 'a task person' or 'a people person'. We see managers that fall into one or other camp. The task person sees the people person as being too weak and the people person sees the task person as being too hard and lacking an understanding of how critical it is to manage and treat people well.

It looks like this:

HANDLING BEHAVIOUR

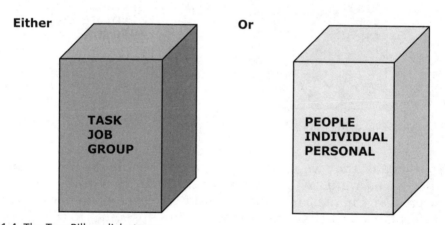

21.4. The Two Pillars dichotomy.

What we believe is that if we are faithful to the Task Pillar or pole then we collapse the People Pillar or pole, and vice versa. This causes us great problems. Often there is no problem and the two are perfectly compatible. But when there is a problem like an incident over behaviour or a case of unsatisfactory performance, like we have been looking at, the clash arises and we collapse one

or other of these pillars. So, you may have a very good relationship with the employee who is performing poorly or with the team
leader who is being aggressive, and you might be afraid of losing
this relationship. Nor do you want to come across as 'doing the
heavy' or bullying. You want to remain friendly.

Recognise this? It happens all the time.

The good news – and it *is* good news – is that there is no need
for this dichotomy at all. We can respect and look after both poles
or Pillars at the same time. We do this by creating and appealing to something that embraces both Pillars, something that is
greater than but actually embraces both Pillars, namely a super-
ordinate goal. By this I mean a vision or goal for the organisation,
as discussed in Chapter 18. This embraces both Pillars so that
what is good for one is also good for the other. It looks like this:

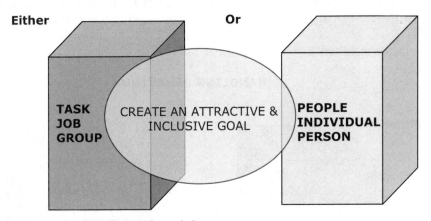

21.5. Managing both Pillars with no dichotomy.

This means that we always operate out of this goal or vision –
what we *all* want, what is good for *all* of us. How this is done is
covered in Chapter 18. How it works in cases of unsatisfactory
performance or behaviour is that you are appealing to this as the
motive for the conversation and for the need to address the issue.
This means that we do not need to neglect either of the Pillars.
We do not need to be unfaithful to the company or the task or
the individual. What is good for one is good for the other. This
allows us to be very tough on the person because what we are
doing is ultimately good *for them too.* This shows not only in how
we think but in the tone in which we direct the conversation. We
can handle it in a very strong and honest way but also in a very

caring way because we genuinely want their welfare as part of our overall goal.

There are times when we are more on one side than on the other. If a person is going through a bad period for work or other reasons then we get closer to the Personal Pillar. But we do not give up on the other pillar; we never forget it. The overall good and welfare of the company will be important for the person at a time like this. On the other hand, when, as in a case like this, we have an issue that affects the company or the job, we get closer to the Company Pillar – but without forsaking the pillar of the person.

Let's see how it would operate in the two cases we have been working on.

If we leave aside for the moment the difference in opinion about the past, the emphasis here would be on the overall goal and how the person's performance is not helping the achievement of the goal and therefore not helping the person themselves.

The conversation with the underperforming employee or the team leader might go a bit like this:

> Manager: I want to raise again the issue of your performance about which we have already spoken and I want to say that I cannot accept your current performance. It is not good enough to achieve our goal, which you understand and which you know is important for all of us and for you too.

Everything the manager says here is important. The manager is saying that he or she cannot accept the current level of performance. It is subjective language and the manager is taking it on him or herself to make this call or judgment. This is the right of the leader or manager. But the reason for the unhappiness or inability to accept the performance is because it is not helping to achieve the goal which the other person understands, has agreed to and sees as being good for them too. The manager handles the whole conversation within the context of the circle, the overall and all-embracing vision or goal, as described above, and goes back and forth between the Two Pillars without ever abandoning either. The manager is in the role of the protector of the overall goal and good of the whole, including that of the individual, the poor performer.

This is so simple and obvious but we often forget it. Let's take a simple example of a band. The members of the band want success, whatever that means in their particular context. They know what this means and they all clearly understand how the success of the band is good for each of them too. They see little divergence between the two. Now, suppose one of the band members, a guitarist, is not playing really well, and is not up to speed with the new numbers the band have taken on. The manager or leader of the band will have to address this issue. In addressing it, the leader talks exactly as we described above. They explain that they are not happy with the recent performance of the guitarist and that this is bringing the whole band down, which is not in the interests of the guitarist either. The leader can stress what is happening to the band in recent performances (Company Pillar) and how that is not acceptable. Then they challenge the guitarist on their performance, their preparation, their commitment and so on. The leader will ask the guitarist what they intend to do to improve their performance and get a commitment from them to do this. The band leader cannot ignore what is happening. In addressing the issue, they are truly acting in the interests of the guitarist as well. To ignore it would mean being a bad friend to them. The leader can quite honestly and justifiably tell the guitarist how good they are and how important they are to the band and recall moments when the guitarist was outstanding and made a great contribution (Personal Pillar).

What happens in work situations is that we forget the circle or it never really existed in the first place. Some kind of vision or goal may have been written up but it has probably become blurred and distant and ceased to play a live part in the daily work of people. As a result, other dynamics enter in – relationships, rivalry, other interests, issues of hierarchy and so on, and these take precedence leading to the need for management to play a false role, as described elsewhere. Even if that has happened, this moment can be an opportunity to address that and to make clear how the good of the organisation is intimately linked with the good of the individual. This needs to be believed and it needs to be practised and built into how the organisation is structured and designed, as described in Chapter 17.

But what if it does not work? And what about discipline?

What if, in spite of doing all those good things, the person still has not changed, has not improved their performance? Are we not going to discipline people in line with established disciplinary procedures?

We will come to discipline later. For now we are pursuing the approach of giving the person every chance to improve. Remember that this is our job as managers and especially as leaders. And if we do that well, they will improve. And we won't need to get into disciplining.

But what if they don't improve?

What if several months have passed during which the actions agreed at the meeting have all been taken but the person remains as they are, with no real improvement?

Yes, we have to deal with that...if it does happen. And we do it through what we call the 'Last Resort Meeting'.

The Last Resort Meeting operates as follows:

1. Spend appropriate time genuinely, honestly, fairly and respectfully trying to get agreement with the person on their performance against the objectives and on the real need to improve. This will have been done during the weeks and months following the first or second meeting, as we described above.

2. Ask the person to another meeting and attempt to get across again what the situation is and why it is not acceptable to you. If this is contested again, explain that the conversation could go on forever without reaching agreement and that you have to move things along and so bring the argument or discussion to a close.

3. Re-state your view, explain your need and what you want and use subjective language ('I believe...', 'I see...', 'I perceive...', 'I can't accept...', etc.').

4. Insist on your right and responsibility to request and require improved performance based on your responsibilities to the business, to your people and to the individual themselves. Get across that you have no choice and that you are doing it out of your responsibility to others and to the person and doing so fairly, honestly and respectfully.

5. Ask the individual to come back with a plan of what they will do to meet your requirements and deliver the kind of performance you and the organisation needs. Put a deadline on this.

6. In a non-patronising way, state that you see the person as a very valuable resource, as a key person in the department or area, and as having enormous potential. State that it is your wish that

this potential be used for the good of the organisation and for the individual themselves.

7. Throughout the meeting, work hard at genuinely caring for the person and being concerned for their real welfare.

There are several important things going on in this conversation that make a great difference to how the meeting goes and how the person responds.

First, the language being used is subjective language. This has several benefits:

1. It cannot be challenged as it is *your* opinion, *your* view, *your* position. No one can challenge your thinking or your conclusions and deny your right to think as you do. If you have reached a conclusion then that is your opinion and no one can take it away from you. This is your judgment of the situation and it is your right and your responsibility to form your opinion and communicate such a judgment. If you are genuinely unhappy with the situation and the person's performance, the other person can't tell you how to feel. It is not contestable.

2. Stating things subjectively is also more respectful. It does not claim that this is how things are or impose your reality on the other person; it merely lets them know how you genuinely think and feel. This gets the same message across but it is easier for the other person to hear.

3. It is focused on the future, what you want and what you want from the other person. The future, unlike the past, is controllable, and can be influenced. It gives the person something that they can do or aim at to resolve the issue.

4. Subjective language is positively focused since it concentrates on what you want and need rather than what the other person is not doing or not doing well enough.

5. It leaves the responsibility with the other person and so invites and challenges *them* to do something.

6. It gives the person the time and space to think about this and to come up with a plan to address your needs. No one likes to be cornered. Any animal when cornered will fight back. This avoids producing a reaction by giving the person space.

7. Giving the person the time and space to decide what to do prevents any loss of face for the person or any sense that they

have lost the battle. There are no winners and losers but the chance for both to be winners.

8. Subjective language is caring. The meeting is handled with care and fondness for the other person, and there is a clearly stated belief in the other person and a real desire for them to be OK too.

9. It respects and holds on to both pillars – the professional and personal – all the time.

10. It appeals to reason, fairness and what is right for and is actually helpful to the other person in terms of changing and improving, which is ultimately the goal.

Well handled as the situation may be by you, there is always the risk of a reaction from people when they feel challenged. This is common and normal. When we challenge and confront people, very often they will:

- Defend themselves
- Give excuses
- Blame
- Bully
- Stonewall
- Threaten
- Deny
- Argue
- Make empty promises
- Complicate
- Undermine
- Lie
- Become emotional
- Take cheap shots

When this happens there is a great temptation or tendency for us to react and to:

- Become defensive
- Challenge and question excuses
- Become entangled

- Score counter points
- Become personal
- Become emotional
- Exaggerate to win a point
- Become sidetracked
- Dominate
- Pull rank

We have to be aware of these dangers and focus on the goal of the meeting, which is to get a change in performance by insisting on the legitimate need for that improved performance and leaving the responsibility with the other person to identify how they will commit to that. Don't get sidetracked!

And will this overall approach always work? And if it doesn't is it finally time for discipline?

No, it will not always work. As long as people are human and free, there is no guarantee that anything we do will work. We can find the most delicious water and bring the horse to it but imbibing it is still an equestrian decision.

Let's see where we may have got to in percentage terms.

Stage 1 – The First Meeting

This was the first meeting or meetings we looked at, which were about making the person aware of what is happening against what is required before moving to the next stage. We said that this stage cannot and should not be taken for granted in a rush to bring things to a head and get into some kind of disciplinary process. We must give it and the person a chance.

This will deal with 90 per cent of people.

Stage 2 – The Last Resort Meeting

We called this the Last Resort Meeting. This involved making the person aware of what is 'not on' – what you cannot accept and will not accept. Ensure they are aware that the situation, whatever it is, is not acceptable to you and that you are unable to tolerate it. They should be given time to digest this and to come back with a satisfactory plan and commitment to improve. This will deal with 80 per cent of the remaining 10 per cent.

So, we can take it that finally now it is time for taking disciplinary action against the remaining 2 per cent? Maybe, but there is still one stage left which we call:

Stage 3 – The Last, Last Resort Meeting

This involves making the person aware of the sanctions that will have to be imposed if there is no change or a real commitment to changing. You make it clear that this is not *your* doing but is a consequence of *their* unwillingness or inability to subscribe to the necessary conditions for operating as a member of the department or organisation.

This may deal with half of the remaining 2 per cent. But you don't issue a threat of action to the person, you point out the consequences.

What's the difference between issuing a threat and pointing out the consequences?

With a threat the emphasis is on what the person threatening will do. And because there is a certain 'dare' in it, the other person may feel aroused to take it on and see if you will carry it through, if only to prove or test something. They don't have to do anything and the onus is on the manager or person issuing the threat. Sometimes the carrying out of the threat can actually create a whole new situation in which the culprit becomes the victim. Some wildcat strikes happen as a result of hearing what they have done to Tommy!

What is being communicated in the Last Last Resort Meeting is not a threat but a *consequence* – the consequence of the person continuing to behave as they are currently doing. It is saying that if you continue to operate like this, here's what will happen, just like if you jumped out of this fourth floor window you would break a leg.

This works really well. I first used this on an assignment with Digital Corporation many years ago. John, a good and important worker in the warehouse section, had got into an unacceptable absentee pattern, mostly on Monday mornings. I coached the person's manager on handling John, who had a frank conversation with him along the lines of:

Manager: John, do you know what happens here when you don't appear on a Monday morning?
John: Eh no...not really.

Manager: Well, when you are not in, there is chaos here. I have to go running around looking for someone to fill in and no one comes near your standard or knows nearly as much as you do. It is mayhem. And I really can't live with this anymore. I am not going to.

So I want you to decide if you want to continue to work here or want to lose your job. Because that is what will happen if you continue to miss Mondays. Is that clear?

John: Yeah, I suppose.

Manager: Good, it is important that you do as it is your decision.

John: OK.

Now, of course there was no guarantee that this would have worked or would work in every case, but it did here. John dramatically improved his attendance at work, kept his job and everyone won.

What made the difference again was the attention to both pillars:

- Letting him know how valued he was (People or Personal Pillar) and

- Letting him know that his behaviour could no longer be tolerated (Task Pillar).

In addition, there was no threat, just a naming of the consequences of his behaviour.

But this seems an inordinate amount of time to get the disciplinary process underway...

Maybe. But look at the advantages of going this road:

1. It will reduce disciplinary situations by a factor of five or ten. This brings enormous gains in terms of time saved alone. Disciplinary procedures especially at the later stages can take days to prepare and can involve very highly paid people from within and without the organisation.

2. The success rate at disciplinary hearing is probably only 50 per cent anyway.

3. There is a great contribution to the improvement of the overall climate of the company from going this route rather than the punishing and disciplinary route.

4. There may be no loss of time at all as most people will recognise and will accept that excellent procedures have been followed and with great care.

5. The chances of winning the disciplinary cases that do occur will be improved enormously from the caring and professional way the situation was handled throughout.

6. It will prevent individual issues escalating and becoming major group issues.

Handling emotions

One of the reasons we shirk getting into these kinds of meetings is because of the emotions that such meetings can produce. The consequences of this are of two kinds:

• Sadness, upset and tears.

• Anger, upset and abusive language.

The first thing on handling emotions is to *expect* them or be ready for them. When we challenge another human being and confront them on their behaviour, it is only to be expected that they may become upset. How we handle it is important. What do we do? Here are some pointers, and I have taken the example of a female who is crying (females *tend* to show their emotions more by crying; men do so by getting angry).

1. Don't be surprised if the person becomes emotional.

2. If they do (e.g. cry), acknowledge it. 'I see you are upset/angry.'

3. Allow space and time for them to deal with it, while...

4. Interjecting with comments like: 'I can understand why you are upset' [silence, sobs or angry language]...'I am sorry you are feeling like this' [more sobs or anger] ... 'It is not easy to hear these things and I understand how difficult it can be to hear them' [less and less sobs and anger]... 'It is not easy for me to say these things but I have to.' etc.

5. Be patient, understanding and tolerant, and get the conversation back on track as soon as you can, at an appropriate time.

6. If they ask to finish the meeting, try to convince them to continue by telling them you would prefer to carry on the meeting if that

is OK with them. Reaffirm that it is understandable that they are upset.

We often act out of a mindset that becoming emotional is bad and is a sign of weakness. We need to drop this way of thinking and make it OK for people to be emotional. What they do with their emotion is what matters – how they handle it and we can help them handle it by our own handling of the situation.

This chapter has been about unsatisfactory performance in the workplace and how to handle it while managing to be human. I hope it is fairly clear that the more human we are, the more effective will be our handling of these situations.

Chapter 22

Deciding in a Human Way, or Making Good Decisions

'Concerning all acts of initiative and creation, there is one elementary truth...that the moment one definitely commits oneself then Providence moves, too.'

– Goethe

Decision making is very often not a problem for us managers. Indeed, we find it easy to make decisions. We often feel that this is what we are for. At times it looks as if there is a sadistic streak in us. The 'No pain, no gain' philosophy, 'Being cruel to be kind' and 'Able to make the hard calls' are often touted as essential qualities for the good manager and we use these as endorsements for taking what sometimes can be hard, cold and cruel decisions. Some companies see these as essential qualities for a manager to have and believe that you need to have a male appendage to make it in the ruthless business world.

If making decisions is not a major issue for many managers, making *good ones* is, I believe, an issue for *all* managers.

But what IS a good decision?

Good question. I suppose it is ultimately only with hindsight that a decision can be adjudged to have been a good one or not based on whether it worked out well or not. So in this chapter I am only talking about upping the chances of making good decisions. I am defining a good decision as *a proposed direction that is the wisest in terms of getting optimum results and stands the best chance of being well carried out.*

And how can you guarantee or ensure that? You can't. One can only increase the chances of it happening. How?

There are various decision-making styles. I narrow them down to four. To understand them, imagine a few decisions that you take or might take at work and apply each of the styles below to them.

- **Decision-Making Style 1**: *'I decide'* – 'I decide that Tom will transfer to the new division, that Teresa will take Tom's job. End of story.'

- **Decision-Making Style 2** is similar to Style 1: *'I decide but I would like to hear what problems my decision might cause, and, if I can, try to resolve them or lessen them or their effects. But I am not changing my decision'* – 'So, Tom goes to the new division but I may try to help him accept it by remaining open about the date or giving some help with a transfer allowance or something. And, yes, Teresa will be given training to help her assume Tom's old job. Clear?'

- **Decision-Making Style 3**: *'I have a very good idea or proposal for this situation and it is what I would like to do, but I am open to other proposals or even improvements to my own. But if I don't hear any better ones, I will go with mine'* – 'Here, I actually think Tom making the move is the best way to go but I *am* open to better ideas if anyone has any. Has anyone any better ideas than Teresa taking over from Tom? I am open to them if there are some good ones. If not, I will go with my own idea.'

- **Decision-Making Style 4:** *'I or we have a problem or decision to take. I would like to hear ideas and suggestions on what to do'* – 'We need someone to handle the new job in Division X. What do people suggest we do?'

So, are you able to apply the different styles to the situations you thought of?

Have you any idea which style is the right or best one? Yes, you're right. They are *all* valid. It depends on the situation. But they are all different in terms of their effects.

Let's look at how they rate in terms of their immediate acceptance or the initial degree of commitment they win. Remember that implementation is one of the ingredients a good decision should have.

The model looks like this:

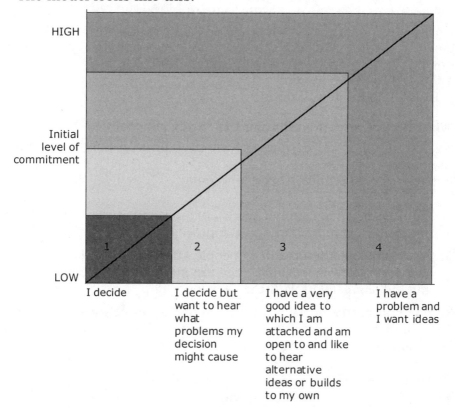

22.1. Decision-making styles.

So, from this you can see that if you go with Decision-Making Style 4, you stand a much better chance of getting support than if you go with Decision- Making Style 1. And, the more we go in that direction – towards Decision Making Style 4 – the greater the level of initial commitment.

So, what about Decision Making Style 1? Is it out?

No, not at all. Have you thought of when and in what circumstances it might be appropriate to use Decision-Making Style 1?

It can be used in two different situations:

1. When the decision is about something of minor importance and is straightforward and so docs not need or will not benefit from the input of others.

2. When it is a difficult or unpopular decision.

It is here that some of those qualities of resolve and strength we mentioned at the beginning of this chapter come into play. Unpopular or tough decisions are not occasions when we should go getting votes. Cutting a team from ten people to eight should not be decided on by a show of hands from the ten in question! *You* need to make the call.

But it has to be well done.

What do you mean well done? Is it not simple?

No, and it is here where most of the problems on tough or unpopular decisions arise.

There are essentially three problems:

1. Your decision might not work out and so you may have to go back on it, reverse it and in the process lose face and time.

2. You may lose the person or people affected – their loyalty, their support – forever because they are so upset or angry, or are in such disagreement with the decision.

3. Apart from the decision itself, you don't handle the communication of it well and so you create a new problem or exacerbate the existing one.

So there are three principles to be observed when taking a decision using Decision-Making Style 1.

1. Be as sure as you can that your decision is a good one and that you will be able to carry it out.

2. Ensure you have a plan or strategy to 'look after' or heal the wounds of those negatively affected by your decision.

3. Give reasons for your decision so that people understand the rationale for the decision, even if they don't agree with it.

Very often – too often – the biggest problem arises from how we handle the *communication* of the decision. We want to avoid a confrontation so we tell people by email or on a Friday evening or send them a letter.

This was the issue behind the suspension of shares of Payzone in January of 2008. The Chief Executive John Nagle was informed through an email on his Blackberry that he was being dismissed from this €400,000 job.

314

Why would people handle unpopular decisions, as in Style 1, poorly?

Managers taking unpopular or tough decisions fear that their decision will be questioned and challenged if they give reasons for it and so they avoid all that by simply informing the person of the blunt decision without any effort to explain why. This, then, becomes a new problem or exacerbates the existing one. It demonstrates or gets used to prove that the decision was a poor one in the first instance.

By giving reasons we are at least giving the person or people affected every chance to understand the decision, even if at that particular moment they refuse to acknowledge the validity of our explanation or see any merit in the decision. Even if this happens, the reasons, if genuine and sound, will continue to work on them after the meeting.

But there is an additional reason for explaining the rationale for your decision – you may want the decision receiver, the person or people immediately impacted by your decision, to implement the decision and to do it wholeheartedly and well. The last thing you want them doing in this instance is simply going along with your decision and telling people that they don't actually agree with it at all but have been asked to implement it.

You might feel that if they don't agree with it, they don't agree with it. There is nothing more you can do. You can't brainwash them. That is true, but you do have to ensure that they run with and communicate the decision because they are in agreement with it.

The question arises – but if they are not in agreement with it, how can they say they are? The answer is because they respect the rules of the game, one of which is that in certain instances you, the manager, make the decision, *you* call it.

And how would I get someone to implement a decision that they don't believe in or agree with?

Here are a few steps you might take that should get you there or at least help to do so:

1. Work out the rationale for the decision – why it is a good thing to do or the right thing to do, or the most meaningful thing to do.

2. Invite the person to share the issue or problem; help them to understand it and to accept that it is problem that needs attention.

3. Explain your reasoning to them – why it is a good thing to do or the right thing to do, or the most meaningful thing to do in your opinion.

4. Work hard to get an understanding of and agreement to this from the other person and engage in real dialogue with them, explaining your thinking and listening to theirs.

5. Be open to being convinced of alternatives or useful and important amendments to your decision.

6. If agreement is reached after this then the decision is a good one and the person will be able to make it happen as their own.

7. If there is not agreement, as the manager, you have to request the person to go along with the decision as their decision also. This has to be done out of respect for the position of the manager or leader. The employee or person involved has to take this on board as part of the arrangement they bought into when they joined the organisation.

8. This has to be done in a truly respectful way and without any hint of threat. It is expected out of a sense of loyalty to the team of which the person is a member.

9. Some points that may help the decision receiver might be:

   - This is how you, as the manager, have to operate on occasion out of respect for your own manager and loyalty to the organisation.

   - It is or should be only an issue in 5 or 10 per cent of cases.

   - Nobody is always right so the chance exists that everybody, including the decision receiver, may actually be wrong, even when they believe firmly they are right.

   - Explain that you, as the manager, have made an honest attempt to explain the reasons for the decision, but, notwithstanding this, it is inevitable that people will not always agree on everything and this has to be resolved.

   - Explain that sometimes people simply can't live with a decision taken as the issue is so serious and the person so certain about their position. Most times in life and in work this is not the case and you certainly hope it is not the case on this occasion either.

- Point out that you, as the manager, have a different and possibly broader perspective on the issue than the decision receiver and it is this that requires you to make the call.

So there is nothing new in this really. I make the call and simply ask the decision receiver to go along with it?

Yes and no. What is or may be different to the usual is that you are making every effort to help the person understand the rationale for your decision, so they understand that you are implementing it for that reason and not just because you are the boss. This is both respectful and helpful to them in going along with the decision, even if they are still not convinced.

But don't we always do that?

It's great if that is always the case. However, I believe that often it isn't. We take short-cuts and use our organisational position or our hierarchical or managerial power to let the person know what we want. We do this in small things, which may be OK, but then we behave the same way on more important issues.

And what of it if we do? Maybe we have to sometimes?

No, we don't have to. And every time we do so we are doing untold damage to the people involved and to the organisation we belong to. This is because we are in fact coercing, even bullying, the person.

That's a very strong word...

I wonder. Whenever we ask someone to do something that does not accord with their way of thinking and we disregard their views and wishes, it is extremely disrespectful, violent and damaging. In essence, we are asking a person to cease being a human being for this particular situation. We know what this leads to and the inhumanity it can produce in extreme situations, like in the cases of those who were 'only following orders' during the Nazi holocaust. But it is always damaging to people to behave in this way, and to us and to the organisation.

How could it damage the organisation?

In two ways:

1. Whenever we do anything that damages the thinking of people in the organisation we are damaging the intellectual strength of

the organisation, and reducing the thinking asset or power in the organisation. It will be a poorer organisation in terms of thinking. We are changing the currency from what makes sense to one based on my hierarchical power. People will stop questioning and will go along with things they should not; they may even do stupid things or not spot things that they should.

2. When we don't give people reasons for decisions to help them understand, we reduce the sense of meaningfulness in the organisation. We need people to feel that what they are doing makes sense. Human beings desperately need this, and if we damage the overall sense of meaning by denying it in particular instances we are reducing the overall meaning of what we are doing and weakening them and the organisation. This will make our overall task more difficult. Every time we don't try to make sense of something to people and don't try to persuade them that something does make sense, we have less to play with in terms of future understanding and commitment. Their own contributions and performance will also suffer because things don't make as much sense to them as before and don't satisfy their innate need for meaning.

But let's recap and check where we are in all of this.

We have been spending time on Decision-Making Style 1 because it is the most problematic one for all the reasons we have mentioned. We know when we should go with that particular style and how to do so well.

To go back to the other styles, as we have said, we do gain more initial support the more we move to the right and involve people in the decision.

But this is not the main reason for doing so.

The main reason is that we will take better decisions if we involve people.

How? Will it not complicate things and confuse people and weaken your authority as a decision maker?

Not at all. None of these things need apply.

We are operating in line with the truth of the situation and of all situations that we will take better decisions if we are better informed. And getting the views and perspectives of people around us will make us better informed. 'None of us is as clever as all of us.' It would be quite foolish not to involve people in the decision when that is needed, as in complex decisions, when, of course, it is not an unpopular decision for some of the people involved. We get more opinions, more points of view and more angles on the issue if we listen to other people. Therefore we will up the chances of it being a good decision, which was our goal at the outset of this section.

I love one part in the book *The Little Prince* by Antoine de Saint-Exupery.

The Little Prince is visiting various planets and then arrives at a very special one with a very special king.

> For what the king fundamentally insisted upon was that his authority should be respected. He tolerated no disobedience. He was an absolute monarch. But because he was a very good man, he made his orders reasonable.
>
> 'If I ordered a general', he would say, by way of example, 'if I ordered a general to change himself into a sea bird, and if the general did not obey me, that would not be the fault of the general. It would be my fault...If I ordered a general to fly from one flower to another, like a butterfly, or to write a tragic drama, or to change himself into a sea bird, and if the general did not carry out the order that he had received, which one of us would be in the wrong?' the king demanded, 'The general or myself?'
>
> 'You,' said the prince firmly.
>
> 'Exactly. One must require from each one the duty which each one can perform,' the king went on. 'Accepted authority rests first of all on reason. If you ordered your people to go and throw themselves into the sea, they would rise up in revolution. I have the right to require obedience because my orders are reasonable.[34]

That's fine. But what if there is not agreement among everyone about what is the right way to go and the best thing to do?

Yes, that may happen but it does not have to happen if the situation is handled well and the right environment is established. If people are listening to each other then there is a very good chance that the truth of the situation will emerge and become clear. The combination of all the different points of view will throw more light on the actual situation and, as a result, it should become clearer.

But what if it doesn't?

It often may not despite the best efforts of everyone. In this case, the manager or leader makes the decision.

Will people not feel disgruntled if, after being asked for their opinions, you, the manager, then go and make the call and take the decision over their heads?

Not necessarily. And it will help if the ground rules are stated and agreed up front, namely that, while all the opinions will be shared and heard, in the event of there being no consensus, you will make the call and decide what is right and best. That this is your responsibility as the manager or leader.

But will some people not feel annoyed if their particular line of thinking or what they really wanted was not followed?

This can happen, especially if people have become attached to their way forward or feel deeply emotional about the issue. For this very reason the manager or leader should:

1. Acknowledge and repeat the valid points of view of those people who want to go an alternative way on the issue.

2. Again re-state the reasons for wanting to go this way.

3. Ask the people in disagreement if they are OK with that and state that you would very much like them to be able to live with the decision taken.

And what if they can't live with it?

They most proably will live with it. If they are shown this level of respect and are helped to understand the rationale for the decision, it is extremely unlikely that they will not be willing to go with the decision being taken.

So, to make this more practical, let us use a simple example.

Suppose you are the manager of a company in London and you have a problem. You need someone to manage an office of the company in Manchester and that someone will be from the company office in London.

Let's look at four ways you could handle this decision.

You could call a meeting of the appropriate people and pose the problem: 'We need someone experienced in our Manchester office because of X. What do you think we should do? Any ideas?' (Decision-Making Style 4). The final decision will be yours, of course, but you want to know what people think and to go with what is best.

You could also call a meeting and tell them about the problem and that you have a good idea to which you are attached, namely that Peter should move to the Manchester office. But you let the group know that you are open to other or better ideas on how to solve it or to improvements to your own ideas. If you don't hear better ideas you will go with this one (Decision-Making Style 3).

You could announce your decision and tell Peter that you want him to go to the Manchester office, with effect from the first of the following month. You tell him that this is your decision, which you will not change, but that you would like to hear if he has problems with the decision that you can resolve (Decision-Making Style 2). These might be about timing or some conditions or career guarantees.

Finally, you could tell Peter and others that you want him to fill the vacancy in the Manchester office with effect from the first of the next month, without the involvement of or any discussion with anyone else on the team (Decision-Making Style 1).

As we have already seen, this decision, which is final, does need to be handled well and so you need to be sure it is the right decision for Peter to go to Manchester. You need to be confident that you can re-build Peter's morale if the decision has dealt it a blow. You also need to give Peter your reasons for this decision and help him to understand them, which does not mean that the decision is still open for discussion. But it will help him to go along with it, even if he is not willing at the meeting, there and then.

A word on Decision-making Style 3 before we leave this chapter. This is a great style to use because it allows you to bring your ideas or proposed way forward to the group and to invite and challenge them to improve it or change it. It is a great way to test your ideas and to enrich or improve them. It also shows real leadership because it means you will have given the topic your best thinking before exploring it with the team. Some managers sometimes abuse teams by failing to do their own thinking before asking their teams for their ideas. Others fear that doing so, sharing their ideas, might inhibit the team. It need not do so if people are clear about the four Decision Making Styles.

I hope I've proved in this chapter that these four styles of decision making are human and respectful. They are also effective, since they will actually lead to better decisions being taken and to more decisions being well implemented.

Chapter 23

Managing Difficult People

'Don't go around saying the world owes you a living. The world owes you nothing. It was here first.'

– Mark Twain

*Everyone said he was the most difficult person they had ever worked with. If he was no good at his job it would have made it easier to complain about him but he was very talented and valuable. But whether it was paranoia, downright insecurity or a cleverly concealed lust for power, he made life nigh impossible for everyone, or at least for those he had his knife in. Though he claimed several had their knife in **him**. Any question of significance that was put to him was taken as a personal attack. Criticism of his work often ended up having to be withdrawn and an apology demanded and given, and reluctantly accepted in a bad spirit. Inordinate amounts of time were spent investigating trivial matters in order to protect his 'good name and reputation'. His vendettas against one or two key individuals, enemies, were notorious and required a lot of managing. These were especially aimed at the Financial Director, who challenged him on claimed expenses for a visit to a plant in Hamburg. The expenses were submitted without any or enough receipts. When he was challenged on it, his good name, reputation and human rights were all dragged into it and the war raged on until the Financial Director was asked to back off for the sake of some peace. But peace there never was as his personal vendetta against the Financial Director was launched there and then and continued endlessly. But not everyone saw him in a bad light. Senior Managers from Head Office were won over by his attention to them when they visited the company and by his loyalty to the company. No one surpassed him in charm when* *the vice-presidents came to town. And many people pointed to his great performance and results. Scarcely had the visitors left when the daggers were drawn once more.*

If there is one thing certain it is that we will find some of the people we deal with in life to be difficult to handle.

To ensure that what I will say here is both relevant and meaningful, why not right now think of some such people or situations in your working life.

When I talk to groups about this topic, I phrase the issue differently. I normally ask the group if they 'know of or have difficult people' in their working lives. It is probably the question that gets the most nodding heads. There seems to be universal agreement that there *are* difficult people in the world and we all get our share of them in our various walks of life.

In these situations, when I look at the group in front of me, I often wonder if some of the difficult people in people's heads are actually in the room. I feel pretty sure that some people have identified as difficult colleagues or others who are in the group. In some cases the 'difficult' people in question may know this. They may have actually selected as difficult the very people who have selected *them*. It's an amusing and interesting dynamic.

I am sure that if we did get all those 'difficult people' in the room, they in turn would identify other difficult people. If we were able to do this on a sufficiently wide scale we might probably find that everyone is a difficult person in some other person's book.

At this point I show them the image of the cat and the dog.

23.1. Taking responsibility for our relationships.

I ask them what is going on and they tell me various things, but they recognise the key message that each one is annoying the other.

The point is that, when we come across a so-called difficult person, we are really talking of how *we* feel, of the effect or impact of that person on *us*. We are feeling something and attributing the cause of that feeling to how another person is behaving. Rather than saying I have someone difficult in my life, it might be more accurate to say there is someone that I find difficult, meaning that I, by my thinking and reacting, find it difficult to deal with them. So because the cat believes the dog will attack, it is feeling fearful, is labelling the dog as an attacker and so becomes aggressive. This in turn leads to the dog, on seeing this aggression, believing that the cat will attack it. The dog equally feels some fear, labels the cat as typically aggressive and so also feels the need to become aggressive. But what starts the whole cycle going are the beliefs, 'prejudices' and feelings of the cat or the dog. It is these that lead them to label the other as aggressive, difficult, dangerous, and impossible to live with.

When I say this to people I know what some will be thinking. They will feel that I am laying all the responsibility for the bad relationship on *them*. They will believe that it is not so in their case. They firmly believe that in their case it is not they who are at fault, but the difficult person in their lives. They will claim that everyone who knows the person would agree with this. Sometimes they will tell stories of the person in question if that is a safe thing to do. They will regale me with examples of how impossible this person is and of how hard they have tried to handle the situation well. They will tell me that 'everyone' agrees with them. If the person is a public *persona non grata* in the eyes of a few in the room, they will turn to the group for support for their viewpoint and so get endorsement for the purity of their intention and action. A gauntlet has been thrown down to me and to my nice little model and theory. They often throw me a sop in the form of agreeing with the overall point I am making, once I concede that there are exceptions to the rule such as theirs.

Now, I am wise enough not to dare take these people on in front of a group. I know I will fail to convince them of how they might be wrong for a lot of reasons – loss of face (for either of us), group support for the individual against the teacher, lack of articulacy on my part, and so on. Even more than any of those, I will fail because it will take a very big jump in honesty and humility on the part of the person to get to the real truth of their situation. And, they will never know anyway until they try a different behaviour with the difficult person. But, let's park that one for now and we will come back to it. Let's return to the general principle with which virtually everyone will agree.

The principle is that very often we react to some behaviour or feature in another person which affects us negatively. In many cases the person is not having nearly the same effect on other people as they are having on us. We can explain this by believing that we are more sensitive or more perceptive than others, but we don't really believe this to be so in all cases. For example, I can regard a colleague in a meeting as dominant because I want to have my say and I lack the confidence to participate in the conversation. What is going on for me is that my own insecurity or lack of confidence is being triggered and I am feeling badly. I label a feeling of insecurity on my part as 'dominating' in the other person. It may be that it is my own need or desire to play a major part or even dominate that is being thwarted by the behaviour of my colleague, but of course I project my own feelings on to him and name him as the guilty and aggressive party.

One of my first reactions when this happens to me is to get confirmation that the problem lies exclusively with the other person. So, I go to those who will sympathise or identify with my point of view and comment to them about how dominating our colleague is. I will cite an example from the meeting to back up my case in order to get cooperation or collusion to label my 'difficult' colleague as a dominator, or show-off or overly ambitious. If we can rope some more people into the jury, all the better. I have begun a mini-war led by me against the other person. Every time any instance of similar behaviour occurs in the future, we will use it as incontrovertible evidence that we are right in our judgment of that person.

What I am after through this action is to increase the pressure for the person I approach, my colleague or friend, to do something about the person's dominating behaviour or whatever behaviour it is that is getting to me. Whoever that someone is, be it our manager or the group as a whole, the one person it will *not* be is me. Through my action I have effectively disempowered myself by disowning any part in the relationship difficulty. My whole campaign has as its objective to make it clear that all the fault lies with the 'difficult' person, the enemy. The more I do this, the more difficult it will be for me to look at how I might be a part of the problem. I have handed over responsibility and power to act to another person, group or authority.

These little tiffs might seem innocuous if they were confined to the level of personalities. Unfortunately, in organisations, they get linked to work and so we use work situations in the war with the other person. We link some work situation to our battle with the other person and it gets charged with all the emotion of the negative dynamic. Others join in or get roped in to the struggle and work gets carried out against this background. Work sinks into the background. Everything gets measured in terms of the part it plays in the personal fight. Company politics often begins with such an episode. There is not one factor in the life of any business that does more damage to the welfare of the company than internal politics. It is a poison that seriously damages the life of the organisation and robs it of energy and synergy. It acts like a demon god that can make good bad and bad good. What would seem like good news for everyone can in fact be perceived as bad news, depending on which faction is seen to gain from it.

I can remember many years ago arriving early to the office in the morning. My manager came in with a glint in his eye. At the time we had one large client on which much of the business depended. Let's call this client Computonics. He stood at the door of my office and announced: 'We have lost the Computonics account! I just got a phone call.' Now this was a minor tragedy for us all. My manager, however, while trying to tell me this with all the tragedy it implied, found it hard to keep the smile off his face. What was going on was that his arch rival in the company was responsible for the Computonics account. He had been warring with him for some time and both of them had clashed over the handling of the account. Now, with the loss of Computonics, he knew that a huge blow had been struck for his cause against that of his rival. This example is far from unique. In my dealings with companies I am generally surprised when I come across a situation where everyone seems to want and rejoice in the same thing. I find the contrary to be more often the case: Good news for one is bad news for another.

Back to our cat and dog. This is where many of these wars begin. At the heart of every issue there will be a personal agenda of some kind – two people driving each other mad and neither one willing or able to break the negative cycle. To break the cycle, the negative dynamic has to be nipped in the bud.

How can this be done? One way is for the person to learn to think about the cat and dog scenario and so whenever any difference arises they can be wise enough to take stock and ask the question: 'How am I a part of this issue?' We are always part of the problem and so must be always part of the solution. This involves getting in touch with your feelings and taking ownership of them. It involves recognising that what the other person has done or is doing is touching or triggering some reaction in me for which I must take responsibility. In so doing, I am stopping at the outset a chain reaction resulting from:

- An event or happening.
- A thought or prejudice.
- A negative feeling.
- Blaming the other person.
- A negative reaction.
- A new event or happening for the other person, and so on.

If I only do this I will at least have prevented some behaviour of mine triggering a similar reaction in the other person and so worsening the situation in a downward spiral. If I realise that my feeling of being rejected by a colleague for not including me in a project is more about my own need for recognition than about a deliberate intention on their part to belittle or punish me, then I will at least be able to refrain from accusing them of being devious or ambitious. I do not take it as a personal attack on me. I am taking responsibility for my own emotions.

This does not mean that I do nothing, that I simply ignore what has happened. It means that, in actual fact, I am in a far better position to deal with it in a more rational, measured and clearer way than if I am lost in confusion about where the real problem actually is. Once I am clear about my part in it or possible part in it, I can deal with it in a truly effective way. Suppose, for example, that I suspect a colleague is deliberately excluding me from some work or project in which I believe I should be involved. I do my work on myself and take on board the fact that how I feel about the situation and how I feel about the other person has a lot to do with me and how I am. Now I am freed up to raise the issue in a very measured and professionally fair way with the other person. Suppose, for the sake of the example, that I don't raise very valid business reasons as to why I should not be excluded from the project and focus on the purely personal or emotional ones. I can still handle it in an easy and acceptable way. It might go something like:

> Me: May I talk to you about something? [Always try to get agreement at every step of the conversation. Here it is agreement to merely have the conversation. That is a help. It *is* an agreement.]
> Colleague: Sure.
> Me: Recently I have noticed that there have been a few projects where I felt I might and should have been included but you did not involve me.
> Colleague: For example?
> Me: Well, the work being done on area X and the new development Y.
> Colleague: Ok!
> Me: On these occasions I felt I ought to have been involved and when I wasn't I felt excluded and ignored. I want you to know that is how I felt when you did not include me.

The conversation can go on from here and may take various forms like the other person giving reasons for why they did not include me, assuring me that that was never their intention. However they deal with it, they are now aware of how I feel about it and are equipped with all the information to handle it differently in future.

They know:

- That there is an issue.

- That they have done something.

- How I felt when they did what they did.

There is no guarantee at all that they will handle it differently in future but at least they now have all the information to handle it in a better and more human way. And, apart from information, they may have some motivation to deal with it differently in future, based on how I handled the situation and that I did not blame them for anything. I took responsibility for my own feelings and made them aware of them.

Had I not taken responsibility for my part in it and for how I felt, I would have ended up blaming and criticising them and probably making the situation worse by creating a new war or exacerbating the present one.

Imagine if I had handled it like this:

> Me: I want a word with you. You are deliberately excluding me from projects just to belittle me and make me feel small. I know what you are at. Well. I can tell you, you will not get away with this. People like you...'

In this case I am throwing all the blame on to the 'dog' for how I feel. And it is extremely likely I will get a strong negative reaction.

When you are aware of the cat and dog dynamic you will spot it all over the place and see it appearing in all kinds of conversations: 'He deliberately ignores me', 'She always puts me down', 'They are very dishonourable', 'We cannot trust people who are dishonest and hide the facts...', and so on.

I worked with a married couple some years ago who were having some trouble in their relationship. When I spoke with the woman about the situation she told me:

'I am at home all day on my own and it can be lonely. I am dying for someone to talk to. But when he comes home in the evening, it's a case of in he comes and picks up the paper or plonks down in front of the television or at the table waiting for his dinner. Never a 'How are you? How was your day?' not to mention a hug or a kiss. Isn't that awful?'

'Yes, awful,' I said.

When I spoke to him he told me:

'I have a very stressful job. I spend all my time listening to people giving out and complaining and generally being so damn negative. When I get home in the evening, I want a little peace. But I barely have the key in the door when I get a torrent of complaints and negativity – 'This is broken', 'I wasn't feeling well today', 'Fiona's baby is in hospital.' I can't take that after a hard day so I just read the paper or turn on the TV or try to have my dinner in peace.'

So what was going on was fairly obvious. She complained to get attention and he would not give her attention because she was always complaining. Each triggered the behaviour they were criticising and disliked in the other. It would remain like this in a form of homeostasis or endless war unless someone broke the cycle. They would each get their witnesses to support them – other women friends on her side and mates in the pub on his side. The more they each did this, the more difficult it would be for them to get to what was really required – each of them to take responsibility for how they were triggering the negative responses in the other person. Sometimes life in the form of a tragedy or an illness will break the cycle for us but we should not wait for life to intervene and bring us to our senses in a harsh way.

The So-Called Exceptions

To get back to the question we talked about at the beginning of this chapter about the so-called exceptions – you know those cases where people believe that what is going on has nothing at all to do with them. Everyone agrees that the person in question is very difficult – aggressive, ignorant, a bully, selfish, devious, manipulative, etc. OK, let's assume that this is the case and that there is a person who is seriously flawed in terms of behaviour or very poor at engaging in healthy and meaningful relationships.

Even if this is the case we can still take the initiative. We can still take responsibility for the situation and, by our behaviour, try to do something about it. This is extremely difficult in such instances where we feel zero responsibility and may even see the person as a hopeless case. It is a situation requiring 'someone' to do something about it, and often we believe that that 'someone' is a person in authority and certainly not *us*.

So, what can we do? Someone who is behaving like this is needy in some way. They are expressing this need in a particular and not very helpful way. What is called for is an accurate reading of what it is the person needs and some understanding of why they are the way they are. Once we have this, we can find all kinds of ways to handle them better in their and our own interests, such as:

- Take an initiative to do something about the dysfunctional behaviour, or

- Take an initiative to be able to make the most of the situation in spite of the behaviour of this person.

There is little point pressing the button on a coffee machine and expecting music or toast to come out. It does not do those things. This also applies to our difficult friend. We should not be surprised when we get a response from them that is not to our liking. We are expecting toast from a coffee percolator. Once we accept this we are half way there and we have at least prevented any worsening of the situation in a downward spiral.

In addition, once we accept the person as they 'are', we will be able to find relatively easy ways to manage them and help them get what they want in a more positive and less dysfunctional way. And, by accepting them as they are, we may be helping them to be better than they are currently being.

A female participant on a programme I was running came to me some time ago and asked me about a colleague of hers who always tried to take the credit for everything and consistently took advantage of her and the other team members. He was impossible to work with, she told me, and everyone in the team agreed. He was a good performer and seen to be such by management. She and some others had tried to raise the issue with their manager but they got nowhere and they were made to feel as if they were bitching and being jealous. It was so bad they had considered leaving the company.

Having listened to her, I knew there was no point in suggesting any more things she could do. Nor did I even dare to talk to her about the cat and dog dynamic. What I did do was get her to understand why this man was behaving the way he was, what the need behind it was. She said that while he wanted to get on in the company and appeared to be strong, in actual fact he was quite insecure. His manoeuvrings and dealings made him feel more insecure and more guilty. He was like a power addict.

Once she got to this understanding, whether it was a perfect analysis or not, she was in a very different place. She now realised that the bigger victim in the whole department was this person – a victim of his own thirst and need for glory. I then got her to a position where she was able to work out a survival plan for herself, built on her new ability to accept the situation and not waste untold energy, time and resources fighting it, criticising it and being endlessly disappointed and angry at it and at him. Huge problems and an interminable process were avoided. Peace reigned.

But surely, I hear you ask, one should not accept a situation like this? Surely one is bound to do something about such abusive behaviour and should not submit to a bully like this.

Giraffes have long necks

This is crucial. By *accepting* a situation like this, I mean that she accepts the reality of the situation, that this person is like this and that this is happening. I am only referring to that kind of acceptance. Giraffes have long necks. There is nothing else for it but to take reality as it is. We can plan later how we will house these giraffes but, for now, we have to accept that they are not like cows or sheep. They have inordinately long necks. Once we accept them for what they are, we can move on and decide what to actually *do* about it. If we spend time lamenting the fact that they are not like horses and become frustrated and angry over our predicament, we are wasting time and energy and avoiding taking action. I know the giraffe isn't an exact analogy for our manipulative, bullying friend because the giraffe can do nothing about its long neck while we believe our man can and should do something about his behaviour. However, it is our 'shoulding' people that trips us up and disempowers us. Our refusal to accept the reality of a situation, be it bad or good, is what blocks us from doing anything about the situation. We get lost in the past, in denial and in negativity.

Look at what happened to my friend who had the overbearing, dominating colleague. Once she came to terms with the reality of the situation, meaning she understood something about the man and where he was coming from, and accepted it as a reality, she changed. She told me she was going to do two things:

1.   Not let his behaviour get to her or unduly bother her.

2.   Call him on his behaviour at times and stand up to him.

I was amazed at the jump she had taken in a very short time. Accepting the colleague as he was, warts and all, freed her up to get on with her life and to be able to take challenge him if she felt the situation called for it. Ultimately it led to her empowerment.

Buying the morning paper

When we react to somebody else's behaviour, we are effectively handing over our power to them. We are letting *them* decide how *we* behave. A colleague of mine tells a story of two people going to work one morning. They stop at a newspaper kiosk and one of them chirpily says good morning to the vendor in the kiosk. All he gets back is a grunt.

The buyer says, 'Can I have my paper please?'

He gets back, 'What paper? How do I know what paper you want? I have a hundred different papers!'

The buyer, showing no upset, says: 'Well I get my paper here every morning...but anyway, it's *The Times*.' The vendor puts the paper on the counter in silence and the buyer thanks him and gives him the money, which gets thrown in the till without any acknowledgement. He again thanks the vendor and wishes him a good day, but the vendor ignores him and has engaged himself with something else.

As they walk away his friend says to him: 'What a rude and ignorant man! Why do you continue to buy your paper from him?' The other replies: 'It suits me. It is on my way. And why should I let *him* decide for me where I buy my paper?' This is what we do when we react to people who get to us; we let them decide how we behave.

I met my friend, the girl with the dominating manager, some time afterwards and I asked her how things were.

'Great,' she said. 'He has changed enormously.'

'He has changed?' I asked.

'Yes,' she said. 'He is much easier to deal with now.'

'How did that happen?' I asked.

'Oh,' she said, 'I called him on a few things and he seemed to realise what he was doing. We have much more respect for each other now and while he doesn't behave well at times, it doesn't get to me any more.'

What had happened was obvious, of course. We all need feedback and he had been getting none or not getting it in a way that he could hear. By having people only complaining about him or failing to let him know in a respectful, strong and adult way what he was doing, he was being given no real chance *or* help to change. It is quite amazing how we can help people to change and transform by how *we* are and how *we* behave. We are enormously powerful. We can even influence people above us in the hierarchy and it is this we will look at next.

For now we know that even with those difficult people we can manage to be human and, in the process, help them to be more human. This, in turn, makes us more human in an upward, ongoing spiral. God only knows where it might end!

Chapter 24

Pub Talk and Managing 'Up' – Managing Your Relationship with Your Manager

'Those are my principles. And if you don't like them…well, I have others.'

– Groucho Marx

'In work we talk about the pub and in the pub we talk about work' was an old adage I heard in my days in General Motors, as I mentioned earlier. In the pub most of what was said was about our managers and not all of it was positive. Much of it was moaning. It was all we could do. There was no other outlet for our gripes and criticisms. Nor did we know of any good way to make an impact on our situation. We were never trained for that. There were so many courses and programmes for managers. Many of these were to help managers manage to greater effect. These programmes were based on the traditional hierarchical model, meaning that the direction they gave was one-way and 'down'. It seems it is deemed necessary to prepare one set of people (managers) to manage or handle another set of people (employees). Is this not unfair? A little unbalanced? To prepare one group, managers, to handle another group, employees, and leave this second group to fend for themselves?

Quite apart from the unfairness of this, it seems to me that all those people – employees over whom managers have hierarchical power – need some help to ensure *they* are empowered. The managed need help as well as those managing. I see a real risk that many people will feel a lack of power over their work lives by virtue of working for people who have complete power over them and take decisions about and for them; people who:

- Take most of the decisions about what happens.
- Hold most of the responsibility for their areas of work.

- Control most of the environment in which they work.

- Do most of the thinking and planning on what is to be done.

In this case there is a strong possibility that many, many of the 'managed' will <u>not</u>:

- Take decisions about what happens but will cede decision making to others.

- Assume responsibility for many things but leave this to those in charge.

- Be proactive about their environment and area of work but become quite passive.

- Give too much time to thinking and planning as others will be doing it.

Isn't that a possibility at least? Haven't you seen instances of this in your company or in your experience?

I come across this very frequently on programmes I run for people in companies. It often comes in the form of a question: 'Will our managers be going through this programme also?' It is the answer to my question about why they are asking this that is most revealing. Generally, it is felt that their managers could well do with a dose of the same treatment and, indeed, could need it even more than they do. Dissatisfaction with how people are managed is fairly common. What is even more problematic for me in my efforts to change mindsets and behaviours is the feeling that, unless their managers change, there is little point asking *them* to change. Sometimes they will simply go along with what I am asking them to do but with little real commitment to follow through on it. Frequently people will hang back and ask me for advice on how they should handle their very difficult managers. I will hear example after example of how difficult their particular manager is and be clearly informed that everyone sees the manager in the same way. If I make any suggestion as to what they might try to do to deal with the situation, it gets batted away with, 'I tried that and it did not work' or 'No, that would not work in this case.' As a result, I have given up trying to give any such advice in these situations. Instead, I address the issue head on and up front as part of the programmes I run. The issue I address is disempowerment or, put more positively, the issue of how to truly empower and to make all people more powerful. Of course this is not easy. But it is important.

I start off by telling them a story: You have bought a house, your dream house, in the country. The deal is done – signed, sealed and delivered. You go to pick up the keys and the former owner hands them over to you and, just as they do, they say to you: 'Oh! One thing I forgot to mention. Sorry! As you know, that woodland there is yours. It goes with the house. But there is a bear who lives in the wood. Now you can't get rid of the bear or kill it. It's a protected species. Anyway, I hope you enjoy the house as much as we did. Good luck!'

So, what do you do?

Of course, you have the option of giving up the house and on your dream, etc.

Let's suppose you don't want to do that. Let's suppose you decide to stay and give it a go. What then? What could you do to make the most of the situation so you can live in your dream house?

24.1. Managing your bear.

Take a few minutes to make a note of at least five things you could do to make life tolerable in your new house with the big bear in the woodland beside you.

I have some options you might look at. However, before we look at them, can we, for the sake of learning, liken the bear to a manager? After all, while managers are not all like bears, many do share some of the bear's characteristics. They have a lot of strength and power. They are used to getting their own way and can like it. They can get upset and angry. And they can be needy.

For that reason it is important to know how to manage them and look after them. How?

Here are a few tips you might try:

1. Accept that you have a bear and that the bear is as he or she is. Don't be surprised.

2. Get to know your bear, what they need, what they like and don't like. Spend time on this and make a list of their needs, charactcristics, strengths and weaknesses. This will help you to understand how they may need *you*.

3. Feed your bear and look after them. Otherwise they may look after themselves. Plan this.

4. Be aware of your bear and the power they have. Learn to deal with this in your own way. Don't underestimate them. Look after yourself.

5. Don't frighten them or surprise them. Bears don't like to be surprised – unless it is with honey.

6. Work hard at building a relationship with your bear – it will make life easier and allow you to do what you want and need to do.

7. Try to set realistic boundaries for yourself and get the bear comfortable with them.

8. Don't set out to take them on or to change them as this can consume a lot of energy.

9. Be wise and your bear can be your biggest ally and will protect you. Not too many robbers are likely to roam around your house.

10. Don't play games with your bear. They won't understand it and won't like it and you may get hurt.

11. Respect them and have confidence in yourself and you may be able to build a relationship of mutual respect where you are able to face them and look them in the eye. Bears, too, have their fears.

12. Try to like them – like us they're OK deep down but are just animals who are looking after themselves and, like all of us, not always doing it in the best way.

So, which of these are applicable in your situation or applicable in general in your opinion?

The main point of this little analogy and exercise is to get people to accept and take responsibility for their situation. No progress is possible until this happens and until people:

1. Accept the reality of their situation in the sense of accepting that it *is* so.

2. Take the responsibility and the initiative to do something about it.

The twelve points are guidelines on how to do that. Let's take a more detailed look at each of them.

1. Accept that you have a bear and that the bear is as he or she is. Don't be surprised

Many of us are actually surprised that our manager or managers are not all they should be. We criticise them, talk about them and, in general, expect a much higher level of maturity and perfection from them than we expect from ourselves or that we are able to live up to ourselves. We somehow tend to imagine that wisdom goes with the position and authority they were given, and also maturity and perfection. So we are repeatedly surprised when we spot the faults in our managers. This first guideline is saying just that and only that. You do have someone very powerful in your life called your manager or boss and that manager or boss is as they are and you have to be realistic about that and not be shocked or disappointed by them. Move on! If you only did that, it would make an enormous difference to the relationship and greatly empower you.

2. Get to know your bear, what they need, what they like and do not like. Spend time on this and make a list of their needs, characteristics, strengths and weaknesses. This will help you to understand how they may need you

This may appear manipulative at first glance, but it is not. It is what we normally do with everyone around us. We do it automatically. Just watch how different you are with your mates or friends than you are with your mother or aunt. You are not being at all hypocritical, only very quickly spotting needs and likes and very skilfully and respectfully responding to these. It is simply relationship-building or managing. But because we attribute perfection to managers we don't make a similar effort in their case. We don't spot where they are needy or what appeals to them or, if we do, we put some negative label on it like 'He is very ambitious', 'She likes to get her own way' or 'She or he likes to get the credit', etc. Basic human, possibly disappointing needs get listed and dismissed as failings that have no right to exist. They then become sources of conflict, disappointment or disenchantment. However, if we see them as human needs, they can be our entry to ways to building a positive and collaborative relationship.

3. Feed your bear and look after them. Otherwise they may look after themselves. Plan this

This is similar to no. 2. Bears need food to survive. It is what they are constantly on the look out for. Managers, too, need food to survive. This food may come in various forms such as success, sense of achievement, recognition, progress, information, security, opportunities and results. These are the staple diet of people in positions of responsibility. They have to have these things. If we can help them get them then they will see us as their allies and friends, and will not only leave us in peace like a well-fed bear might do, but will actually look after us.

4. Be aware of your bear and the power they have. Learn to deal with this in your own way. Don't underestimate them. Look after yourself

This makes sense in terms of grizzly bears and, yes, not all managers are grizzly. However, they do have power and it is good to remember this. Many of them are fine until cornered and then they can become quite ferocious and dangerous. A very good chief executive I once had was accustomed to being accosted and challenged when socialising in pubs with staff. He always stopped his attackers with the invitation: 'Why don't you come to my office on Monday morning and tell me all this?' He did this to mark people's card and remind them that they were talking to the boss, to their bear. So, while it is important to work to build up a good relationship with your manager or boss, it is important also not to be naïve or to forget that managers sometimes have difficult decisions to make and can be strong and sometime ruthless in how they make them.

5. Don't frighten them or surprise them. Bears don't like to be surprised – unless it is with honey

You know what this means, of course. Don't land them in it. Managers like to be forewarned of problems. They are often one step removed from the nitty gritty detail and so need to be kept up to date and not have bombshells go off around them, at least not without some forewarning.

6. Work hard at building a relationship with your bear – it will make life easier and allow you to do what you want and need to do

This does not mean that one has necessarily to be friends with one's manager; however, a good working relationship is important and will make life easier. This will not happen automatically and often needs work. Two different human beings thrown together in a stressful and challenging situation will not always get on well together. Like many relationships, it needs some work.

7. Try to set realistic boundaries for yourself and get the bear comfortable with them

This can make life so clear and straightforward for all kinds of bears, be they animals or managers. What it means in the work context is that you clarify what is expected from you by your manager. This may mean straightforward things like results, reports and updates. It could mean conversations, meetings and visits. It can be done easily and smoothly: 'Would you be OK with my giving you a weekly update on sales results?' 'It would be great if we could sit down once every two weeks to check how things are going. Would you be ok with this?' 'How often would you like to come and visit the office or sit in on our meeting?' Good boundaries make for good neighbours and also for good relationships with one's manager.

8. Don't set out to take them on or change them as this can consume a lot of energy

This can be the number one pastime or task in some companies – getting rid of your manager. That's great if you can pull it off, but be 100 per cent sure you can. Bears are pretty powerful and you underestimate them at your peril. Trying to force someone to change in this life is a nearly impossible task and will be doubly so in the case of your manager. On top of that, it consumes a lot of energy and focus and you may lose out in the process from not fulfilling your own role.

9. Be wise and your bear can be your biggest ally and will protect you

Without pandering to your bear or getting into any form of licking, a good relationship with your manager can be a great help to you in getting your job done. Strong managers are great resources to have and will reduce the number of lone battles you will have to fight to get your job done and to get what you want. A good relationship with a strong boss can also give you the freedom to take some risks and so enjoy more freedom and latitude in what you do. They will cover for you and, if you have a relationship of trust with them, they will stand by you.

10. Don't play games with your bear. They won't understand it and won't like it and you may get hurt

Politics and politicking can be great fun and very exciting. It can also be dangerous and a huge waste of time and life. Often we get it wrong. We can overestimate our own strengths and under-estimate those of the other side. This can be particularly so in the case of managers who are not too bad at politics if they have survived and thrived thus far. And if you once get caught playing games, you may never live to fight another day.

11. Respect them and have confidence in yourself and you may get a relationship of mutual respect where you are able to face them and look them in the eye. Bears, too, have their fears

This is important. There is no reason at all why you cannot build a relationship of mutual respect with them. This does call for some courage and risk-taking on your part, but your manager will respect you for it. In addition, they may come to respect you and your strength and see you as a formidable ally and not want to see you as an enemy. Once achieved, this will create a healthy relationship of equals.

12. Try to like them – like us, they're OK deep down but are just animals who are looking after themselves and, like all of us, not always doing it in the best way

This just refers to basic understanding of the humanity behind all the huffing and puffing. None of us is perfect, so being able to understand and forgive is a critical skill to have.

As I already said, these points are not so much intended to be a prescribed list of actions you should take but attitudes you can develop regarding your manager. They will greatly empower you. They will also make life so much more enjoyable and pleasant.

When dealing with human beings it is always important to treat them like human beings, even if they are managers. If you can manage that it will make a great difference to your working life.

Chapter 25

Bullying – Managing the Bear within Yourself

Bears don't know they're bears. They see other animals around them but they are not aware of what or who *they* are from an objective standpoint. Being a bear is all they know and they just get on with being a bear and using their bear qualities. Many managers – if not all of us – don't know they are bears either. Because of this, while managing our bears – our managers – is challenging, managing the bear in *ourselves* is even more challenging. It is easier to deal with the bear or potential bully in others because we can see it. We very often don't even recognise it in ourselves.

For this reason when we talk of bullying, we talk of the effects of being bullied or what to do when you are bullied. Rarely do we talk to the bullies themselves to tell them not to bully or to stop bullying and how to do so. Most times this is because the damage has already been done. The person has been bullied and the so-called bully is being accused of or has been taken to task for bullying.

Another reason why we don't talk to the bullies and tell them to stop is that the so-called bullies either don't accept they are bullying or don't even know they are bullying.

Rarely will a bully actually accept they are one or that they have been bullying. Often they are dragged through HR departments, courts, tribunals and investigations in an effort to get them to accept that some behaviour of theirs was wrong and is regarded as bullying. Rarely are these efforts successful. Managers and others accused of bullying fight to the death in an effort to protect their good name.

This may be understandable and we will come back to it later in this chapter but how can it be that people accused of bullying are not aware that they are behaving in a bullying way?

There are several reasons why this may be so. The most common one is that most of us are not aware of the effects of our actions. We think that what we do and how we behave is fine and we are not aware of how negatively others may see what we do. It is simply the gap between intention and effect. Our intention in doing something may be entirely positive but the effect of what we do may be negative, i.e. have a negative effect on other people. And we are in part at least responsible for the effects of what we do. Good intentions are not enough. We have to take responsibility for the effects of what we do or at least be fully aware of the effects we are having on others. The important question to answer is why managers may be even less aware than others of behaviours of theirs which might be regarded by others as bullying.

Much of this comes from the kind of power that managers have. This is usually some form of hierarchical power by which a manager has the right to take decisions that affect the lives and actions of other people. We take this situation for granted and see nothing wrong with it. Some of this comes from the world of the military where orders are issued and have to be obeyed. Different ranks of official have the right to decide for those below them and their orders are not to be questioned.

Of course it is not exactly like this in the world of business or in organisations in general, but at least some of this way of relating does get carried over and practised. What it means, in effect, is that when a superior gives an order they expect it to be followed purely because *they* have said they want it done or followed. This seems OK and it would appear that that is the right of a superior. Just having authority gives us, as managers, the right to tell others what to do.

However, it is not as simple as that. What this means in effect is that a person is doing something purely because they have been instructed to do it and this is not acting rationally. They are doing it, not because they believe it is the right and reasonable thing to do, but because someone else has told them to do it. Except for very minor matters, it is not right to ask a person to do something without their understanding the reasons for doing it. This is simply asking a human being to behave in an inhuman way. We already dealt with this in Chapter 23 where we said much of management actually operates in just this way. Is it any wonder people feel bullied?

Add typical human flaws to this and we have a very dangerous cocktail indeed. Take a certain percentage of people who have an undue quota of ego or insecurity, or anger or fear, add in the right to take decisions for people and to instruct people and you have a recipe for trouble and for bullying. Many managers are not aware of how powerful they are and that they often abuse that power. Annoyances, frustrations, fears and anxieties can get expressed through instructions, or by handling people in an abusive way. Kicking the cat when one is cross can take other forms when managers have subordinates around them. Many managers are oblivious to what is going on in themselves and so are quite taken aback when they are challenged about their behaviour or accused of bullying. What they are doing seems normal to them. They see their own behaviour as being fine and the basis for their orders and instructions as being sound and justified.

In summary, much of normally accepted management is built on a wrong and outmoded form of power devoid of rationale. In many cases this form of power gets coupled with human weaknesses and this leads to various forms of abusive behaviour and bullying.

What can we do about this? Well, we can educate people about all of this and support them in recognising their behaviour, but even then it may be too late and it may not be accepted by the person in question. A better approach might be to try to nip it in the bud and help managers to be sensitive to the pitfalls associated with managing and by so doing avoid the error in the first place.

What follows are ten things managers can do to avoid slipping into bullying or accusations of bullying.

In the previous chapter, we, perhaps unfairly, likened managers to bears in that they have a lot of power and can hurt people as well as do them a lot of good. If this is true of our managers then it is also true of us as managers.

So, what do we do about the bear in us as managers? How can we ensure that we do not treat people badly and so run the risk of bullying people?

Here are more bear guidelines, this time to be applied to ourselves:

1. Understand that you are a bear. This might help you understand people's behaviour around you

As managers we do not always realise how powerful we are. We take ourselves for granted and forget that people can be nervous in our presence. We forget that our growls can be taken seriously,

25.1. Managing the bear in yourself.

more seriously than we intend. Even what we might regard as mild blows, like being abrupt or sharp with people, can have devastating effects on people. So we need to be aware of what we do and say and of the effects these have on other people. We need to be more sensitive about this than we might be in other parts of our lives. The lack of awareness of this can lead to managers being greatly surprised when they are accused of bullying. They simply are not aware of how powerful they are and how seriously they are taken by people around them.

2. Understand that people, at least some people, may be afraid of you

You might be surprised to hear that. 'Who? Me?' you might say. Bears can be unaware of how afraid they make people. Of course they know they can make people afraid but oftentimes they do it inadvertently, unconsciously. So, as managers, we do not have to change what and who we are but simply be aware of who might be afraid of us. This will help us to get our messages, words and tone right with these people. It will also prevent us from being surprised at accusations of bullying and abuse.

Who might be wary or afraid of you? If you can't think of anyone, ask some people around you who might fall into that category. There will always be some. It's not good to have people afraid. Fear damages people and performance.

3. Don't underestimate the power you have – to do good things and to damage people

As a manager you have a lot of power. This power can be used well or badly. It should not be taken lightly. Just as it is easy to damage people with a wave of a hand or stroke of a pen, so too can you achieve great things for people. Careers have been ruined, people damaged and growth stunted by the careless actions of managers who acted without regard for the effects their actions might have. Board members and executives can act in cold and cruel ways and just see cold and cruel actions as good business decision making. You have power, so watch how you use it. It is a privilege to be a manager but it brings responsibilities with it.

4. If you once maul people they will find it hard to trust you in future

We can fly off the handle. We can take our frustration out on someone. We can lose patience. We can be unfair to people. We can let a bad mood spill over into abuse of someone. Whenever we do this, we are doing damage. We are creating wounds and leaving scars, and it may be hard to heal them and win back that trust. People will fear they might get another mauling. Saying sorry may not always be enough. Like people bitten by a dog, the fear that it will happen again always remains. So we need to be careful not to let our emotions get us into trouble, and if we do slip up we need to be ready to work very hard to undo the damage. A quick and sincere apology will help and can work. Difficult as it may be, it will avoid greater difficulties later on.

5. Understand people's boundaries and respect them as much as you can

Everyone needs space. Not just space in terms of room, that too, but psychological space within which they have the freedom to work, think, and take decisions and initiatives. Sometimes we can over-manage people and deprive them of the freedom and autonomy they need. So we need to find out where their boundaries are, where they want to put their fences up, and try to respect these. This will mean clarifying things like reporting, responsibilities, projects, tasks and above all using the coaching approach and philosophy as much as possible (see Chapter 13). Doing this will give people greater confidence and comfort, and remove or reduce unnecessary fears.

6. Look after people and they will look after you and feed you

Bears need to be fed. They can feed themselves but it is better and safer for everyone if they are fed. It is also easier for you. Being fed in this case means getting what you want, what you need to get your job done. If you care for your people and look after their needs they will reciprocate and look after you. So be a good bear and you will be well fed. It is OK to be independent but we are better when we are surrounded by allies and friends, so it pays to look after your people. And it is the best and right thing to do anyway.

7. Use your power to protect your people. They will respect you for this

People need protecting sometimes. Work organisations can be threatening places for some people. People can feel insecure and can also be afraid to take risks and fail to live up to their true potential. As a manager, you can use your power to protect them, ride shotgun for them and cover for them. This will give people great confidence and they will be loyal to you in return. And you will get more and better work from people.

8. Be aware of what annoys you and that this may be more about you than about the actual situation. Bears should occasionally take a look at themselves

We are all human and have our moments and our moods of weakness. Sometimes when we get upset we can think it is about some person and take it out on them. We can abuse our strength and not want to examine our motives. People with little or no hierarchical power would not get away with taking their moods out on others. Managers can sometimes treat people at work in ways in which they would never treat people outside of work or get away with outside of work. In positions of power, we can take the liberty of mistreating people who work for or with us. We need to be aware of this. If we are really aware of ourselves and of our moods and reactions, we will avoid abusing people and we will grow in the process. Others around us will grow too – in respect, confidence and performance.

9. Beware of throwing your weight around, bullying and wanting to get your own way always. It is not good for you or for anyone else

Getting our own way can become a habit. We can also believe that that is how things should be – that our word has to be final, that we need to be always right. While some of this can come from straightforward ego and security needs, some of it can also come from how we see our role as a manager. We can feel that to be wrong, be seen to be wrong and admit to being wrong can mean a loss of face and a consequent loss of respect. The opposite is, in fact, the case. First of all, we will *not* be always right. There are times when we will make mistakes and get things wrong. Others will have better ideas than we have. If we don't recognise this and admit it, people will see what is happening and lose respect for us. They may go along with it out of fear but we will have lost their respect and good will. We will then never know when we are right or wrong because people will be afraid to tell us. People will admire the lovely clothes we, as the emperor, are wearing when they know very well we have none.

When we admit that we were not right or that some other idea or proposal is better than ours, we not only win respect but we take a better decision and do a better job. We need to ensure our power does not block us getting feedback, input and criticism from our people.

10. Clever and powerful as you are, you have a lot of other clever people around you. Make the most of them and they will make life much easier and better for you and for everyone

While we really need to see ourselves as different and apart from our people, we need to make sure that we do not believe that we are independent and autonomous. Strong as we are, we will always depend on others to get things done. Powerful as they are, bears need bees to make honey for them. Our very strength can be a weakness if we try to go it alone and fail to recognise our dependence on our people and those around us. We do this, not to make people feel good, but because it will make our own life easier and better. In the process, of course, we do gain their favour and support as well. Strong as we are, when we use and involve other people we become stronger.

There is little doubt that if managers were more aware of how they can abuse their power or wield a wrong kind of power it would greatly reduce the instances of bullying.

We can't get everyone to behave well and not bully but we can practise awareness of ourselves and so begin a whole new wave of good healthy management. We have no idea where the effects of our awareness and good behaviour may end. We will be exemplifying and modelling a non-bullying approach.

So, even if we are a bear, we can still behave in a human way.

Final Word

A beggar sat on a box on a street asking passersby for some money. As he saw a man approach, he began his plea for some help.

The man stopped and explained to the beggar that he had no money on him, but the beggar persisted, asking for just a little help.

The man asked the beggar what was in the box on which he was sitting.

'I don't know,' answered the beggar. 'I've never looked.'

'Why don't we have a look?' said the man.

Between them they struggled with the box that hadn't been opened for a long time and was quite stuck.

When they finally got it open, they discovered that there was gold in the box.

My aim throughout this book has been to try to get across to you that you are sitting on gold. I mean this in two senses:

1. You are sitting on gold in terms of the enormous wealth in the people, in the resources and in the opportunities within your organisation.

2. You are sitting on gold in terms of the enormous potential and richness that exist in you as a human being, which you may not have fully realised or appreciated.

But, apart from helping you to realise that you have this gold within your reach, I have tried in this book to give you the tools and wherewithal to access that gold. I hope that the many insights I've shared have made sense to you and I hope that you can put them into practice. This is the only way that you will know how well they work. It is a case of 'I'll see it when I believe it', rather than the other way around. Managing in a human way does require some courage because we have to abandon many of our traditional props and ways of doing things and let go of some of these sometimes false and deceptive comforts. It is true that 'Risk and reward ride side-by-side. Avoid the first and the second will pass you by.' And the rewards, in this case, are very great. They include having a more successful but also a more sustainable, healthy and happy organisation.

I hope this book has given enough clues about how to allow and develop real intelligence in every part of your organisation. When you do this, not only will it reduce problems and the need for supervision and correction, but it will create a real vibrancy in every part of the company or organisation. Each section and each person will know the creative input that they need to make for the welfare of the organisation of which they are a part and from which they benefit. And they will really want to make that input because it makes sense to them.

The key to achieving this is to make the switch from using hierarchical or positional power to using the power of meaning, of what makes sense and what is good for everyone. As Richard Rohr says: 'The soul can live without success, but it cannot live without meaning.'

I have tried to explain how the power of meaning can be put into practice in all kinds of work situations and my hope is that you will put it into practice. Everything I have said in this book I have put into practice in all kinds of work situations, and I try to apply it to every aspect of my life.

Notes

1 Rosamund Stone Zander and Benjamin Zander, *The Art of Possibility: Transforming Professional and Personal Life*, US: Harvard Business School Press, 2000.

2 Zander and Zander, *The Art of Possibility*, p. 128.

3 Marianne Williamson, *A Return to Love: Reflections on the Principles of a 'Course in Miracles'*, US: Harper Collins, 1992, pp. 190–191.

4 Tracy Huston, *Inside Out*, US: The Society for Organizational Learning, 2007, p. 4.

5 Joan Manuel Serrat, *En Transito*, Spain: Estudios Eurosonic de Madrid, 1981.

6 John Ralston Saul, *Voltaire's Bastards: The Dictatorship of Reason in the West*, UK: The Free Press, 1992.

7 Claudia Koonz, *The Nazi Conscience*, US: Harvard University Press, 2003.

8 Gitta Sereny, *Into That Darkness: From Mercy Killing to Mass Murder*, UK: Pimlico, 1974, p. 207.

9 Keith Schneider, 'Uranium Miners Inherit Dispute's Sad Legacy', *New York Times*, 9 January 1990.

10 Jonah Lehrer, *How We Decide*, US: Houghton Mifflin Harcourt, 2009.

11 Terry Eagleton, *After Theory*, US: Basic Books, 2003.

12 Nelson Mandela, Statement from the Dock at Rivonia Trial, South Africa, 1964.

13 Viktor Frankl, *Man's Search for Meaning*, UK: Hodder & Stoughton, 1989, pp. 27–28.

14 Frankl, *Man's Search for Meaning*, p. 17.

15 Frankl, *Man's Search for Meaning*, p. 78.

16 Rosa Parks, *My Story*, US: Penguin Group, 1999.

17 Jack Houlahan, *A Ghost in Daylight*, Ireland: Veritas, 2006.

18 Margaret Wheatley, *Leadership and the New Science*, US: Berrett-Koehler, 2006, p. 23.

19 Eckhart Tolle, *A New Earth*, US: Penguin, 2005, p. 9.

[20] Eckhart Tolle, *Touching the Eternal* (DVD), US: Eckhart Tolle Teachings, 2007.

[21] Gary Hamel, *Leading the Revolution*, US: Harvard Business School Press, 2000, p. 57.

[22] Hamel, *Leading the Revolution*, p. 58.

[23] Hamel, *Leading the Revolution*, p. 59.

[24] Charles Handy, *The Empty Raincoat: Making Sense of the Future*, UK: Hutchinson, 1994; Charles Handy, *The Hungry Spirit: New Thinking for a New World*, UK: Arrow Books, 1998.

[25] Jonathan Gatlin, *Bill Gates: The Path to the Future,* US: Perennial Currents, 1999.

[26] Ulric Neisser and Eugene Winograd, *Remembering Reconsidered: Ecological and Traditional Approaches to the Study of Memory,* US: Cambridge University Press, 1995.

[27] Jonah Lehrer, *How We Decide*, p. 218.

[28] Antoine de Saint-Exupery, *The Little Prince*, UK: Pan Books, p. 18.

[29] Jonah Lehrer, *How We Decide*, pp. 254–255.

[30] Ellen MacArthur, *Taking on the World*, UK: Penguin Books, 2002, p. 330.

[31] Ellen MacArthur, *Taking on the World,* p. 330.

[32] Mihaly Csikszentmihalyi, *Creativity: Flow and the Psychology of Discovery and Invention*, US: Harper Collins, 1996, p. 72.

[33] Mihaly Csikszentmihalyi, *Creativity,* p. 20.

[34] Antoine de Saint-Exupery, *The Little Prince*, p. 38.

Bibliography

Adams, John D., *Transforming Work*, US: Miles River Press, 1984.

Agassi, Andre, *Open*, UK: Harper Collins, 2009.

Allende, Isabel, *The House of Spirits*, UK: Alfred A. Knopf, 1985.

Amado, Jorge, *Tent of Miracles*, UK: Alfred A. Knopf, 1971.

Andricopoulos, Yannis, *In Bed with Madness*, UK: Imprint Academic, 2008.

Annunzio, Susan Lucia, *Contagious Success*, US: Penguin, 2004.

Appleyard, Bryan, *Understanding the Present*, US: Doubleday,1993.

Ariely, Dan, *The Upside of Irrationality*, UK: Harper Collins, 2011.

Assagioli, Roberto, *Psychosynthesis*, UK: Psychosynthesis Research Foundation, 1965.

Ball, Alan, *American Beauty*, UK: FilmFour Books, 2000.

Bandler, Richard and Grinder, John, *The Structure of Magic*, US: Science and Behaviour Books, 1975.

Barbery, Muriel, *The Elegance of the Hedgehog*, UK: Gallic Books, 2008.

Barker, Joel Arthur, *Paradigms*, US: Harper Collins, 1992.

Barry, Brunonia, *The Lace Reader*, US: Harper Collins, 2006.

Bauby, Jean-Dominique, *The Diving Bell and the Butterfly*, UK: Fourth Estate, 1997.

Berg, Art, *The Impossible Just Takes a Little Longer*, UK: Judy Piatkus, 2002.

Berger, John, *Hold Everything Dear*, UK: Verso, 2007.

Berger, Peter L., *The Homeless Mind*, UK: Penguin Books, 1973.

Berry, Thomas, *The Dream of the Earth*, US: Sierra Club Books, 1988.

Bohm, David, *Wholeness and the Implicate Order*, US: Routledge Classics, 2006.

Bonhoeffer, Dietrich, *Letters and Papers from Prison,* UK: Fontana Books, 1959.

Borges, Luis, *Fictions*, UK: Penguin Books, 1999.

Boyle, Nicholas, *Who Are We Now?* US: University of Notre Dame Press, 1998.

Boyne, John, *The Boy in the Striped Pyjamas*, UK: Random House, 2006.

Capra, Fritjof, *Uncommon Wisdom,* UK: Century Hutchinson, 1988.

Cartwright, Justin, *The Song before It Is Sung,* UK: Bloomsbury Publishing, 2007.

Castaneda, Carlos, *A Separate Reality*, UK: Penguin Books,1973.

Catford, Lorna and Ray, Michael, *The Path of the Everyday Hero*, US: Jeremy P. Tarcher, 1976.

Chabris, Christopher and Simons, Daniel, *The Invisible Gorilla*, US: Random House, 2010.

Chardin, Teilhard de, *The Phenomenon of Man*, UK: William Collins Sons, 1959.

Chopra, Deepak, *The Way of the Wizard,* UK: Rider, 1996.

Conrad, Joseph, *The Secret Agent,* UK: Penguin, 1994.

Covey, Stephen, *Principle-Centred Leadership*, US: Simon & Schuster, 1990.

Csikszentmihalyi, Mihaly, *Creativity*, US: Harper Collins, 1997.

Csikszentmihalyi, Mihaly, *Flow*, US: Harper Collins, 1990.

Davies, Robertson, *The Deptford Trilogy*, UK: Penguin Books, 1983.

Dawkins, Richard, *The Blind Watchmaker,* UK: Penguin Books, 1988.

De Geus, Arie, *The Living Company*, UK: Nicholas Brealey, 1999.

De Mello, Anthony, *Awareness*, UK: Harper Collins, 1990.

De Mello, Anthony, *Wellsprings,* US: Doubleday, 1986.

De Pree, Max, *Leadership Is an Art*, US: Dell Publishing, 1989.

Deutsch, David, *The Fabric of Reality*, US: Penguin Books, 1998.

Diamond, Jared, *Guns, Germs and Steel*, UK: Vintage, 1998.

Dillard, Annie, *The Maytrees*, UK: Hesperus Press, 2007.

Dillard, Annie, *Pilgrim at Tinker Creek,* US: Harper Perennial, 1990.

Dillard, Annie, *Teaching a Stone to Talk*, US: Harper Perennial, 1982.

Donohue, John, *Anam Cara,* UK: Bantam Press, 1997.

Dostoyevsky, Fyodor, *The Brothers Karamazov*, UK: Penguin Books, 1958.

Douthwaite, Richard, *Short Circuit*, UK: Green Books, 1996.

Dyer, Wayne W., *Your Erroneous Zones*, UK: Sphere Books, 1977.

Eagleton, Terry, *The Meaning of Life,* US: Oxford University Press, 2007.

Eagleton, Terry, *After Theory*, UK: Penguin Books, 2004.

Ferguson, Marilyn, *The Aquarian Conspiracy*, US: Jeremy P. Tarcher, 1980.

Fisher, Roger and Ury, William, *Getting to Yes*, UK: Hutchinson & Co., 1983.

Frankl, Viktor E., *Man's Search for Meaning*, UK: Beacon Press, 1962.

Freire, Paulo, *Pedagogy of Hope*, US: The Continuum Publishing Company, 1997.

Fritz, Robert, *The Path of Least Resistance*, US: Ballantine Books, 1989.

Fromm, Erich, *To Have or to Be*, UK: Jonathan Cape, 1978.

Fromm, Erich, *The Fear of Freedom,* UK: Routledge & Kegan Paul, 1942.

Fukuyama, Francis, *Our Posthuman Future*, UK: Profile Books, 2002.

Fukuyama, Francis, *Trust*, UK: Hamish Hamilton, 1995.

Gaddis, William, *Agape Agape*, US: Viking Penguin, 2002.

Gallwey, Timothy, *The Inner Game of Work*, UK: Orion Business, 2000.

Garaudy, Roger, *The Alternative Future*, UK: Penguin Books, 1976.

Gardner, Howard, *Leading Minds*, US: Basic Books, 1996.

Gatlin, Jonathan, *Bill Gates: The Path to the Future*, US: Perennial Currents, 1999.

Gelb, Michael J. and Buzan, Tony, *Lessons from the Art of Juggling*, UK: Aurum Press, 1995

Gendlin, Eugene T., *Focusing*, UK: Random House, 2003.

Gibran, Kahlil, *The Prophet*, UK: William Heinemann, 1991.

Glasser, William, *Reality Therapy*, US: Perennial Library, 1990.

Gleick, James, *Chaos*, UK: Penguin Books, 1988.

Glover, Jonathan, *Humanity*, UK: Jonathan Cape, 1990.

Goldratt, Eliyahu and Cox, Jeff, *The Goal*, UK: Gower Publishing, 1989.

Gordon, William J., *Synectics*, US: Macmillan, 1961.

Grayling, A.C., *The Meaning of Things*, UK: Weidenfeld and Nicholson, 2001.

Greenberg, Gary, *Manufacturing Depression*, UK: Bloomsbury Publishing, 2011.

Greenberg, Joanne, *I Never Promised You a Rose Garden*, US: Signet, 1989.

Greene, Graham, *Brighton Rock*, UK: Penguin Books, 1943.

Grey, Mary, *The Wisdom of Fools,* UK: Society for Promoting Christian Knowledge, 1993.

Haley, Jay, *Uncommon Therapy*, US: W.W. Norton & Company, 1986.

Hamel, Gary, *The Future of Management*, US: Harvard Business School Publishing, 2007.

Hamel, Gary, *Leading the Revolution*, US: Harvard Business School Press, 2000.

Handy, Charles *The Hungry Spirit,* UK: Random House, 1997.

Handy, Charles, *Beyond Certainty*, UK: Arrow Books Limited, 1988.

Harris, Thomas A., *I'm OK – You're OK*, UK: Jonathan Cape Ltd, 1970.

Harte, Mickey, *Harte*, Ireland: Poolbeg Books, 2009.

Haughton, Rosemary, *The Passionate God*, UK: Darton, Longman & Todd, 1981.

Hawkins, David R., *Power Vs Force*, US: Hay House, 2002.

Hederman, Mark Patrick, *Kissing the Dark*, Ireland: Veritas Publications, 1999.

Herrigel, Eugen, *Zen in the Art of Archery*, US: Vintage Books, 1971.

Houlahan, Jack, *A Ghost in Daylight*, Ireland: Veritas Publications, 2006.

Huston, Tracy, *Inside Out*, US: Society for Organizational Learning, 2007.

Huxley, Aldous, *Brave New World*, UK: Vintage Books, 2004.

Illich, Ivan, *Shadow Work*, UK: Marion Boyars, 1981.

Ionesco, Eugéne, *'Rhinoceros', 'The Chairs' and 'The Lesson'*, UK: Penguin Books, 1962.

Jacobs, Jane, *Dark Age Ahead*, US: Vintage Books, 2005.

Jaworski, Joseph, *Synchronicity*, US: Berrett-Koehler, 1996.

Kabat-Zinn, Jon, *Full Catastrophe Living*, UK: Judy Piatkus, 1996.

Kafka, Franz, *Metamorphosis and Other Stories*, UK: Penguin Books, 1961.

Kafka, Franz, *The Trial,* UK: Penguin, 1935.

Katie, Byron, *Loving What Is*, UK: Random House, 2002.

Kay, John, *Obliquity*, UK: Profile Books, 2011.

Keen, Sam, *The Passionate Life,* US: Harper & Row, 1983.

Keirsey, David and Bates, Marilyn, *Please Understand Me,* US: Prometheus Nemesis Book Company, 1978.

Kelman, James, *How Late it Was, How Late*, UK: Vintage, 1998.

Kenneally, Christy, *Life after Loss*, Ireland: Mercier Press, 1999.

Kimmage, Paul, *A Rough Ride*, UK: Yellow Jersey Press, 2007.

Klein, Naomi, *No Logo*, UK: Harper Collins, 2001.

Kohn, Alfie, *No Contest*, US: Houghton Mifflin, 1980.

Koonz, Claudia, *The Nazi Conscience*, US: Harvard University Press, 2003.

Kriegel, Robert J., *If it Ain't Broke...Break It*, US: Warner Books, 1992.

Kubler-Ross, Elisabeth, *On Life after Death,* US: Celestial Arts, 1991.

Kundera, Milan, *The Unbearable Lightness of Being*, US: Harper & Row, 1984.

Kushner, Harold S., *When Bad Things Happen to Good People*, US: Avon Books, 1981.

Laborde, Genie Z., *Influencing with Integrity*, US: Syntony Publishing, 1987.

Laing, R.D., *The Divided Self,* UK: Penguin Books, 1960.

Lambe, Wally, *I Know This Much Is True,* US: Harper Collins, 1999.

Lawrence, D.H., *Women in Love*, UK: Penguin Books Ltd, 1995.

Le Carré, John, *Absolute Friends*, UK: Hodder & Stoughton, 2004.

Le Carré, John, *The Constant Gardener*, UK: Hodder & Stoughton, 2001.

Le Carré, John, *Tinker Tailor Soldier Spy*, UK: Hodder & Stoughton, 1974.

Lehrer, Jonah, *How We Decide*, US: Houghton Mifflin Harcourt, 2009.

Liedloff, Jean, *The Continuum Concept*, UK: Penguin Books, 1986.

Llosa, Mario Vargas, *Conversation in the Cathedral*, UK: Faber & Faber, 1993.

Llosa, Mario Vargas, *The Time of the Hero*, UK: Picador, 1986.

Llosa, Mario Vargas, *Aunt Julia and the Scriptwriter,* UK: Faber & Faber, 1983.

Lorenz, Konrad, *On Aggression*, UK: Methuen, 1996.

Lovett, Brendan, *A Dragon Not for the Killing*, Philippines: Claretian Publications, 1998.

Lovett, Brendan, *It's Not Over Yet*, Philippines: Claretian Publications, 1990.

Lovett, Brendan, *Life Before Death*, Philippines: Claretian Publications, 1986.

MacArthur, Ellen, *Taking on the World*, UK: Penguin Group, 2003.

McCabe, Eugene, *Heaven Lies about Us,* UK: Jonathan Cape, 2005.

McEwan, Ian, *Saturday*, UK: Jonathan Cape, 2005.

MacMillan, Margaret, *Paris 1919*, US: Random House, 2002.

Maher, Barry, *No Lie*, US: Barry Maher & Associates, 2006.

Morgan, Gareth, *Images of Organization*, UK: Sage Publications, 1986.

Marquez, Gabriel Garcia, *Love in the Time of Cholera*, UK: Penguin Books, 1988.

Marquez, Gabriel Garcia, *No One Writes to the Colonel*, UK: Jonathan Cape, 1979.

Marquez, Gabriel Garcia, *One Hundred Years of Solitude,* UK: Penguin Books, 1972.

Martel, Yann, *The Life of Pi*, UK: Canongate Books, 2002.

Martinez, Mario E., *The Man from Autumn*, US: Llumina Press, 2005.

Maturana, Humberto R. and Varela, Francisco J., *The Tree of Knowledge*, US: Shambhala Publications, 1987.

Mayer S., Bernard, *Beyond Neutrality*, US: Josey Bass, 2004.

Mengestu, Dinaw, *Children of the Revolution*, UK: Jonathan Cape, 2007.

Minstry, Rohinton, *A Fine Balance*, UK: Faber & Faber, 1996.

Moore, Sebastian, *God Is a New Language,* UK: Darton, Longman & Todd, 1967.

Moriarty, John, *Dreamtime*, Ireland: The Lilliput Press, 1994.

Murdoch, Iris, *The Sovereignty of Good*, US: Routledge Classics, 2007.

Naisbitt, John, *High Tech High Touch*, UK: Nicholas Brealey, 2001.

Neisser, Ulric and Winograd, Eugene, *Remembering Reconsidered*, US: Cambridge University Press, 1995.

Nolan, Vincent, *The Innovator's Handbook*, UK: Sphere Books, 1987.

Nolan, Vincent, *Open to Change*, UK: Password Publications, 1984.

Nouwen, Henri J.M., *Reaching Out,* UK: William Collins Sons & Co., 1976.

Okri, Ben, *Astonishing the Gods*, UK: Phoenix House, 1995.

Owen, Harrison, *Leadership Is*, US: Abbott Publishing, 1990.

Palmer, Helen, *The Enneagram in Love and Work*, US: Harper Collins, 1995.

Parks, Rosa, *My Story*, US: Penguin Group, 1999.

Phillips, Adam, *Going Sane*, UK: Penguin Books, 2006.

Phillips, Nicola, *Reality Hacking*, UK: Capstone Publishing, 1997.

Pirsig, Robert M., *Zen and the Art of Motorcycle Maintenance,* UK: The Godley Head, 1974.

Powell, John, *Through Seasons of the Heart*, UK: Fount Paperbacks, 1986.

Pressfield, Steven, *The Legend of Bagger Vance*, UK: Bantam Books, 2001.

Prince, George, *The Practice of Creativity*, US: Macmillan Publishing, 1970.

Putnam, Robert D., *Bowling Alone*, US: Simon & Schuster, 2000.

Riso, Don Richard, *Personality Types*, UK: The Aquarian Press, 1987.

Robinson, Marilyn, *Home*, UK: Virago Press, 2008.

Rozier, Gilles, *Love Without Resistance*, UK: Little, Brown, 2005.

Runciman, David, *Political Hypocrisy*, US: Princeton University Press, 2008.

Saint-Exupéry, Antoine de, *The Little Prince*, UK: Pan Books, 1982.

Saint-Exupery, Antone de, *Wind, Sand and Stars*, UK: Pan Books, 1975.

Saul, John Ralston, *Voltaire's Bastards*, UK: The Free Press, 1992.

Schlink, Bernhard, *Homecomings*, UK: Weidenfeld & Nicholson, 2008.

Schlink, Bernhard, *The Reader*, UK: Phoenix House, 1997.

Schneider, Keith, 'Uranium Miners Inherit Dispute's Sad Legacy', *New York Times*, 9 January 1990.

Schumacher, Christian, *God in Work*, UK: Lion Publishing, 1998.

Senge, Peter, *Presence*, US: Random House, 2004.

Senge, Peter, *The Dance of Change*, UK: Nicholas Brealey, 1999.

Sereny, Gitta, *Into that Darkness*, UK: Pimlico, 1974.

Serrat, Joan Manuel, *En Transito*, Spain: Estudios Eurosonic de Madrid, 1981.

Shah, Idries, *Wisdom of the Idiots,* UK: The Octagon Press, 1969.

Shaw, Patricia, *Changing Conversations in Organizations*, US: Routledge, 2002.

Shirky, Clay, *Cognitive Surplus*, UK: Penguin Books, 2010.

Stacey, Ralph D., *The Chaos Frontier*, UK: Butterworth-Heinemann Limited, 1993.

Stacey, Ralph D., *Strategic Management and Organisational Dynamics*, UK: Pearson Education, 1993.

Stacey, Ralph D., *Managing Chaos*, UK: Kogan Page Limited, 1992.

Steinbeck, John, *The Pearl*, UK: William Heinemann, 1948.

Steiner, George, *Grammars of Creation*, UK: Faber & Faber, 2001.

Storr, Anthony, *Music and the Mind*, UK: Harper Collins Publishers, 1997.

Storr, Anthony, *The Integrity of the Personality,* US: Ballantine Books, 1960.

Szabo, Magda, *The Door*, UK: Vintage, 2005.

Taleb, Nassim Nicholas, *The Black Swan*, UK: Penguin Books, 2007.

Tannen, Deborah, *You Just Don't Understand*, US: Ballantine Books, 1991.

Thompson, D'Arcy, *On Growth and Form*, US: Cambridge University Press, 1961.

Thouless, Robert, *Straight and Crooked Thinking*, UK: Hodder & Stoughton Ltd, 1930.

Toffler, Alvin, *Future Shock*, UK: The Bodley Head, 1971.

Tolle, Eckhart, *A New Earth*, UK: Penguin Group, 2005.

Tzu, Sun, *The Art of War*, US: Shambhala Publications, 1988.

Wall, William, *The Map of Tenderness,* UK: Hodder & Stoughton, 2002.

Watzlawick, Paul, *Ultra Solutions,* US: W.W. Norton & Company, 1988.

Watzlawick, Paul, *The Situation Is Hopeless But Not Serious*, Canada: Penguin Books, 1983.

Watzlawick, Paul, *Pragmatics of Human Communication*, Canada: Penguin Books, 1967.

Wells, H.G., *The Country of the Blind*, UK: Penguin Group, 2005.

Wheatley, Margaret J., *Finding Our Way*, US: Berrett-Koehler, 2007.

Wheatley, Margaret, *A Simpler Way*, US: Berrett-Koehler, 1996.

Wheatley, Margaret, *Leadership and the New Science*, US: Berrett-Koehler, 1992.

Wheen, Francis, *How Mumbo Jumbo Conquered the World*, UK: Harper Perennial, 2004.

Whitmore, John, *Coaching for Performance*, UK: Nicholas Brealey Publishing, 1992.

Williamson, Marianne, *A Return to Love: Reflections on the Principles of a 'Course in Miracles'*, US: Harper Collins, 1992.

Zander, Rosamund Stone and Zander, Benjamin, *The Art of Possibility: Transforming Professional and Personal Life*, US: Harward Business School Press, 2000.

Zizek, Slaoj, *Violence*, UK: Profile Books, 2008.